PAGAN PARENTING

Spiritual, Magical & Emotional Development of the Child

KRISTIN MADDEN

2000
Llewellyn Publications
St. Paul, Minnesota 55164-0383, U.S.A.

First Edition
First Printing, 2000

Book design and editing by Connie Hill
Cover photo © by Kevin Radford/Superstock
Cover design by Anne Marie Garrison
Herbal Consultant: Elizabeth Ann Johnson

Library of Congress Cataloging-in-Publication Data
Madden, Kristin
   Pagan parenting : spiritual, magical & emotional development of the child /
Kristin Madden
      p.   cm.
   Includes bibliographical references and index.
   ISBN 1–56718–492-8 (pbk)
      1. Witchcraft.   2. Family—Religious life.   3. Child rearing—Religious
aspects—Goddess religion.   I. Title.
BF1572.F35 M35   2000
649'.1'0882999—dc21   00-062327

Llewellyn Publications
A Division of Llewellyn Worldwide, Ltd.
P O. Box 64383, Dept. 1-56718-492-8
St. Paul, MN 55164-0383, U.S.A.
www.llewellyn.com

Printed in the United States of America

For Karl

I love you with all that I am

Also by Kristen Madden

Shamanic Guide to Death and Dying

Contents

Acknowledgments

Karl is the reason this book exists. Since before he was born, our son has been a teacher and a friend to me. My every action is based on how it will affect him, and I am a better person through striving to be the best mother I can be. Karl, I am blessed, humbled, proud, and honored to be your mother.

I am so honored to have had my Mom and Woz as my parents. Their total support and willingness to explore allowed me to grow up without ever having lost touch with my interconnections. Their honesty and courage set role models that I continue to use as a guidepost. I feel truly blessed to have you both in my life.

My husband, Dave, is my lover, my partner, and the best friend I could ever dream of. Your love and support make all things possible. I respect you more than anyone I have ever known. And you are the best Dad!

Thanks also go out to all the parents that have shared their stories with me and to all those that have created message boards, chat rooms, and websites devoted to pagan parenting and to the legal issues involved in living a pagan life. We all need support and camaraderie. We also need guidance and to know that we are not alone in this. Your work and dedication is a gift to all of us.

I gratefully acknowledge Llewellyn Worldwide and their entire staff, especially Ann Kerns, Nancy J. Mostad, and Connie Hill for their support and assistance throughout the process. Once again, the cover truly impressed me and I have Anne Marie Garrison to thank for that. It is an honor to work with all of you.

Preface

Having grown up well outside mainstream religion, I have a unique perspective on the experiences and issues facing pagan families today. While I would never desire to change how I was raised, I cannot say that it was all fun and harmony. My family had many of the same issues that most modern families have. In addition, I had to deal with issues of conformity, and often loneliness as one of the few children on the "lunatic fringe" of the late 1960s through the 1980s.

Now that I am a mother, I want my child to have the same support for his psychic abilities and paranormal experiences that I was blessed to have. I want him to have fun in all aspects of his life. I want to support him in continuing playfulness and exploration throughout his life. Most of all, I want him to be able to choose for himself what path is right for him. The best way for me to do these things for my son is to set an example and to allow him to explore to his heart's content.

I first wrote a small article on "Children's Psychic Skills" for the Family Focus section in *Circle Network News*. Much of what I wrote in the first few paragraphs of this book is from that article, published in the fall of 1997. I was surprised at the response to that article and began to wonder if there was a need for a book such as this. I was very surprised to find a huge interest when I began talking to other pagan parents.

It seemed that there were plenty of parents who wanted to share their activities and what they were learning with their children but did not feel that adult workshops were appropriate. Some of them had attempted to alter some of the exercises in adult books to little success, depending on the age of the child.

Many people, especially those that are relatively new to a metaphysical path, were unsure when their children were ready for certain experiences and how to communicate their own new understandings to their children. Even some parents who were involved with a religious path such as Wicca were having difficulty creating age-appropriate training systems for their children.

In addition, I heard from many parents who had concerns for their children with regard to "psychic stuff." The most prevalent of these concerns is a fear that our children will be ridiculed, snubbed, or worse because they are different from the majority of mainstream society. While the New Age and pagan movements have made great strides, things are not always easy for children raised in these types of families. I learned at a very young age to keep my mouth shut about the alternative activities of my family and I lived a double life for many, many years.

Times have changed, but not so much that all pagan families can feel comfortable blatantly discussing our family's spirituality or metaphysical beliefs with just anyone. We don't want our children to be ashamed of our lifestyle, but we would be foolish not to recognize the need to be discreet. This is something I want to address in this book, in the hope that by bringing these issues into the open and offering suggestions I may be able to support and assist other families so they do not need to learn everything the hard way. It is also my hope to let other families know that they are not alone.

One note on some odd literary licenses I have taken with capitalization and italics in this book. In most cases, I use italics to denote anything outside physical reality. For example, there is a difference between physical sensory feeling and psychic *feeling*. The few examples of unusual capitalization reflect similar meanings. The main use in this book is that of Other worlds or realities. I could have just used the usual "other" but I want it to be clear that these are dimensions of altered states or realities that stand outside our everyday experience.

The identities of some of the individuals who offered their stories for this book have been changed to protect their privacy.

In reading this book, please take the time to have fun with the games and exercises. Go easy with yourselves and your children. Don't expect phenomenal success with all the exercises from the beginning. Sometimes, these things take time. Also, please keep in mind that different people tend to manifest abilities in different areas. I will explain this in detail in the following chapters. There are many factors that go into whether or not someone "gets it." The key with this book is to play and talk and have fun learning with your children. Enjoy!

Introduction

As pagan parents, we are pioneers, in a way. Certainly, many of us were raised pagan, or with metaphysical influences in our families, but there are significantly more pagan parents and children in society today. Estimates of the numbers of pagan families range from 100,000 to more than one million throughout the world. Our ranks seem to be growing by the day.

All pagan parents are finding their own ways to introduce their children to their spiritual beliefs and religious paths. At the same time, many are just learning to develop their own psychic and/or magical abilities. Furthermore, most of us must walk a daily tightrope of honesty versus secrecy about our practices and beliefs.

Pagan parents generally recognize the innate wisdom in their children. We understand that these beings do not belong to us. We know that they are here, sharing their time with us, for their own soul growth as well as for ours. Our children are far more than their bodies and the names we have given them, and we have much to teach each other.

It is my belief that we are all born with psychic potential and an innate spirituality that is not defined by belief systems. While it is true that some of us openly exhibit these tendencies more than others do, we all enter this incarnation open and connected to Spirit. Most young children see auras, are empathic, and have "invisible" friends who are more than mere imagination.

With age, our consciousness becomes more limited within our belief systems. In an attempt to gain acceptance into a largely conformist society, many of us block these psychic connections. Those of us bringing children into pagan families have the opportunity to bring up a new generation without many of the blocks and fears our generation had.

From the moment of birth and earlier, new parents are aware of the psychic bonds between them and their infants. Some parents may experience this simply as a growing love and emotional attachment. Others become intensely aware of the presence of the incoming spirit and *feel* the strengthening of psychic ties. Many people may even *see* a psychic, or energy, umbilical cord connecting mother and child, and usually also father and child.

These bonds remain part of us throughout our lives. Frequently they will connect us to our parents beyond physical death. As I discussed in my book, *Shamanic Guide to Death and Dying* (Llewellyn Publications, 1999), these are the connections through which an after-death communication is often attempted. Infants can enter this incarnation still connected to past friends and family members.

Although past-life connections are rarely a problem, we need to be aware of these bonds. Pagan parents should keep in mind that these other beings might be present and be respectful of their love for your new baby. The soul inhabiting this infant body does not belong to you or to them. In truth, this being is far more than merely your child, the personality incarnating in this current body.

Many psychically aware parents find themselves playing out of body or sharing dreams with their young children. Often a parent will feel drawn to a child's room at night, or believe the child called out, only to find that child sleeping peacefully. I would caution you to be sensitive to the possibility that your child is traveling out-of-body. The child may need reassurance from you, particularly if they have followed you into their own room.

It can be a shock to young children (really to anyone who is new at astral travel) to see their physical bodies from the outside. If a child has not been prepared for the possibility, he may fear that he has died. If handled with confidence and honesty, these nighttime (or naptime) forays can become a fun, safe place for our children to learn to use their nonphysical abilities. It can also be a unique outing for parents and children to take together.

I also believe that psychic abilities are just another step in our evolution as a species. According to many researchers, the brain forms new connections between neurons during our early years and throughout any kind of learning process. Over time, these connections become more defined and change their strengths, depending on the need for each.

It is my opinion that psychic abilities are nothing more than generally unused neural pathways. This would explain why these abilities tend to run in families. I believe we are genetically passing on the potential to our children. Eventually, I expect the hundredth-monkey phenomenon to occur and all of humanity will exhibit this as normal functioning.

As our children grow, their energy bodies develop along with their physical bodies. With the maturing connections between the physical and energy bodies, we naturally develop the potential to utilize these magical abilities. Whether this potential lies dormant or is actualized depends largely on the environment within which the child is raised.

Children generally have less defined and less shielded energy fields than adults do. As parents, we need to be aware of this, so that we may effectively support their total growth and safety. In Barbara Brennan's book, *Hands of Light* (Bantam, 1987), she states that the chakras of children under age seven have no protective film to filter and screen out incoming psychic influences. She also points out that often when a child settles into the lap of a parent, he or she is being shielded from outside influences by the energy field of the adult.

I have observed children who have been abandoned and abused. From an emotional point of view, some of them appear to have developed some incredible shields. They seem to be very tough and hard, almost unemotional. On a spiritual level, these children exhibit significant soul fragmentation, soul loss, and damaged chakras.

From a shamanic perspective, trauma can fragment the soul. Soul parts are then hidden from one's conscious mind or lost in the shamanic Other worlds. The fragmentation of the soul results in a significant loss of personal energy and power. When fragments are retrieved, they may return as a lost power animal, an archetypal image, or a different aspect of the Self. Some may return spontaneously when the individual is strong enough and ready for the reintegration, but most require the assistance of a shamanic guide or counselor.

These lost fragments will often be stored within the chakras, or in other areas of the body. People often exhibit physical symptoms at the point where these fragments are located in the physical body. We may also carry over fragments from past lives that will be similarly stored in the current body.

The chakras of abused or abandoned children will almost always appear damaged in some way. The colors will be murky or dim. Often, they lack energy and seem to drift listlessly. Holes may appear or the chakra itself may be disfigured. Sometimes, the chakras may actually stop spinning or spin in the opposite direction.

This is one reason why we must be careful what we expose our children to. While we may want our children to share in all aspects of our religion and spirituality, there are valid reasons for following a process of training and awareness. The phrase, "Just because we can, does not necessarily mean we should," applies quite well here.

We must be careful not to fall into the sooner-is-better trap of modern society. How early our children develop in any area is not a reflection on us, nor is it any measure of their abilities. If we guide them lovingly and move them along when they are truly ready, they will be better able to reach their potential.

In my experience, the best way to encourage the development of a child's psychic and magical skills is to keep it fun. I loved to play with psychometry, visualization, and telepathy when I was young. It was almost always a game and I could play for hours. My recommendation to other parents is to have fun with your children. Accept this as a renewed opportunity to play with your own abilities, without any purpose other than joy and exploration. In teaching, play, and guidance, we learn a great deal (much of the introduction to this point is reprinted as first published in the Fall 1997 issue of *Circle Network News*).

Children have an innate sense of spirituality. They don't need ritual or formal meditation groups to connect with Other dimensions. We don't really need to teach them to respect and find wonder in the natural world and Other realities. Unfortunately, they also learn disrespect and fear, and to block the full experience of this and Other realities.

Much of what we pass on to our children is not consciously learned. We may have limiting beliefs that remain in spite of the work we have done on ourselves. Children also learn unconsciously. They pick up our reactions and beliefs through body language, tone of voice, and psychic impressions. Not only are they living and sleeping in our homes, which are imbued with our energy, but when they are young they continue to receive a significant amount of our personal energy through the psychic umbilical cord.

In order to do what is best for our children, we must do what is best for ourselves—on a spiritual level. This does not mean running from reality and hiding away in a temple or out in the wilderness somewhere. This means facing up to the responsibility we accepted when we chose to have children. This means facing our dark sides and our fears and moving through them; clearing them so that we do not pass on destructive patterns to our children. It also means living a sacred life and setting an example of strength mixed with sensitivity and intelligence.

Then there is the question of honesty versus secrecy. By this, I mean the dilemma every pagan faces when deciding whether to be completely open and honest about one's lifestyle and beliefs or to pretend to conform with mainstream expectations. This is not an easy issue and the responses vary widely among pagans.

When my mother was growing up, there was no question about it. One just didn't talk about it to anyone outside the family, and there were those within the family who didn't want to hear about it either. Things were only slightly easier for me as a child. While things are much more open today, there is still a majority within modern society that either has no idea what paganism is, or truly believe that it is evil and our sorry souls need to be saved before we roast.

While I will deal with this in detail in a later chapter, the truth is that we all must find an acceptable comfort level. The choice of openness or secrecy will depend on many factors and will vary according to the situation. We need to remain flexible.

However, we must take care not to teach our children that the beliefs of their families are wrong or are something to be ashamed of. Our beliefs and practices are beautiful and powerful. They are also protected under United Nations law and under the federal laws of many of the countries in which we live.

The issue is not within our families, but rather with an ignorant and fearful public. It is in everyone's best interests for us to maintain the higher road. To react with hostility in the face of fear and ignorance is to be pulled down to that level. While this may be an honest reaction for many pagans, it does nothing to assist our children in creating a safer and more tolerant future. It gives our critics the power to control our behavior, which does not serve the common good.

I define the term "pagan" as "a follower of any of the Earth-based religions or spiritual paths." Most of the ethical principles discussed in these pages are common to these paths and are frequently a matter of common sense. Followers of other magical practices and religions may not subscribe to the ethics presented here, particularly when it comes to the free will of other people. These people may or may not be pagans. It is certainly also true in any path that there are individuals who may espouse one thing while exhibiting very different behaviors. That is part of life and growth. In this book, I am writing from a general Earth-Nature-based spiritual perspective.

This book is intended to be an "owner's manual" of sorts. Its goal is to offer pagan families a better understanding of the spiritual and physical development of our physical bodies, thereby assisting us in raising happy and healthy pagan children. It is also my hope that this book will provide some helpful suggestions for issues regarding mainstream society and everyday life. At the same time, I want other pagan families to know that they are not alone in their concerns or experiences.

Life is a journey of learning, challenge, and change. Although there are certain things about our physical reality that we cannot change, we do have the power to control our experience of this reality. We can live in fear and anger, reacting from our repressed shadow sides and living in hiding. Or we can choose self-knowledge and balance, acting with the wisdom of our higher selves and spirit guidance. In living this type of life, we create a better reality for all—the choice is ours. The things that we teach our children, through both words and actions, will have a dramatic impact on the realities of the future.

Incarnation

The process of incarnation begins well before conception and continues beyond birth. It is this process that largely determines one's emotional, mental, and spiritual development at any given age. This is vital information for the pagan parent (or for any parent with metaphysical interests). An understanding of this process allows us to determine how best to introduce certain religious or spiritual elements to our children, and when. It is also extremely valuable to keep in mind when creating a safe and healthy environment for our children.

In this chapter, I will deal with incarnation with regard to the integration of the spirit essence and physical body after the decision to incarnate has been made and before birth into this reality. Certainly, the spirit is the enduring and pre-existing energy that animates the physical body. That spirit greatly influences the physical body, just as the body and life experiences influence the spirit.

However, the energy systems that develop while we do inhabit a physical body would not come into being without that body. It is a little like trying to decide whether the chicken or the egg came first. The creation of the physical body combined with the process of incarnation is what catalyzes the creation of those energy systems that are specific to this physical plane of existence.

Many people agree that the two systems begin to manifest at the moment of conception, or when the spirit decides to incarnate into a body that has already been conceived. From conception on, the spirit begins the process of integrating with the body. When the initial contact between spirit and developing body is made, an energetic link is established between the two. Some people see an energetic womb created around the embryo at this time; others see the beginnings of an aura.

As the baby's body develops in the womb, the link between spirit and body is strengthened. The spirit becomes more and more bound to the body. This dramatically affects its spiritual energy. The point of total integration seems to vary. Some psychic healers have stated that this occurs instantaneously around the time of the quickening, or when the mother first feels the baby's movements. For many women, this is the case. However, for just as many other women, this process is a more gradual experience that may not be complete until the third trimester.

The mere act of physical conception does not necessarily mean that a spirit has decided to incarnate into that potential body. Conception is, at its most basic level, a physical process that may be the result of a variety of influences. Women who abort or miscarry may or may not have had a spirit waiting for that body. Frequently, if a being was intending to enter that particular family, it will wait for another opportunity with the family. Sometimes these beings will be around for years, through several pregnancies.

For example, my friend Kethry was aware of the spirit who would become her oldest daughter, two years before her daughter's conception. When I asked Kethry if she knew back then that this being would be a child of hers, she said, "I knew her, her name, her personality—even what she looked like. It was pretty spooky."

During the course of a pregnancy, the incoming spirit is generally present in the home and/or anywhere the mother-to-be goes. The spirit may show up at any point, even before conception.

However, it is much more common that the child-to-be settles into the home during either the first or second trimester.

Many preconception communications have some purpose to them; and they are not limited to the mother. A large number of fathers-to-be have contact with the incoming spirit both before conception and during pregnancy. While some of these contacts are simply the awareness that a spirit has chosen its intended parents, others have a definite intent. Sometimes the purpose of these contacts seems designed to bring future parents together. Other communications are more specific, often regarding a name for the baby.

One woman shared the story of how her son was with her four years before his body was conceived. The first time she was aware of his presence, she had just been in a very bad sailing accident. She heard a voice saying "But you're my mommy! I haven't had my chance to be born yet." She felt her body filled with a powerful, healing energy and she survived what should have been a fatal accident.

This woman had no more concrete contact with this spirit until she delivered her son. While nursing him soon after they came home from the hospital, she had a vision of that night and became aware of his "plan." For reasons of his own, he desperately wanted her to be his mother. He had stepped in when it looked like his plans would never materialize. If she had died, he would never be the child he wanted to be; with the parents he wanted.

This type of prenatal communication clearly has a purpose to it. I have heard from several mothers and fathers who reported similar types of contacts, from days to even years before the birth of a child. In most of these cases, when the parents finally did meet their new baby, they knew without a doubt that this was the same being that had communicated with them before.

While I had no preconception contact with our son, I had constant communication with him during my pregnancy. Our contact began with a dream I had of "the baby" when I was about one-and-a-half months pregnant. I could not tell if it was male or female but it was blonde with blue eyes and beautiful.

This is the perfect description of our son. He has the most amazing blue eyes.

I wrote in my journal, "We were out somewhere; it [the baby] was approximately four months old. I was speaking to someone and the baby spoke to me, helping me to explain something. I was amazed that it spoke like a very wise adult so early." I went on to have several more "speaking" dreams of our son. As time went on the dreams became more involved and intense.

As my pregnancy progressed, so did my contact with Karl. He began to be a very distinct presence in our home at around four months of pregnancy. He was a huge and imposing mass of energy with a reddish tinge in our home. The color was very interesting, particularly since my parents and I *saw* it as red or reddish hair during dreaming. I generally *saw* it as strawberry-blonde. He has an incredibly strong life force that, even now, can manifest as a beautiful true red in his energy field.

In shamanic societies, it is common for the baby's name to be received by the mother, usually through dreams. If the parents do not receive a name for the child, the shaman will often go in search of the child's name through dreaming or shamanic journeying. In my family, a child's name is often received as a *knowing* during pregnancy.

In speaking with other metaphysical mothers, I have discovered that this is far more common than we may realize. Many mothers tell me that both they and their husbands or mates have received the names of their children well before delivery. This occurred in a variety of ways, including dreams, visions, meditations, and simple intuitive feelings.

Like many new parents, my husband and I were having difficulty deciding on the right name for our son. Karl made it all very easy for us. When I was between six and seven months pregnant, I began thinking of adding the name Carl to the list. We had never considered this name, but I had the distinct feeling this was the baby's idea. I was ambivalent toward the name but appreciated that it was also a family name on my mother's side.

One night around this same period of time, I was awakened in the middle of the night. As I walked through the hallway, I met the huge presence that had taken up residence in our home during my pregnancy. He was adamant that his name must be Karl and it must be spelled with a "K." There was no questioning his insistence and the fact that it was obviously very important to him. That was the end of that.

Although the gestational periods of physical incarnation do vary, it is most commonly during the third trimester that the spirit actually begins to merge with the energy field of the mother. When this occurs, the spirit becomes far less apparent as a separate being within the home. Psychically sensitive mothers will often report experiencing a feeling of dualism, similar (but much more integrated) to that of the merging between person and spirit guide among shamanic practitioners and the merging of God and Goddess among priests and priestesses of other paths.

As the energy field of the mother alters to accommodate the incoming spirit, her energy is dramatically altered. In addition to hormonal changes which, in the opinion of many, are interrelated with these energetic changes, a pregnant woman must deal with an expanded energy field and opening chakra systems. As her energy, or aura, opens to merge with the incoming spirit, she is also open to the energies in her personal environment

This opening, coinciding with increased hormone levels, can lead a woman to be more emotional than usual. As is true when a woman is menstruating, we are energetically open to everything. We can easily pick up the feelings or thoughts of others without recognizing them as separate from us. Even if a woman has done a fair amount of spiritual work on herself, she can react to these outside influences as though they were her own feelings.

It is for this reason that we need to maintain a personal environment that is as consistently balanced and supportive as possible during pregnancy. Not only is the mother vulnerable to stress and destructive energies, but it is also true that the incoming spirit has not yet developed the necessary psychic shields to prevent the spiritual and physical damage that can result from an unhealthy atmosphere.

Many mothers will experience one or more kundalini risings during this time period. Throughout my second and third trimesters and particularly during my last two months of pregnancy, the kundalini energy was very active along my spine. It was uncomfortable for me to lie down in certain positions because the energy moving up my spine was so intense.

This activation of kundalini energy accompanies the opening of the chakras and an increased receptivity to alternate realities. Many pregnant women often report that they are considerably more psychic or intuitive during pregnancy. This is beyond the connection to the unborn child, and carries over to all aspects of their lives. This receptivity also appears to increase as the pregnancy progresses.

Although I had always been very psychically sensitive, in my journal I recorded that I was becoming even more so throughout my pregnancy. There was a dramatic increase in telepathy and intuition during my third trimester. This coincided with Karl's integration into his physical body. It seemed that as I expanded to accommodate his energy field, I was wide open to other people's thoughts and energies.

Not all women experience an increase in psychic awareness during pregnancy. Some women find quite the opposite is true for them. The reasons for this will vary according to the individual woman. However, it is most frequently the result of one of two situations. In many cases, and particularly when the incoming spirit fully merges with its body at a very early stage, all of the mother's energy is focused inward. Her energy is not directed outward, but is rather almost entirely involved in protecting the fetus and growing the new body.

This protection is the other main reason for a shutting down of psychic awareness during pregnancy. A perfect example of this situation is demonstrated by another of my friend Kethry's stories. Kethry is very aware that she was pregnant with this being she had met two years earlier at one point, and miscarried. Several months later, she became pregnant with her daughter-to-be again. She shut herself down psychically in order to protect both herself and her baby from another miscarriage.

To make matters worse, when she was in California during a serious earthquake, Kethry felt her psychic shields shatter and effectively buffered herself and her unborn child by shutting down completely. This psychic buffering in not uncommon among pregnant women, especially in times of crisis. Kethry notes that her second daughter began the process of unwinding her from her "cocoon."

Although many women experience the integration of the incoming spirit at an early stage of the pregnancy, the third trimester is when the majority of the women I have spoken with felt the presence of the baby-to-be shift from an external spirit to a being within their own bodies. Some women became very afraid when they noticed the lack of that external spirit. Some were frantic that something had gone wrong with the pregnancy. A few women even went in for an additional medical examination to be sure the baby was still alive.

Seven days before the birth of our son, I wrote in my journal that he had been hanging around a lot less recently and seemed to be more in his own body. It was an unusual feeling. I went from having a constant companion outside to carrying a being in transition within my body. As he integrated into his body, his energy was completely focused on becoming that new person.

Karl had an enormous energy field when he showed up at our house. It seemed to be difficult for him to fully compact himself in that tiny body. It is interesting to note that toward the end of that time period, my uterus grew twice the normal rate in one month. My doctors were concerned enough about this growth spurt that they had me go through the full eight-hour test for gestational diabetes, which might explain an unusual increase in the size of the baby. We also got to see another ultrasound of him. All the tests were normal. Karl had decided that it was time to move in.

Prenatal Attunement

Even during pregnancy and early infancy, our children respond best to sensory input and symbolic images. Thanks to ultrasound, we now have scientific evidence that fetuses as young as seven weeks react to external stimuli.

Many people, from scientists to parents-to-be, have experimented with reading stories or playing music to babies in utero.

My husband and I did the same. In the beginning of my third trimester, my husband sang and spoke to our son through my belly. Our baby definitely moved in response to Dave's voice. When Dave switched sides, Karl moved toward his voice. When Dave sang, Karl squirmed.

There are several books out these days that focus on prenatal stimulation and beginning to develop a relationship with your child before birth. Most of these recommend using guided imagery, music, and voice to stimulate an unborn child early in the pregnancy. I have found these methods to be valuable, not only as an early "educational" tool, but also in strengthening those energetic connections we have with our children and in developing our own intuitive abilities.

You may want to just seek attunement with your unborn child at first, especially if it is early in your pregnancy. Some books direct parents to practically quiz the unborn baby with psychic games. Certainly, these tests can be beneficial in developing your own intuition. However, unless the baby is far enough along for you to ask it to kick or move as an answer, there is no easy way to be sure whether the images you are receiving are from the baby or from your own intuition.

We are the ones who need validation for extrasensory perception. These incoming beings may find games amusing or play along for our benefit, but they need no training to communicate outside everyday physical reality. What will benefit both parents and child most is the fostering of an early relationship built on love and trust. The ability to use nonphysical senses can only strengthen that relationship and make communication more effective, throughout the lives of all involved.

With that in mind, I have outlined several exercises and guided visualizations for use during pregnancy. These need not be limited to the pregnant woman, but anyone else planning to use these exercises should let the mother-to-be know before beginning. If she is unaware that someone is working with the child within her, she may be unnerved or even disturbed at the additional presence or energy changes that may occur. If the child-to-be is present within your home but not yet integrated into the body, you may also wish to use your own practice of meditation or shamanic journeying to communicate with this being.

Attunement to the Baby in the Womb Exercise

Initially this exercise needs to be done in a safe space where you will be undisturbed for at least an hour. Once a connection is made, the exercise may be done anywhere and anytime. It is beneficial to use during times of stress for mother or child; or in uncomfortable surroundings.

If you would like to do this exercise with a partner, choose one of you to lead the exercise with spoken directions or tape it to play back during the meditation. Hold hands or sit very close to one another throughout the exercise. While this exercise may be done by more than two people at a time, I would recommend beginning with one or two, until you and the child get comfortable with each other. The security of the child, whether real or perceived, is of utmost importance.

> Make yourself very comfortable. Take care of any bathroom or food needs ahead of time. Light some incense or candles. Cast a Circle or simply call in the Spiritkeepers of the directions, if you feel more comfortable this way.
>
> Take a deep breath and relax. Count yourself down from ten to one, stopping periodically to remind yourself to take a deep breath and go deeper. Visualize a bubble forming just before your face. Blow all your fears, stresses, irritations; any negative energies you may be carrying around, into this bubble. Watch the bubble grow and begin to rise. Blow the last of these energies into the bubble and watch as it flies off toward the sun, carrying these things away from you. Feel very centered and relaxed.
>
> Feel the energy of the Earth, flowing up through the soles of your feet (or the base of your spine if you are seated on the floor). Feel and visualize this light

filling you completely. It flows out your pores and your eyes and out through the top of your head.

Become aware of the energy of the universe flowing into you through the top of your head and filling your body. Feel and visualize this light filling you completely. It flows out your pores and your eyes and down through the soles of your feet (or the base of your spine).

Visualize and feel these energies flowing through you at the same time. See them as balanced and centering you. You are energized and revitalized.

Now, turn your attention inward to your womb. Be aware of any sensations or images that come to mind. Send a gentle stream of love and peacefulness to the child within you. Visualize an image of you, smiling and happy with this child in your life.

If you are practicing this with a partner, both of you should visualize the same images together. Follow the image of mother with an image of the partner.

As you progress with this exercise; and as your pregnancy progresses, you may choose to use this exercise to introduce your child to the rest of the family. They do not need to be present, only in your mental images. You may also use this exercise to learn more about your child, by being very aware of images or thoughts and by asking questions. Feel free to experiment and discover what works best for you.

Dreaming Exercise 1:
Meet Your Unborn Child

Keep a pen and paper beside your bed so that you may write down your dreams as soon as you wake up. Keep in mind that you may awaken during the night and should write down any dreams before falling back to sleep.

As you lie down to go to sleep, count yourself down from ten to one, stopping periodically to remind yourself to take a deep breath and go deeper. If you find you are still tense from the day, count down again from ten to one. When you are very relaxed and nearing sleep, tell yourself with belief and intent that you will meet with your unborn child this night during dreaming and that you will remember it upon awakening.

Turn your attention to the child in your womb. If you are not the mother, focus your attention on your image of the baby and continue as directed. Visualize your intention to meet with this being in a dream that night and send it with the feel of a question. Be specific that you are asking the child to meet you in a dream.

Allow yourself to fall asleep.

Dreaming Exercise 2:
Meet Your Unborn Child

Keep a pen and paper beside your bed so that you may write down your dreams as soon as you wake up. Keep in mind that you may awaken during the night and should write the dream down before falling back to sleep.

Depending on how far along you are in your pregnancy (if you are the mother), you may choose to use only a half- or quarter-filled glass of water to prevent awakening for a bathroom run.

Before going to sleep, count yourself down from ten to one as usual. Once you are relaxed and centered, take up a fresh glass of water between both hands and hold it just above eye level. With eyes closed, energize this water with your intention to meet with this child during dreaming. State specifically that you will remember the dream(s) upon awakening and then drink the water.

Allow yourself to fall asleep.

Pathworking Exercise:
Meet With Your Unborn Child's Spirit Guides

Allow at least one hour when you will not be disturbed for this exercise. You may wish to use a shamanic-journey drumming tape in place of the ten-to-one countdown. This exercise can also be done using either of the dreaming exercise techniques.

> Make yourself very comfortable. Take care of any bathroom or other needs ahead of time. Light some incense or candles. Cast a Circle or call in the Spiritkeepers of the directions, if you feel more comfortable this way.
>
> If you are experienced with the shamanic journey, follow your usual method of journeying and go to whatever World you feel drawn to. Otherwise, go to your favorite place of relaxation. This may be a real or imagined place, but it should be somewhere that you feel perfectly safe and comfortable.
>
> Call upon your own spirit guides to join you in this journey to establish a connection with the guides of this child. Be aware of any images or thoughts, as well as what guides show up. It may help to imagine a doorway or an elevator for your guides to use as an entryway, if they choose.
>
> Speak with your guides and let them know exactly what your intentions are during this journey. Ask their guidance, protection, and assistance.
>
> Say to yourself and your guides that you will now go to meet the guides of this child. With this intention in mind, allow yourself to be taken wherever you feel drawn. Keep in mind that these guides may choose to come to you.
>
> When you meet with a being, ask for confirmation that this is one of the guides of this child. You may receive confirmation as a feeling, or as an indication from your guides or the being in question.

Take a good look at this being and ask who it is (or what it is). Accept whatever is given in response. Ask any questions you may have regarding this child or your relationship with this child. You may choose to ask what you can do to help this child succeed with the current life plan, or about a past-life connection. You may also want to ask for their assistance in creating a safe, healthy pregnancy and delivery for both you and your child. Ask whatever you feel compelled to and accept whatever is given in response.

Thank this being (or beings) for meeting with you. Tell them of your love for this child and that you are open to them in any way that may benefit this child. Say your goodbyes and thank them once more.

If they have come to you, see them leave now. If you have gone to them, return to your favorite place of relaxation. You may wish to review this experience with your own guides before returning to everyday reality.

If you used a countdown, count yourself back up from one to ten. If you are using a tape, allow the drumming to return you to this reality.

One last note, before we move on to the child after birth: I highly recommend keeping a journal of these exercises, as well as any dreams or other experiences you have. This is an excellent way to record your experiences and your development on these levels of being. It can be invaluable in determining your personal symbolism as well as honing your accuracy. You may wish to keep separate journals for each child—to be given to them along with other baby books when they grow up.

2

Development of Energy Systems

Along with the physical body, the human energy system develops as a child grows. The two are vitally interconnected. It is commonly accepted that the physical body is the manifestation of an energy template, but to decide which is responsible for the creation of the other is rather like discussing whether the chicken or the egg came first. That debate is not relevant to the work at hand. However, an understanding of the development of the human energy system can be extremely beneficial, not only when working on a metaphysical level but also during everyday activities. Our energy systems influence and are influenced by everything in our environment: mental, physical, emotional, and spiritual.

When a child is born, all of its spiritual energy is fully integrated into its body. This energy begins to mesh with the physical energy starting at the head and moving down through the body. The fontanels, the "soft spots" that must be protected on a baby's head, are the physical manifestation of the wide-open crown chakra through which this spiritual energy has entered physical form. As a child grows and becomes more grounded in their body, the root chakra opens up and the crown chakra closes down a bit, to balance the other energy centers.

As a result, the infant is not yet fully connected to this reality. He or she is still very open to other dimensions and usually retains memories of past lives. Infants may continue to be in contact with friends and relatives from the past, either from past lives or between lives. It can sometimes be difficult for them to let go of these relationships. As parents we need to be understanding of this, even as we encourage the transfer of these emotional bonds to the current family.

Before birth, an energetic umbilical cord is created between mother and child, and similarly between father and child. As I wrote in *Shamanic Guide to Death and Dying*, "It is a similar connection to the cords we form in any relationship, but tends to be much deeper and stronger. . . . As a result of this connection, the process of pregnancy and birth can open a Gateway similar to that of the death experience. Pregnant women and new parents frequently experience heightened psychic sensitivity . . ."

This heightened sensitivity among new mothers can be attributed both to the gradual process that separates the mother's energy from the child's and to the development of an independent energy system in the newborn. Many new parents, not just mothers, experience a continuing Oneness with their newborns. Some people have experienced a physical feeling of inhabiting the body of the newborn: seeing through the child's eyes or sensing a sudden snapping back into the parent's body when they realize their perspective of a baby's stretch is from the baby's body.

I experienced these types of perspective shifts when my son was born. I also experienced a series of popping sounds as our energy separated or as we returned to this reality from interdimensional journeys. These were very similar to the sound a balloon makes when it breaks and it always shocked me quickly back into this reality and my own body. Once the separation of our energy fields was complete, the pops ceased.

When children are very young, a significant amount of the parents' personal energy flows into them through this energy umbilical cord. This energy is used to support the healthy development of their energy systems, as well as for protection from external influences. As they grow and their energy systems stabilize, they no longer need such an intense connection to their parents, and the cord becomes less pronounced.

The infant sleeps much of the time, waking mainly for food and diaper changes. During this sleep time, the astral body, or what many shamans refer to as the free soul, occupies the higher energy centers, and their associated energy bodies. In a way, infants are half in and half out of the physical body during infancy.

Some infants do seem to have lost their conscious awareness in the womb and are truly reawakening as new beings in the physical world. However, many infants at this time struggle not only to release interdimensional loved ones, but to separate who they were in past incarnations from the current life. Some may resist being limited once more by a physical body; or they may have changed their minds about this incarnation. Any of these issues may result in illness, extreme colic, or disease.

While the free soul handles interdimensional issues, the body soul (which is generally associated with the lower chakras) is occupied with building the physical body and grounding the rest of the energy to the physical plane. The spinning of the chakra vortices plays an important part in keeping the physical and energy systems intact.

This can be a difficult process as the spirit attempts to fit its entire energy field into the very small infant's body. Because our son had an enormous energy field when he arrived at our home, he had some difficulty integrating and grounding all this energy into his physical body. The lower-chakra difficulties manifested as digestive problems that he grew out of as soon as he fully integrated into his body.

As the infant grows, this separation of energy fields and the integration into the physical body is accompanied by the ability to recognize and respond to his or her own name. Children begin to learn the language of their family and attempt to communicate in this way. They begin to show signs of thinking and will experiment with the things in their surroundings as they learn how this world works.

With each new milestone, or each experiment and change in awareness, babies' auras and chakras become slightly more defined. As they focus on a new toy or begin to find a partially hidden object, their auras seem to color more brightly. Colors are deepened or new colors are added with each new experience. Their energy fields—their auras—tense and stretch toward the object they focus on. When their attention shifts their auras return to relatively indistinct states, no longer stretched toward the object.

The color of the aura, or energy field of most babies tends toward pastels. It is interesting that our society views pastels as baby colors. These are the colors that most infant clothes come in. In fact, it can be difficult to find baby gifts in any colors other than white and pastels. This often pastel field is rather amorphous and undefined. Those who can *see* the individual energy bodies or energy centers usually perceive infants' chakras to be less rigid than those of adults.

An adult chakra is relatively fixed, whether it is damaged or not. It occupies a specific place in the body and has a definite shape. The chakras of the infant and young child reflect their greater connection to the amorphous world of Spirit and their relative lack of defining belief systems. As the child grows and learns more of our world, assuming more indoctrinated beliefs, the energy systems become accordingly more fixed within an adult shape.

It appears as though both the physical and spiritual bodies develop along with the individual's belief systems. This accompanies the integration into a limited third-dimensional reality. As the energy systems become more rigidly defined, so does the physical body become less that of the chubby baby, distinguishing itself as a specific type of individual. As our chakras firm up, so do our bone structures, and our personalities begin to show in our physical forms.

While these chakras are developing, the energy field is wide open to external influences. This is yet another reason to maintain a healthy and honest environment around our children. They can and do pick up the psychic and emotional atmosphere of the family, even repressed or hidden issues.

Any conflict or violence in their environment has the potential to damage the chakras of both children and adults and cause blockages or soul loss. I believe that much of the juvenile crime and teen pregnancies we see today are the result of generations of wounded souls, reacting out of their own pain and numbness. These children are no longer able to feel a connection to their expanded selves, other beings, or the natural world. As a result, respect and honor have no meaning.

Children know instinctively to go to a trusted person for comfort and protection from these influences. When we hold our children, we are effectively shielding them with our energy fields; much like a mother does when still pregnant with her child. We provide the buffers they need until they develop their own. When a child has no buffers, the wounding can be extreme.

I have known children who were raised in extremely violent and nonnurturing environments. Some of these children saw loved ones killed before their eyes when they were very young. Most of these children had no adults to love or shield them. By the time their own shields developed, several of these children no longer really needed them. They learned to completely shut down all but those chakras essential for physical survival.

Many of these children have grown up to be wonderful people. They love children and several of them now work toward global protection of children. But I can still see the intense need for approval and love whenever I am with them.

Many of them also retain another side, with a tough outer shell that can be impenetrable if they feel the slightest threat. They often react to perceived threats by lashing out and shutting down. These individuals have some of the strongest self-protective mechanisms I have ever seen. And they remind me that too many children in the world today have developed similar measures to protect themselves from the continual assault on their developing systems.

Being exposed to very strong emotions, such as rage, uncontrolled lust, and deep depression within a child's environment can shock a young child's energy systems, much like physical trauma shocks the body. Physical shock jars the body. It can lead to a depressed physical condition.

Occasionally, shock causes one's necessary blood flow to be withdrawn from the extremities. This survival mechanism is designed to sacrifice "nonessential" body parts to prevent the death of the organism. Shock may even shut down physical systems, often leading to death if untreated. Energetic shock is experienced in a very similar manner and can directly affect physical, mental, and emotional behavior.

Children that are exposed to this type of environment have no way to filter these impressions. They cannot really understand these emotions, yet they receive them with full force and must deal with them in some way. Some children are fairly good at automatically grounding some of this energy out, if it is not continuous.

However, many children cannot handle this influx of extreme adult energy. They react with nightmares, insecurities, hostility, and other behavioral problems that are the result of shocked and damaged chakras. From a shamanic point of view, these children experience soul fragmentation. They may also exhibit physical problems in the area where the damage to the energy field has occurred.

Obviously, these children need help. Medical or psychological help may be necessary, but they need more than that. They need energetic healing and soul retrieval by someone who is experienced and qualified to do so. Beyond that, the cause of this damage must be resolved for any long-term healing to occur. If parents and guardians won't get help for themselves, perhaps they will when they realize what their unspoken hostility, constant fighting, or other personal issues do to their children.

As the baby develops into a toddler, she or he begins to separate even more from their parents. I have observed that this type of separation is often forced upon children who enter a fulltime daycare situation as infants. Many young children will develop similar energetic bonds to their daycare teachers. A thin etheric cord can be observed between these children and their teacher or teachers. In the infant and toddler rooms of some daycare centers, I have perceived this to be an energetic umbilical cord, very similar to that between parent and child.

These children can become very upset if their usual teacher is out sick or moves on to another job. Children may experience a separation anxiety that has been transferred from the parents, or added, to the usual daycare teacher. Slightly older children, particularly toddlers, may feel betrayed or abandoned if their teacher is seen working with other children in another room.

In some cases, children do not handle this well and cannot form the necessary bonds with a teacher. Most children will at least attempt to go to the teacher for protection—to be held within the teacher's energy field. But the chakras of other children are so shocked that they can do nothing. These are often the children that either cry all day long or isolate themselves and shut down their emotional reactions.

There is another issue involved with the emotional response to being left at daycare. Most of these children have formed significant bonds with their parents. When the parent leaves, the child not only loses a familiar buffer from outside influences, but she feels a tearing or stretching of the cord that binds her to her parent. This can be felt as a physical pain, as that cord is forced from the chakra binding it to the child. We may know this as that heartbreaking feeling when a lover breaks up with us, or when a loved one passes over.

Our energetic bonds to our children are never really broken, nor do they disappear as we get farther physically from our children. Much of our energy is still flowing into our children while they are very young. That is diminished when we are no longer in their proximity and are fully focused on other things. It is this that they are usually reacting to.

I do not include this to make any parent feel bad about using a daycare center. Daycare is a necessary, and often beneficial, fact of modern life. This is merely what I (and others) have observed. I include it so parents can make an informed choice. It is my intent to provide this information so parents can recognize these issues if they arise and handle them appropriately. My goal is simply to make you aware of the possibilities that may be causing changes in your children's behavior. Perhaps they need some additional time while you focus solely on them. They may need more physical contact or your undivided attention as they recount the events of the day.

Behavioral changes and issues do not mean a child is bad or that this is how the child will grow up. Certain changes are normal and necessary. Other changes may need to be addressed by some means other than punishment and Prozac.

Our son began attending daycare one day a week when he was two years old. We decided to gradually increase his days there. In this way, his system was not overly shocked by immediately jumping into full-time daycare. Furthermore, he was able to gradually develop bonds to his teachers and some of the children.

It took a while to find a center where he felt comfortable and could form these bonds to his teachers and to other students. I did pull him out of one center where the children were neglected and where he was obviously unhappy. But our children need to assimilate into our culture. We felt it would be a greater shock to his system to throw him into kindergarten after having had interaction only with family members.

We all do what we must and what we feel is best—as parents and as individuals. There is no point in second-guessing decisions that cannot be changed. However, we should be able to recognize when our children are in need spiritually, as well as physically.

For example, our son is very attached to me. Among other things, we have conjunct Moons in Pisces, which creates an intense and unavoidable psychic and emotional bond. He needs some additional Mommy-time when he comes home from daycare. Sometimes, all it takes is a few extra hugs; other days he needs some extended time and physical contact with me.

I would encourage all parents to have their children's astrological charts cast and interpreted. I would also caution you not to view astrology as a mere divination tool or as an absolute pre-determiner of personality. I have found that astrology is best used as a tool for determining tendencies, karmic patterns, and energies that will be impacting one's life, as well as for finding the best ways and times to communicate with certain individuals.

Some children need more recharging and comfort from a parent's energy field than others do. At this young age, it is counterproductive to pressure our children to toughen up. It is far more beneficial to their developing energy systems, as well as their emotional and psychological well being, to give them the comfort and support they require—within reason. Parents need down time too.

In any event, all children reach the point where their stuff is "Mine." This often accompanies the beginnings of imaginative play. By this time, they are fairly well integrated into their bodies and their lower chakras are beginning to develop. Toddlers now understand that they are individual beings. As a result, they begin to assign ownership to people, animals, and things.

Toddlers go through a constant struggle between being an individual with a defined personal auric field and being psychically connected to other life forms, as they were as infants. They are testing the waters of individuality. Sometimes your two-year-old will amaze you as she or he shares and offers certain toys to a playmate. That will change from minute to minute. Five minutes later, you may hear screaming because they decided that the toy is theirs, even if they do not want to play with it at the moment.

Remember how the infant's aura stretched out toward the things it focused on? This is taken to a new level in the toddler years. That stretching continues, but filaments of the child's energy field surround anything (or anyone) he or she decides belongs to them. These filaments remain attached to these things, becoming a part of the child's energy field. He or she feels the tearing or hole in their aura when these things are lost or taken away from them. To a child this young, psychic wounds are no different than physical wounds. They are felt just as intensely. Furthermore, physical wounds generally create auric wounds, and vice versa, thereby doubling the pain.

When a child is approximately seven years old, filters begin to form over their chakras, buffering the energy that flows into the child. No longer is the child open and vulnerable to all outside influences with no protection. As humans grow up, these filters strengthen.

Some of us learn to consciously use our chakra filters. However, most people in modern society are unaware of these shields. They are unable to use them for their own protection and may experience significant jars to their auric fields. As a result of shocks to the physical and energy bodies, one or more chakras may be partially blocked, fully closed, or even stuck wide open.

The child at this age no longer needs constant adult buffers. He or she has developed a distinct personal energy field. As their chakra filters form, children feel much safer away from their parents. They may spend more time with friends, visiting their houses or traveling about the neighborhood. They may even get involved in extracurricular activities at this point. Their energy fields are more protected and they are comfortable exploring their individuality.

By age seven, children have learned much of what is acceptable in society. They have assumed many of the cultural belief systems in their immediate environment. Depending on their society's culture, they may begin to block their interdimensional awareness. They are often involved in fitting in with other children, school, play, and television. Those other senses we all possess tend to be pushed into the realm of the unconscious in modern, mainstream families.

This is the perfect age to begin to encourage your children to use these abilities, before they are completely blocked. It is also a good time to begin some form of training program, as long as it is fun and does not evolve into work for the child. In many pagan traditions, children are dedicated to the path of their parents at this age and may begin to participate in some ritual workings, other than holiday celebrations. There are a number of metaphysical children's courses, like the Silva Method, that accept children beginning around this age.

The key is not to rigorously train our children, putting their self-esteem on the line and attempting to create superkids. Any training system begun with a child of this age should focus on learning to use these innate abilities, just as we learn to walk or talk. This should be a time full of fun and games and family involvement. Look at it as a way to play and be young again yourself, as you explore with your children.

As a child progresses in school and adapts to a modern technological society, their mental chakras begin to develop. This is not as pronounced in certain other cultures, but in our culture, the child learns to think and use their mental capacities from a very young age. Not only does this allow them to succeed in school, but it also provides fodder for active young imaginations.

Elementary school children are masters at make believe. They truly seem to create whatever it is that they are pretending. The influx of mental energy at this point only adds to their creative abilities. This also contributes to the productivity of any spiritual training process, and this is how we determine what elements to include for each age group.

In general, infants cannot be "trained," but they can be exposed to elements of the family religion and/or spirituality. This is the best way for children to grow up feeling these ways are natural and normal. However, it is very important that infants not be exposed to potentially dangerous or extreme magic. It is sufficient for them to attend holiday celebrations, Naming ceremonies, or other celebratory rituals that do not include strong magical forces.

Toddlers must be protected from similar types of energies. They gain the most benefit from holiday celebrations and they tend to enjoy these immensely. This is also the age where bedtime prayers and special stories make a big impact. Little ones (who are past the point of putting everything in their mouths) can be encouraged to collect stones and feathers and amulets. Be aware that possession of most wild bird feathers is illegal—this does not merely apply to birds of prey or endangered species. Domestic bird feathers, like turkey or goose, are wonderful beginning ritual tools for toddlers.

The toddler age is the time to introduce the concepts of faeries or angels and other helping spirits, respect for all life, and the fact that the Earth itself is alive too. This is a very active age, with a very short attention span. As a result, physically active rituals and exercises are essential. Beginning yoga, dances, songs, and easy games are favorites among children at this age. Toddlers also respond very well to introductory ritual elements, such as smudging, charging liquids, and saying thank-you to the Great Spirit/God/Goddess or spirits of the directions.

When the chakra filters of a child have begun to form, they may participate in more directed training. It is vital that we not only keep this training fun, but that we also refrain from pushing children to do anything that they strongly prefer not to. At this age, we use the ever-present make-believe focus to the child's advantage. We begin to use visualization games and exercises to help the child gain access to their own inner self, as well as develop stronger connections to helping spirits.

Young school age children excel at most of the games and exercises in this book. They may love to create their own altars and they take the initiative in many holiday celebrations. While some people have had success meditating with children as young as three, it is normally most productive beginning in the early school years. Keep in mind the attention span of each individual child as you meditate along with her or him. As long as you allow for giggle fits on occasion, it can be a truly wonderful practice to share with your children.

As children grow, so does their ability to focus for extended periods of time. Their abilities to ground and protect themselves also increase dramatically over the school-age years. Depending on the individual child, more focused meditations and simple rituals may be introduced. Participating in Moon rituals and assuming roles in holiday celebrations increase a child's independence and self-confidence. Children may take an interest in a specific deity or path. This should be encouraged whenever possible. Assist them in creating ritual clothing or tools.

Eventually your child reaches puberty and you wonder where your little boy or girl went. Some parents feel they don't even know their children and cannot understand them at this age. The truth is that sometimes your children don't know themselves either. A tremendous amount of change is occurring on all levels of being throughout adolescence. It can be a challenge for all involved just to get through it.

It is the opinion of many of us working in the metaphysical and alternative-healing fields that hormonal changes are directly related to spiritual changes. In fact, all physical events are preceded by a spiritual cause. With regard to puberty and the teenage years, the hormonal imbalances that make kids and their parents so crazy are related to another period of flux in the personal energy field.

Popularity and fitting in become even more important when one reaches puberty. Suddenly, the opposite sex (for most teenagers) is the most important thing in the world. They cannot stop thinking about their appearance, whether they are cool enough, if they hang out with the right crowd, and if that special someone likes them back. They seem to make a big deal out of everything and even a hair out of place is treated with absolute horror.

Teenagers sometimes become like toddlers once more, except to a much more complex degree. What may seem trivial to an adult is a matter of huge importance to a teen. Losing a boyfriend or girlfriend is accorded a similar reaction to that of the toddler whose favorite toy is taken by a playmate.

In fact, this is a similar event on an energetic level. Those filaments that attached toddlers to the people and things they decided were theirs are still around. And they still get attached to people and things that are "owned." This is not something that most people grow out of. To some extent, we all have these filaments connecting us to our people and our stuff.

With all the spiritual and physical changes going on in the body of an adolescent, the loss of a person or thing of importance can cause a very real wound in the personal energy field. An auric hole is opened up whenever one of these cords is torn free. This is particularly true when it comes to relationships with romantic interests and the very public nature of junior high and high school relationships.

Once again, the child is struggling with individuality and connections to others. This time, the individuality issue is more about being somewhere between child and adult, as well as establishing one's self in relation to peers. The chakras are fairly well defined by this time, but this is not the time to get children deeply involved in magical or psychic work. While they are connecting and testing their places within the community of other teens, they tend to be highly open on an emotional level. They frequently waver between experiencing wide-open heart chakras (and sometimes lower chakras) and shutting down in self-defense.

They do not have enough control over their emotions and their energy systems to handle the influence of everything they may encounter on a magical or psychic level. They may be ready for more advanced work, but they are still children. They continue to need the guidance and protection of a parent or guardian.

And so it is with these stages of development in mind that we will proceed with this book. There are no hard and fast rules and the development of the individual may vary slightly from what I have discussed here. The best way to know when your child is ready for something new is to get to know your child and develop your own intuition. As parents, this is a relatively easy task, since we are already connected to them on a psychic level.

3

Innate Psychic Abilities

With an understanding of the human energy systems, it should be clear that psychic abilities are a natural and innate part of the human condition. We all possess these abilities to some degree and use them at a very early age. It is only through the indoctrination of limiting beliefs and the total immersion in this three-dimensional reality that we block our interdimensional, or extra-physical, perception.

I prefer not to use the term "extrasensory perception." The implication that these senses and abilities are in some way "additional" precludes the possibility that they are a natural part of the human experience. In my opinion, it is our refusal to accept and develop them that is unnatural.

Few of us in the modern world take the time to be silent or alone. Most of us require continual background noise, even when we are just hanging out or working around the house. When we have nothing better to do, we watch television or surf the Internet. All of this interferes with our awareness of Self and Spirit.

This interference is one reason why many of us continually barrage ourselves with electronic noise and keep ourselves busy for all of our waking hours. These are blocking mechanisms that we have created to prevent us from having to face our inner selves. Too many of us have no real understanding of who we are, many of us do not know why we react as we do, and most of us don't really want to know. Facing the truth of oneself, with all that it may entail, is possibly the most frightening task of one lifetime.

Shamans and many other pagans work intensively with their shadow sides. The shadow side is that place within each of us where we hide all of our weaknesses, fears, embarrassments, etc. This is that dark place, deep within, where we keep all those aspects of Self that we do not want to acknowledge and do not want other people to know are a part of us. Unfortunately, repressing and denying these sides does not make them go away. Quite the opposite, it gives them even more power over our lives.

These repressed aspects become our unknown urges and the uncontrolled reactions. We may experience them as behavior or feelings that we have no control over. These aspects refuse to be denied and will use any opportunity to get us to face them. They manifest in all aspects of our lives, attracting situations that may be used as opportunities for growth. Often these situations are difficult and we cannot understand where they came from. We can move out of town, dump our current relationships, and switch jobs, but those uncomfortable patterns follow us everywhere.

Why do I bring this up in a book on pagan parenting? I do so for two very important reasons. The child who learns at an early age to know him or her Self and to act with wisdom, rather than react from ignorance, grows up to be a much happier and healthier adult. These are the children who will have the power to recreate our society and bring us into balance once again. As parents, an understanding of these issues allows us to be better guides for our children. The other reason may not be so obvious.

Anyone who works on a psychic level without clearing their own shadow issues will have difficulty *seeing* clearly and accurately. The shadow side will show up in all aspects of our lives.

This includes all levels of being. Repressed issues or memories can alter our perception on all levels.

These issues may show up (on all levels) as external beings or forces. Many of the frightening images that are encountered during dreaming and the early stages of shamanic journeying are simply the projection of our inner selves. These can also manifest in the people and situations around us. Our communities truly are mirrors of our selves.

It is for these reasons that I encourage people to maintain a balance between inner work, such as meditation and shamanic journeying, and outer work, like magic and ritual. As parents, it is our responsibility to guide and protect our children. This includes getting to know our Selves. When considering involving children in any type of metaphysical working, we need to make our decisions based on what is best for their total soul growth. Imbalance does not lead to healthy development. Self-knowledge leads to true wisdom and power.

We know that children begin this incarnation more connected to the other dimensions than this one. We also know that as we grow, our focus shifts to a three-dimensional perception, altering our experience, but what does this mean in terms of usable abilities?

Generally speaking, these "extra" senses and levels of being are just like the physical in that they are usable to the extent that we develop them. They can be compared to an unused muscle that gets stronger and more flexible with use. It is also true that our individual talents may differ.

For example, a great baseball player is not necessarily a great violinist, although he or she may be. Willow may be fantastic at entering deep trance and returning with accurate and pertinent information. Shadowhawk, on the other hand, may struggle with trance but may be very telepathic in everyday life. It is important to keep this in mind when working within a specific path or with a certain area of psychic ability.

Few of us are highly talented in every area of life. I was a good pilot, a fair swimmer, and really bad at throwing a football. Such is life this time around and I work within my talents. This does not mean that I do not have a lot of fun playing with the areas where I am less talented. But to put pressure on oneself to achieve greatness in all areas, or perfection in any one area at all times, is counterproductive.

Set realistic goals for yourself and your children. Do your best to laugh at your mistakes and play with your successes. Use each experience as an opportunity for growth and learning. Support each other in the process. I strongly suggest that you work to develop your own way of *seeing*.

Seeing and *sight* are generic terms used to describe the ways in which we receive telepathic, prophetic, or Otherworldly information and communications. Literally, it means the perception of visions or the ability to perceive spirits. But our perception of these things differs. Just as we differ in this reality between being predominantly visual, auditory, or sensory, these tendencies carry over into the psychic realms.

One person may receive visions or see spirits, almost as if with his physical eyes. Another individual may hear voices resulting from a telepathic link. She may hear voices or other sounds indicating the presence of spirits or an overlap of realities. Still another may perceive these things with some type of feeling. These feelings may be physical sensations, such as a chill or tingling, or they may be simply a *knowing*. When we receive communications or impressions in this way, we just *know* what the spirit wants to communicate, that there is someone "else" present or what another person is thinking or feeling. The key is to determine in what area your strengths lie and to separate your own stuff from that of others.

The goal, whatever it may be, is a wonderful thing to set one's sights on. But the process, the journey, is really the place to be. Being present, in the now, is the only place we really can be. Living in the future or the past is an avoidance tactic. So I invite you all to become explorers, rather than seekers.

Our children are great explorers and we can learn a great deal from them. Rather than seeking and looking for something "out there" that we feel is missing, children explore what is present right now. Fully experience the place you are in and the growth potential you are presented with each day. In this way, you become a shining example for your children and all those around you.

With all that said, let's get on with learning to develop our own talents (and of course, those of our children) and to use them for our greatest benefit. I have separated what one might term "psychic" abilities into subsections of this chapter. Each subsection contains a description of the ability and exercises or games that will help in developing that strength. Parents should be encouraged to play along with children. Make it a family affair and have fun with it.

Also, be aware of what areas your children prefer and encourage them to develop those areas. Areas in which they are ambivalent or that they dislike should not be pushed. They may just have no interest in these areas, or perhaps their intuition tells them that their strengths lie in other areas. Perhaps they are just not ready for these areas yet. Whatever the reason, we do not want to create blocks or resistance to these areas. Go with the flow, as they say.

Breathing

Breathing is certainly an innate ability. We all breathe, but why discuss it in this type of book? Because it is incredibly important in our abilities to remain focused, emotionally stable, and to assist us in attaining trance states. (Much of this section is reprinted exactly as it appeared in *The Shamanic Guide to Death and Dying*.)

As stated in *Shamanic Guide to Death and Dying*, we can see the impact of the body on the breath, and the breath on the body, during an emotional outburst. When we are frightened or very upset, we begin to breathe more quickly and from the chest. Unfortunately, chest breathing is quite common during normal functioning in our society. The shallowness of chest breathing reduces our oxygen intake and fatigues the body-mind. This effectively puts our body and mind in a state of constant anxiety and stress.

On the other hand, when we are calm and centered, such as we are when meditating, our breathing is significantly different.

During these times, the breath fills us from the diaphragm through to our shoulders. We breathe slowly and deeply. It is no surprise that when we want someone to calm down, we inevitably tell them to "take a deep breath" and relax.

The control of the breath is an integral part of most spiritual, shamanic and magical training. Through the breath, we can regulate our systems to allow ourselves to slip easily into trance. *Pranayama*, put very simply, is the yogic practice of breath control.

Prana, meaning the flow of energy of the universe, is the link between body and mind. This flow of energy is vital to health and life. Prana moves through the breath. As Swami Rama describes in *Science of Breath*, the "science of pranayama is thus intimately connected with the autonomic nervous system and brings its functioning under conscious control through the functioning of the lungs."[1]

This is the one exception to that rule we were all taught in high school biology: that the autonomic nervous system processes are involuntary. This is also where a student of any pagan path derives the greatest benefits, and this is one of the simplest and most powerful tools a parent can offer a child.

Through the conscious variation of inhalation and exhalation, and through maintaining diaphragmatic breathing during everyday life, we can regulate our responses both to everyday reality and to our Otherworldly experiences. Rather than instantly being thrown into a fight-or-flight fear response, which can paralyze the mind and spirit, we have the ability to step back from the situation. Through the simple control of the breath, we can remain calm and centered, then view things from a much more confident and expanded perspective. This is also what enables us to enter trance states at will and with full control.

While it sounds simple, this may take some practice. The breath does not stop when we forget about it. It automatically kicks in and continues our habitual breathing patterns. Life has

---

1   Swami Rama, Rudolph Ballentine, M.D., and Alan Hymes, M.D. *Science of Breath* (Himalayan International Institute of Yoga Science and Philosophy) p. 95.

a way of taking one's focus away from the breath. This is usually when the shallower chest breathing returns, along with its associated tension and stress.

For children, developing an awareness of the breath and working with its control can be extremely beneficial in assisting the release of attachments and fears, as well as centering and opening to spirit guides. It can prevent unnecessary outbursts and arguments. It has the potential to greatly increase a child's control over their own behavior and help them to see situations with much wiser perception. It would be beneficial to encourage your children to include breath control when working with the games and exercises outlined in this book. I also suggest guiding children in an awareness of how they are breathing in everyday life, how it makes them feel, and how to change their breathing at will.

When I was in elementary school band, our teacher showed us a wonderfully simple way to determine just where you are breathing from and how to be sure you have switched to diaphragmatic breathing. Lying on your back, place one hand (or a light book) over the center of your chest and one on your abdomen. As you inhale, whichever hand rises indicates where your breath is entering your body. Deeper and slower inhalations bring more oxygen, more energy, and less stress. This type of breathing, called diaphragmatic breathing, invigorates the body.

Once we have developed an awareness of this, we can move on to slowing the breath. According to *Science of Breath*, it is considered the average to take between sixteen and twenty breaths per minute.[2] While pranayama is an involved discipline that also takes years to master, I will make two suggestions for exercises to practice with children. Both of these exercises are very simple and will encourage the experience of calm and balance. These are particularly recommended for anyone who is experiencing pain, fear, or any type of emotional distress.

---

2 Ibid., p. 109.

Breathing Exercise 1

Place your full attention on your breathing. Do not attempt to alter it, just observe for a few moments. Where does your breathing seem to come from? How do you feel at this moment? If there is any tension in your body, where is it localized?

Slow your breathing. Count to three on each inhalation and again, on each exhalation.

Breathe deeply, filling your lungs from the bottom first. Feel your diaphragm stretch and expand as your abdomen moves out. As you exhale, feel your abdomen contract as the breath leaves from the bottom of your lungs first.

Breathe into any areas of tension or stress. Feel your breath fill and relax these areas. With each breath, tension and pain melt away.

Once you feel comfortable with this exercise, increase the count for inhalations and exhalations.

Practice this several times a day, particularly when you are feeling stressed or are in pain.

Breathing Exercise 2

Recommended only for older children, or for those who have easily mastered Breathing Exercise 1.

Beginning with Breathing Exercise 1, begin to alter the count of inhalations and exhalations.

Starting slowly, work toward a 1:2 ratio between inhalations and exhalations. For example, if your inhalation lasts for four counts, your exhalation will last for eight counts.

Do not increase this ratio too quickly. If you are gasping for air and desperately sucking in the inhalation, you should return to Breathing Exercise 1.

Dreaming

One area in which kids tend to be way ahead of adults is dreaming. Young children have not yet assimilated those blocks and limiting beliefs that most adults have. As a result, they remember vivid and clear dreams. Many children will remember several dreams from the previous night. How many adults can say that?

Don Juan Matus said that dreaming is one of the two main avenues to power; the bridge between our tonal and nagual selves.[3] The art of dreaming and dream interpretation was of particular importance to most ancient cultures. Dreams captivate us with possibility and wonder. In dreams, it seems, all things are possible.

Dreams are not only bridges to our inner selves and our subconscious issues, they are frequently out-of-body journeys. Teaching our children to utilize these abilities is, in effect, giving them the tools to self-knowledge and power. An individual that is able to master the dual nature of dreaming can do and create just about anything.

Individuals that work intensively with dreaming learn to create and alter realities. They develop the ability to completely attune themselves to spirit guidance. They are shamans, in a sense, in that they gain an experiential understanding that life is not what it appears in this reality through their conscious and deliberate journeying between worlds.

Dreams are a fun way to play with abilities without any pressure. It is part pretend, part exploration and investigation. Kids who are still masters at imaginative play are sure to be dream masters too. Learning your own symbols is like cracking a code. It can easily be made into a game with plenty of story telling involved.

Dream Interpretation Exercise

To teach dream interpretation, encourage your children to keep their own dream journal. If they cannot read and write well

---

3 Don Juan Matus was Carlos Castenada's mentor. Reprinted with permission from *The Teachings of Don Carlos* by Victor Sanchez (Santa Fe: Bear & Co.), pp. 175–177.

enough to do their own, you may want to keep one for them at first.

> Begin by simply writing down everything that happened. The goal is to get into as much detail as possible. Asking questions as the child relates the story will help them access details they may have missed.
>
> Try to cover the following aspects of each dream: Who or what was in it? What time of day or night did it take place? Where did it take place? What happened? When and where did each event take place? What was said or heard? How did the child feel at each point? See if you can get very specific about clothing, colors, sounds, smells, feelings, and the size and placement of people and things in the dream.
>
> Once your child (or you) can access the details, move on to taking each piece of the dream as a symbol. For example, say the dream contained a big blue bus driven by a mouse. What is the first thing that comes to mind when you think of blue, a bus, big, a mouse, driving, etc? What types of things do you associate with each element? Then, do the same exercise for the whole picture, and the whole dream. We want to see the dream holistically, as well as broken down into individual parts.

Encourage your children to share by setting aside a time to hear everyone's stories. Make it fun and be honestly interested in hearing what they have to say. Reciprocate and teach by example, through sharing your dreams as well. Allow your children's interest to stimulate your own openness and creativity, and to help you regain control over your own dreaming. As we all know, parenting is a two-way street; a give-and-take relationship, in which we learn and grow at least as much as our children do.

Sometimes, a dream will appear to be so real that it couldn't be "just a dream." Occasionally, you will be aware that you are dreaming during the dream. These dreams are probably astral travels, or out-of-body journeys. This is also what is referred to as lucid dreaming.

The astral body is akin to the shamanic free soul. It is part of one's total energy: an energy body that is free to travel without the physical body. People have many differing beliefs regarding this. Some see it as a separate energy body that actually leaves the physical body and journeys to other realities.

Some people believe this is not truly another body and that we don't "go" anywhere, but our perception is sufficiently altered that we have access to Other realities. There is no time or space, except in our own mental constructs in our three-dimensional experience. How you choose to view it is irrelevant, as long as it works for you.

Children will almost always perceive this as a double body that is free to travel around without the physical body. When explaining this to children, be sure to let them know that the astral body is connected to the physical body by a silver cord. As a result, the child cannot get lost outside the body. They can always find their way home by following that silver cord. I have included a Silver Cord Game in chapter 4.

Keep in mind that our perception of reality is defined by many things. In this reality, and while associating ourselves with the identities of this incarnation, we do not see the full picture. Much of our experience is colored by our beliefs. These beliefs are responsible for how we create our experience of this reality.

My point is that our children learn by how we describe things and how we react. If we teach them that they can always get home by following that silver cord, they will believe that. We can be very convincing when our actions show that we believe it as well. In this way, the protection of the silver cord will become real for them. They will be comfortable traveling out of body and they will never get lost.

This is more than indoctrinating a beneficial belief. It is providing a tool to create realities and to manifest what is needed. We are giving them a head start on magic. For after all, what is magic but the ability to effect change on one's reality?

It is not uncommon for parents and children to share dreams and to journey out of body together. My son and I have shared dreaming since he was born. We have been able to use this to move him past some difficult past-life memories that created nightmares when he was approximately one year old. I remember clearly playing and traveling with my mother when I was a child, while our physical bodies slept.

There is one night from my childhood that I remember vividly. I had been up and about at night as usual, without my physical body. I went to the foot of the couch where my mother was reading. I called to her. She whipped her head around to stare at me with wide eyes and got up to check on me (my body). I remember following her into the doorway of my bedroom. The sight of my physical body, in bed without me, was very unsettling. I was so startled that I was pulled immediately back into my body.

Parents need to keep this in mind when responding to perceived calls in the night from their children. Frequently, our children are wandering around without their physical bodies. This is normal and is nothing to be concerned about. Sometimes, they will come to us looking for comfort or play, or whatever they usually come to us for while they are awake. When we respond by going to their rooms, and find they are still sleeping soundly, it is a good idea to send them some extra love. The first time anyone sees his or her physical body from the outside can be very unnerving.

Our son comes to me less frequently now than when he had just moved from the "family bed" into his own room. It was always quite clear to me when he was present as his free soul alone. I made it a practice to curl him up into me, as I do when we are awake and hugging or cuddling. We cuddle for a while and I take him back to bed, as I always do when he physically falls asleep in my arms. I gently place him down with his body and kiss him goodnight. In this way, the nightly excursions are not something unusual to which I react with ignorance or fear. He gets his love and comfort and goes back to bed as always. Consistency and calmness are the key.

Lucid dreaming has become so much a part of our collective consciousness, as a concept if not a reality, that it has found its way into some surprisingly mainstream arenas. I was very pleased to see that the *Blue's Clues* television show that my son loved so much actually had an episode devoted to changing dreams, specifically taking the scary objects out of nightmares. This is a wonderful, empowering example for children. It also brings this topic into the mainstream, allowing children to openly talk about it without fear of ridicule.

To help our children work with lucid dreaming, we must do two things. First and foremost, we must support and encourage them unconditionally. Our children need us to believe and become excited right along with them, and it certainly doesn't hurt to play dreaming games with them.

Second, we must work to be the best guides we are capable of being. Start simple and direct your explanations to the language level of each individual child. If your children have nightmares, begin by having them practice calling in a spirit guardian or a parent. Also, have them experiment with changing the dream. Perhaps they can walk out a door into a happy place or make friends with the monster. Then pay attention to your own dreams as well. If your child calls you, you may remember the experience.

Lucid Dreaming Exercises

If your child is not experiencing nightmares, have him or her play with their dreams. They can experiment with going to places they know. If you want to, you may be able to verify their information the next day. Have them meet with spirit guides or change objects in their dream. Encourage them to allow their imagination to run wild. Give them the freedom to create what they will. This is a stepping stone to creation in our reality, as well as being one of the keys to self-knowledge.

Depending on the severity of a nightmare, we can play with changing these, as well. You may want to begin by having your child practice being able to recognize she or he is in a dream and wake from it. This way the child is out of the dream and develops confidence in their abilities during dreaming.

The easiest way to do this is to establish a dreaming cue. This is a sign to the child that will indicate that he or she is really dreaming. This often takes the fear out of a nightmare and allows control to be regained. People who practice looking at their hands in a dream often use this as a cue. They have inserted a hypnotic suggestion that, upon seeing their hands in a dream, they will realize they are dreaming and will be able to wake up whenever they choose. You might choose something fun or unusual for the child, perhaps the sight of a yellow balloon or a purple stop sign.

Dreaming Cue Exercise

To create an image as a dreaming cue, all you need to do is guide your child through a simple meditation.

> Count them down from ten to one in your usual manner. Remind them periodically to pause and take a deep breath; that they are going deeper into relaxation. At the count of one, remind them that they are perfectly relaxed and comfortable.
>
> Guide them to their favorite place of relaxation, either imagined or real. Once there, have them imagine falling asleep. Have them feel going even deeper. If they do actually fall asleep, continue with the meditation. They are still able to follow your voice. You may choose to repeat this at another time when they are more able to stay awake throughout.
>
> Suggest to them that they are now dreaming. Get all their senses involved by asking them to feel the temperature, hear the sound of their footsteps, see where they are, and smell the air. Then have them visualize the cue you have decided upon.
>
> Again, get all their senses involved in really creating this cue. Spend some time making this visualization

and experience as real and clear as possible. Now, ask them to say (mentally, if you both prefer) after you, that whenever they see this image (be specific) they will instantly recognize that they are dreaming. Repeat this twice. Continue by saying that whenever they see this image and realize they are dreaming, they will be in total control of the dream. Repeat this twice. Say together, that they can awaken themselves whenever they choose and can change or end the dream in any way they want.

Have them return to their favorite place of relaxation. Tell them that they can always return to this place whenever they need to and they will be safe and comfortable here. Then, count them up from one to ten, in your usual manner. Stop periodically to remind them that they are coming up slowly and that at the count of ten, they will be wide awake and feeling great.

Shared Dreaming Exercise

A great exercise for parents and children is shared dreaming.

Decide to meet each other one night. Discuss how you will set up your dreaming and what you will tell yourselves before falling asleep. See the section on "Problem-Solving Through Dreams" for a simple way to set up dreaming. You may wish to begin by deciding on a familiar place to meet.

The next day, share your experiences. See how many details you can remember and how many images you share, even if your initial images do not include each other. Don't be discouraged if your memories don't match up. Either you have not yet learned your personal symbols or you just didn't remember that particular dream experience. Practice will improve your memory and ability.

Another wonderful way to work with dreams is use them for problem-solving or guidance. We have used dreaming to find lost objects, to gain guidance in making decisions, and just for fun. This can be done in one of two ways.

Answer Faeries Exercise

This exercise came out of my own experience with helping spirits, what my Saami ancestors call *saivo* spirits, and it has been adapted for dreaming. The saivo are generally Nature spirits, although they can be little people who live in the Earth. They act as helpers and go-betweens for us when we need assistance.

I chose to use faeries for two reasons. First, because they have become a common element in our culture. And second, because they are often related to Nature and they are completely non-threatening. Those of you who are well versed in the various kinds of faery folk may want to distinguish these faeries as devas or Nature elves, as opposed to the Great Elves or the Sidhe of Celtic paganism.

> First, count down from ten to one, in your usual manner, just before going to sleep. You may either do this for your child, or older children may do this for themselves. In that calm, relaxed place, have them call on the Answer Faeries to come join them and help them answer their questions.
>
> Give them a few moments, and then ask them what the faeries look like. Ask them how many have come to play with him or her tonight. Have them greet the faeries and thank them for coming to help. Even if you are not really aware of the faeries, greet them and thank them yourself. Now, guide the child to tell the faeries what it is that he or she wants help with. Help them get as specific as possible. You may wish to discuss this in advance.
>
> Guide the child to ask for the faeries' help tonight and get an answer to him or her within a specific

amount of time. Some people believe that three days, or seventy-two hours is a magical period of time. It doesn't really matter, unless you believe it does. Asking for an answer by the following morning works just as well, although, some very involved issues may take some time before a complete answer is received.

Problem-Solving Through Dreams Exercise

In order to set up dreaming, count down from ten to one just before going to sleep. In that calm, relaxed place, get a clear picture of the question or problem you are seeking to solve in your mind. Tell yourself that you will have a dream tonight that will give you the answer or some guidance to find the answer to resolution. State, with intent, that you will have the answer to your situation, or a path to this answer will be apparent by the following morning—and you will remember and understand it. Allow yourself to fall asleep. Although it may take some practice and a degree of trust, it really is as simple as that!

With all dreaming exercises, I highly recommend keeping a pad and paper right beside your bed. It is a good idea to write down (or use a tape recorder) everything you remember as soon as you wake up. Throughout the course of a day, or even just through the process of waking fully, many people will lose details of a dream. The entire dream itself may actually be forgotten as time passes.

There is one other possibility in dream recall. Some dreams may not be immediately accessible to the conscious mind upon awakening. For this reason, I suggest that older children and adults carry their pad and pencil with them throughout the day. It is quite common for a dream to be spontaneously remembered later in the day. It is also very possible that something you see or hear may spark the memory of the dream. I have had dreams brought to mind by billboards along the road, things people around me say, and even television commercials.

Telepathy

Telepathy is generally defined as the ability to communicate on a nonverbal level. Some people may think of it as the ability to read minds. Telepathy is often distinguished from empathy as being more mental, while empathy is more emotional. Personally, I perceive the only real difference to be how the individual receives psychic information.

A person who tends to be highly mental, or even auditory, may pick up impressions from those around them in a "mind-reading" kind of way. These people may receive words or pictures. Someone who tends more toward feeling is more likely to be empathic (not empathetic) and receive these impressions as emotions or sensory feelings. The telepath may know what someone is thinking; the empath feels their emotions and may even experience similar physical sensations.

We are all interconnected by Spirit. Some modern physicists believe that reality is really a holographic matrix of frequencies. We create our own reality by focusing on specific frequencies, thereby making them "real." Some modern physicists have described subatomic structures as a web that interconnects all entities. Pagans describe this as the Web of Life, and we do not limit it to physical life.

Our thoughts and emotions are out there in the Web for anyone to pick up on. Some of us shield ourselves better than others do, but there are plenty of people who unknowingly pick up on these psychic impressions. There are also those who would probe an unsuspecting person for information or simply for entertainment.

Why do pagan parents care about developing telepathy, or any of these psychic abilities in themselves and their children? There are innumerable reasons that will vary according to the individual. However, these are abilities that expand our own experiences of our spirit guides, the God, Goddess, and the

Great Spirit. They also increase our effectiveness in divination and healing.

So what are the ethics involved in telepathy or empathy? Do these ethics differ from those we apply to psychic/magical healing? And how does this vary from reading a person's tone of voice or body language? These are complex questions that could probably take up a book on their own.

Suffice it to say that we must do what we feel is right for us. In cases like this, the Wiccan Rede, "An it harm none, do what ye will," is a good guideline. In truth, the idea behind the Rede has its roots in many cultures and religions. However, your use of this as a guide will depend on your definition of harm and whether an invasion of privacy is applicable. Generally, we can go by spirit guidance or intuitive/gut feelings. If you question it or wouldn't be comfortable telling others about it, don't do it.

Some people make a distinction between reading what is out there for all to see and probing for deeper, more private information. In general, I tend to agree with this distinction. I believe that it is unethical and harmful to expect people to shut off their innate telepathic or empathic impressions for fear that they may learn something beneath the surface. If we are to go to this extreme, we may as well refuse to acknowledge any body language or tones of voice in communication. We may as well rely solely on email, where to go on there are only the words given in a message.

This is a tricky area for parents, especially psychic parents. In chapter 2, we learned that we are connected to our children from pregnancy by one or more energy cords. It is through these cords that we intuitively *know* when our children are upset or injured. We often receive telepathic or empathic impressions through these connections.

Some parents will know exactly what a child is thinking, as though the child spoke the words. I will often ask my mother to at least let me say it on occasion before she answers me. Similarly, I had to consciously stop answering our son's telepathic communications and make him speak to me when he was learning to talk. It had become far too easy to communicate on a purely psychic level and he was not verbalizing enough when I was around.

We receive these impressions in different ways. Most of us tend toward one or two areas, with less emphasis on the third. Many parents *feel* their children's wounds, whether physical or emotional, as though they were their own injuries. Others *see* visions of their children; or *hear* a child cry or call the parent's name.

Most people who live together will develop a basic telepathic link. This is when we finish each other's sentences and just *know* what the other person is thinking and feeling without needing to say a word. Living together, especially as a family, harmonizes our energies and strengthens those energetic cords. So, working with your own children in this area is merely developing and honing interactions that are probably already occurring without your conscious recognition. This usually makes things very easy.

Telepathy can be a fantastic game to play with families. By the time I was a teenager, my mother and I had gotten so good at *reading* each other, we would joke about maybe using the telephone once in a while. The following are some of my favorite games from childhood, plus some new ones we have devised. They are listed in order of increasing age level.

Find Your Photo Game

This is a silly game that reminds many people of the testing games played by psychic experts on television shows. It can be played for prizes or simply for fun. As the parent, it is up to you to decide whether receiving a prize for giving correct answers would create an issue for your child. If there is any doubt, it is probably best just to play for fun. For some children, there is likely to be enough competition, even in the absence of other players, without adding the element of a prize.

> Start out by assembling some photos in manila
> envelopes. Include some of places your child has never
> seen (in this lifetime), one current one of the child or
> children, and a few of people, places, or animals that
> the child knows well. You can proceed in one of two

ways. You can play double-blind, so that neither of you knows which photo is in which envelope, thereby eliminating the possibility that the child is picking up the image from your mind.

Or you can number the envelopes, keeping a list of what photo is in which number envelope. Then when you ask the child what the picture is, you can immediately gauge their accuracy and possibly coach them along. This is a good way to develop telepathy between the two of you and to establish a common set of symbols. This will also aid you in dream interpretation. Furthermore, it is an excellent tool for developing the clarity you may need if you ever receive disturbing impressions about your children.

Story Time Game
This can be a really fun and creative game.

Begin by making up a basic outline for a story. You may wish to write it all down as you play. Have one person be the StoryWeaver and start the story by telling a few sentences to get things moving. The StoryWeaver will then step back from the game and begin to send one image at a time to the group. This is the person who will direct the storytelling, through projecting images and by jumping in verbally to get things moving again, if necessary.

Encourage the other players to say whatever pops into their minds spontaneously and weave that into the story. Allow yourself, as StoryWeaver, to pick up impressions from the other players and incorporate these, as well. It may be necessary to create rules for the game, like taking turns.

The Newspaper Game

Using an unread newspaper, have each person select a page. Work with partners or in a group. Have the "sender" focus on a specific article at a time from their page. The "receiver(s)" communicate anything that comes to mind. Feel comfortable enough to communicate whether the sender needs to focus more or if the receiver(s) are "hot or cold." This is another fun way to work on accuracy and personal symbolism.

The Doctor Is In Game

This game is similar to the Newspaper Game in the partnering and receipt of psychic impressions.

Each person will come to the game with one or more "patient cases." These cases are either people that the guiding individual knows, but the doctor-partner does not, or people from the news or other media, who are in need of some type of healing. This does not need to be limited to physical healing.

The guiding partner will count the doctor down from ten to one and then give the doctor only the patient's name. As the doctor receives impressions, the guide continually meditates on the case at hand. The guide either confirms the doctor's findings or states that this information is unknown.

We rarely have complete and total knowledge of any individual and we do not want to tell the doctor that he or she is wrong unless we are absolutely certain of our facts. Information has come out of these sessions that was previously unknown, even by an individual's physician.

The doctor is encouraged to go with any impressions he or she receives, even if they do not initially appear to be related to the patient. As these impressions come through, the doctor may perform any healing he or she feels is necessary, from visualizing the patient healed to sending specific energy. The guide is also responsible for maintaining a grounding energy for herself and the doctor.

When the session is complete, the guide will either count the doctor back up for a debrief or continue with another patient. This is a choice to be determined by the parents and should be based on your child's ability to ground energy, maintain personal shielding, and his or her level of endurance. This game should never tire anyone out or leave someone feeling irritable or ill.

The debrief is a perfect way to end this type of game. It allows the situation to be discussed and the number of hits and misses to be evaluated. Sometimes, what may initially be regarded as a miss will be recognized as a hit, when viewed from another perspective.

A perfect example of this is a story from my own experience with this game. I was approximately thirteen years old and playing this game with a friend of the family. When we got to my second patient, I could not get a clear image of anyone but a friend from school. I could not get her out of my head. Sometimes, this is because another person requires our attention at that time.

In this case, it was a question of symbolism. I said to my friend that I was getting nowhere and could not get past this other friend with brown hair, who had just gotten a new hairstyle. I said I must need a break. My friend was astounded because the patient also had brown hair and had just gotten a haircut the previous day, completely changing her hairstyle.

Psychometry Game

Psychometry games should always be played with other well-known and trusted individuals, especially when playing with children.

> Pass around personal items until no one is sure whose item they are holding. Have each person share what he or she is receiving from the item. Communicate any feelings, thoughts, mental pictures, etc., that the item triggers. This is an excellent way to hone accuracy and develop personal symbolism.

Working with the Aura

The aura, as most of us are aware, is the human energy field. All living things produce an electromagnetic energy field that can be measured or *felt* in various ways. I highly recommend the works of Barbara Brennan and Rosalyn Bruyere for anyone interested in working with the aura or energetic healing.

The aura is comprised of several levels, each corresponding to a chakra and an energy body. You may perceive all seven chakras within each individual energy body, as opposed to only the chakra associated with that level. The auric levels generally alternate between the amorphous masses of color and the more defined, almost web-like bodies. The following descriptions are my own perceptions of these levels. You and your children may *see* them differently. Your perceptions may differ slightly. Please keep in mind that each of these levels, while different, is interconnected with all other levels, including the physical.

Within a few inches of the physical body is a web of white or blue-white energy. This seems to be easiest to see around the head. Over that is an amorphous mass, often initially *seen* as colorless. This is the emotional level, and with practice, one can perceive varying colors that can change according to one's emotional state. It is at this level that we first observe individual colors associated with chakras. Next is another web, this time a white-yellow energy grid. This appears to be a mental level and

changes in thoughts will alter this level. These three are generally believed to be those levels most involved in the creation and
maintenance of the physical body.

The heart level is the point of balance, the first level above the
physical. This is the level of the astral body. It appears to be very
similar to the emotional body, but the colors are often more
vibrant or intense. Above this are the three spiritual bodies. The
fifth level is also called the light body. It is generally seen in varying shades of blue and white, usually much deeper than the first
level and vastly larger. This body is not limited to the physical
form and expands into one of the first egg-shaped bodies.

The sixth level is often called the celestial body and is related
to the third eye. This is like a star of colored light. Finally,
beyond the celestial body is the ketheric level. Kether is the
Kabbalic crown and this level is associated with the crown
chakra. This is the golden luminous egg described by shamans
and psychics, and is quite likely the basis of the heavenly halo
shown in paintings of Jesus Christ and the Christian saints.

I give this basic description as a guide. I also offer these words
of advice: to *see* the individual levels takes a great deal of practice
for most people. It may take a lifetime for most people to be able
to separate these levels and to *see* all of them. However, there are
many people who easily perceive the first few levels at different
times, depending on a number of factors. This guide should help
those people to understand what they are *seeing*.

Shake Hands Game

This is one of the simplest and most profound ways to learn to
feel the human energy field.

> It may help to rub your hands together before and
> after. If you wish, you may count down from ten to
> one beforehand, but this is usually not necessary.
>
> Sit or stand together. Hold out your hands, as
> though you were going to shake hands. Stop just
> before actually touching the other person's hand.
> Notice any feeling or impression you get when your

hands are very close together. Many people will feel a warmth, tingling, or resistance similar to touching two north (or two south) poles of a magnet together.

Now, play with this by slowly moving your hands further apart and then closer together. Be aware of any feelings or impressions that either person receives. Learn to trust your instincts. Practice this at different times to get a feel for how the aura changes. It will normally *feel* different after work or school than it might after meditation or ritual.

Movie Star Game

What child doesn't love to play movie star, even if it is just for family? Playing movie star is a great way to learn to *see* the aura.

Take turns standing before a plain, solid-colored wall, or movie screen. The "audience" should center themselves as much as possible. In the beginning, it is a good idea to count down from ten to one, or play this game after meditation.

Pay attention to the edges of the body of the movie star, particularly the head. Try not to fix your eyes on any one spot, but see if you can blur your vision, or simply gaze at the star. As the star moves, you may notice an image that remains or follows behind his or her motions. Some people find this easier to recognize in the beginning as a true afterimage. They will watch, then close their eyes and see an image or colors in the basic shape of the person.

If the movie star is into acting, he or she can call up different emotions, or play various parts for the audience. You might want to try this before and after a meditation or ritual. Watch to *see* the changes in size, shape, and color or the aura. If you do not *see* color at first, or even for a long time, do not be concerned. Many people do not and it is not important. There are other ways to gauge the condition of energy and the aura without the *sight* of color.

This is an exercise or game that is wonderful to play any time you are listening to a speaker. Speakers and lecturers tend to project a great deal as they speak, especially around the head. Again, do not stare or fix your eyes at any one spot, but watch and be aware of any images, particularly those around the edges of your visual field.

The Plant Experiment Game

I expect that many pagans have played this game in one form or another, with one's own energy, with crystals, pyramids, Moon blood, or ritual magic. The basic idea is that plants respond to changes in the universal energy field. We can directly affect this field by directing our personal energy with a specific intent, so it is really plant magic.

> In a distant approximation of scientific method, we will use a test subject and a control subject. Choose two plants of the same species, preferably the same age and condition. Do not change anything in your behavior or the environment of the control plant. The test plant will also remain in the same environment and receive the same food and water as the control plant. The only change will be energy directed to the test plant.
>
> Since, as pagans, we would never intentionally harm a living being, we direct healing and loving energy to the test plant. Do this on a regular basis for a period of at least six months. Keep track of any changes in either plant. You will most likely notice an increase in growth or a deepened color in the test plant. There are certainly other variables that may interfere, especially when this experiment is performed in a home, rather than a completely controlled

laboratory environment, but some type of change should be noticeable after six months.

There are a great number of games to play in this chapter, all having to do with some type of psychic ability. I offer these as suggestions for you to have fun and develop as a family. Don't attempt to do all of them at once. If this becomes at all stressful or ceases to be fun, put it on hold and go take a walk, or play a mainstream game.

As pagans, we seek balance in all things. Psychic work must be balanced with ritual and physical work or play. A full day of meditation may be wonderful, but it is even more special and valuable if balanced with a bike ride or a game of baseball in the park. We do not serve our soul growth if we neglect one aspect of Self in the hope of developing another, and our children need to be allowed to be children. In fact, we adults need to be allowed to be children too.

4

Protection and Grounding

As parents, it is our both our desire and our responsibility to protect our children. We do whatever is necessary to keep them safe and healthy so that they may grow into happy, healthy individuals. As pagan parents, we recognize that this protection must extend beyond the physical realm.

Pagan parents are very aware that nonphysical energies affect our children, whether these energies come from other people, the natural world, or from the Otherworlds. In order to best guide and protect our children, we must educate ourselves. Not only should we learn various protection methods, but we also must develop an understanding of the realities of these additional influences.

We lead by example. When it comes to protection and guidance, particularly in the magical/psychic realms, we can do more harm than good if we allow our own imaginations and subconscious fears to get the better of us. It is essential that we work through our own stuff before we needlessly frighten our children.

I have known pagan parents to react to unknown energies in ways that caused unnecessary fear and nightmares in their children. Often, these were during rituals that had frightening connotations to the uninformed, usually Voudoun or ceremonial magic. Individuals that are completely new to the energies and experiences of these types of deities and religions can easily overreact. I have seen parents misinterpret the effects of certain rituals to the point that they were asked to leave.

I remember one night in particular when several friends of the family were invited to observe a specific African ritual. One young man's parents were so wrapped up in their fear of the unknown and the associated beliefs that this ritual had evoked some destructive energies that they were utterly unaware that they had terrified their son. He ended up sleeping with my family that night for protection. The reality was that these parents were unaccustomed to the feel of this particular pantheon and still held on to stereotypes about the religion involved. What occurred was normal for the ritual.

It is certainly true, and not necessarily harmful, that many people in our society love to be scared. The adrenaline rush from risky sports and horror movies can be addicting. Kids love ghost stories, and quite often so do their parents. The more realistic, the better. Plenty of people get together to share wild stories and personal experiences, especially when these people are relatively new to metaphysics.

This is fine and it can be great fun. However, when we allow this to carry over into our behavior with our children, it has the potential to be damaging. Our children look to us to be brave and strong. They expect us to understand the world and the things we expose them to. They expect us to act accordingly.

When we behave like children who have heard too many ghost stories and overreact, whether out of real fear or for the attention of others, our children experience these situations as real and frightening. They learn about the world through our behavior. We do them a disservice if we do not keep this in mind whenever we are with them.

The nonphysical world can become something to be feared and mistrusted for children whose parents react in this way. If it is enough to freak out their parents, then surely it is truly frightening. Suddenly, the child finds something to fear every-where. The physical world is frightening enough, but now the nonphysical world holds the potential to become a horror movie. These fears will continue to affect the experience of these children.

There is another drawback to permitting our imagination and fear to get the better of us. We are then limited, and potentially paralyzed, in our abilities to protect our families. Fear can create tremendous blocks. In many cases, it seems to short-circuit the brain, preventing us from using the abilities we have. Fear clouds the ability to see things as they really are, rather than how they appear through the filter of our fears and beliefs.

How does one learn to separate perceived threats from the real thing? Only through personal exploration and clearing one's shadows—and through experience. The more familiar you become with other paths and Other worlds, the more comfort-able you will be. This familiarity will allow you to determine what is a real threat and what is not. It will also provide the clar-ity to recognize the threats from within (the projections of our own shadows) from those originating somewhere outside of us. As a result, you will develop a measure of strength and confi-dence that will diminish the number of perceived threats and increase your abilities to react appropriately in all realities.

Among some pagan groups and individuals, there is an over-emphasis on spells and outward-directed magic. I use the term "overemphasis" because some individuals do not balance this with inner, personal work. The shadow is completely external-ized and all magic is directed outward.

I definitely understand the reasons people avoid facing their innermost selves and accepting responsibility for their lives and experiences. However, I must stress the importance of doing just that. There is a danger in relying solely on spellwork to create one's reality and to handle all issues that arise.

Our power flows through us. The power to create one's life and to create effective spells flows through us. We can liken the body to a garden hose. The hose itself consists of the physical and energy bodies, especially those associated with the physical realm. Unresolved issues create energy leaks and blocks. As power flows through us, it is lost through these leaks and is restricted by our blocks. Blocks can often create more damage than leaks as the building energy needs to find an outlet. The more issues we carry around, the less power we have available to us for creation.

This is the main reason for doing Shadow Work. As we face and clear these issues, we become more complete beings, with significantly more energy to work with. We are stronger after having faced our own shadows. As a result, we frequently find less to fear outside our selves. Far less of our own stuff is being projected onto the worlds around us and suddenly we find ourselves in a new, more comfortable reality.

With this increased energy comes an increased capacity for understanding and protection. Now, we are better able to discern the real threats from the projections of inner fear. And we have the necessary power available to protect ourselves and our loved ones when we need it.

There are several good books available on psychic self-defense. This topic, even from a purely pagan perspective, could easily take up an entire book. Therefore, I will concentrate on the basics of protection and grounding as it applies to parents and children.

The first part of protection is the maintenance of security and the creation of a safe, sacred space. In our family, we follow up particularly difficult days by smudging the room and ourselves before lying down to sleep. We call in the Spiritkeepers of the directions, asking for their guidance and protection.

At the age of three, our son had his own feathers to move the smoke around while I held the burning herbs. He continues to learn to offer prayers of thanks to the Great Spirit and to be respectful during ritual and meditation. By three and a half, he was allowed to hold a wrapped smudge stick. By four years old, he had created his own smudge fan and began to join me on sagebrush picking expeditions, which will be discussed in a later chapter. In these ways and others, he is learning to bolster the energy of security and to create his own sacred space.

We have created our home and yard as a sacred space by regularly honoring the spirits and each other. In doing this, we not only give back something of what we receive throughout our lives, but we continue the cycle of energy. This enables the flow of guiding and protective energy through our home. It makes for a very calm, centered energy.

Before I get into specific methods of protection, I would like to discuss the effects of resistance during any form of psychic attack. Many pagans believe that they must always offer some type of barrier or perform some sort of spell to protect their families. This is not necessarily the case. Resistance itself brings additional and undesirable energy to the situation.

The effects of resistance can be likened to an encounter with an annoying or pushy individual. When confronted by someone like this, sometimes the best course of action is not to get defensive or upset. Many times, the best way to handle these people is to simply let it go and walk away. The offending individual is then immersed in his own drama. He has no response from us to latch onto and use. Energetically, this is frequently the case as well.

Often, the best thing we can do is recognize that unwanted energy is there and simply allow it to pass through us. Resistance and fear create obstructions that hold this energy within our own auric fields. Our emotional reactions to this energy, and our often incorrect assumptions about its intent and source, appear to be almost sticky, like glue or gum. This not only holds onto any energies directed at us, but it attracts and binds to any passing thoughtforms that may be similar to the energy we are resisting.

Teaching children to trust in the God and Goddess or Great Spirit and in their helping spirits can reduce the possibility that they will automatically create this type of block or "glue." This is the first best defense against psychic attack. Children that are able to honestly release any attachment, any resistance, to incoming energies will not provide the opportunity for these energies and thoughtforms to stay with them. Lacking energy to feed off, they will simply pass by that child in search of another source of emotion.

Shielding

In a way, the other side of telepathy is shielding. This can take many forms, but shielding, as it relates to telepathy, involves learning how we leak or broadcast our thoughts and emotions. It also means developing the ability to create boundaries and to plug up the leaks in our energy fields.

Not only does this give us a degree of privacy but it also increases our personal power. When we continually leak energy, we allow holes to remain in our energy fields, our auras. That garden hose I described earlier loses energy through these holes.

Furthermore, other people can drain one's energy much more easily when the individual being drained is unaware of the condition of his or her auric field. Without a conscious awareness and ability to control our own energy fields, we open ourselves up to psychic vampires, as well as to psychic attack.

Psychic vampires are commonly known. They are people who need everyone else's energy constantly. We may feel tired or depleted around them. Often, they will create minor crises in order to get the group energy level higher. They tend to be what my husband and I call the long-huggers. They seem to hang on for dear life and for an eternity, sucking your energy as they hug you.

Most of the time, psychic vampires are adults. Unfortunately, since they are generally unaware that this is what they are doing, they will drain anyone, including children. Children are vibrant and full of life. They exude the energy flowing through them effortlessly. Like strong adults, children often attract people who are no longer able to feel that life force flowing through them.

Some of these vampires may even be parents who have become so beaten down by life or so hurt that they effectively switch places with their children. They depend on their children for their own emotional well-being. Frequently, they will live vicariously through their children, having no social life of their own. They unconsciously maintain an emotional (usually guilt-driven) hold on their children that can prevent their children from fully living their own lives as adults.

Psychic attack most often takes the form of unconscious destructive energies that may or may not be directed at us. Although many people believe they are consciously attacked, this is rarely the result of a directed magical attack. It is far more commonly directed via anger or unpleasant thoughts.

When we allow holes to remain in our personal energy fields, we leave the doors open for any passing energies to enter our fields. Whether conscious or unconscious, the thoughts and feelings of other people, even if they are not related to us, can affect us if we remain unaware of these factors. Children, especially very young children, are particularly susceptible to this because of their relative lack of chakra filters.

It is a very good idea for parents to teach their children how to shield and how to call in protective energies whenever they feel uncomfortable. Below I have outlined some great ways for kids to shield themselves and to call in protective energies.

But first, I want to talk about infants and toddlers. Any child whose language and comprehension skills have not yet developed to the point where she or he can understand your descriptions of shields, let alone understand what the point of the shields is, is obviously not ready to learn these techniques. Until our children are ready to handle it on their own, it is our responsibility as parents to do it for them. To be honest, I don't know too many parents who stop doing it, even when their kids can do it for themselves; that's just what parents do.

Earlier in this book, I explained how the energy field of a parent shields and filters outside energies when a child is in contact with them, such as sitting in the parent's lap. I also described how as children grow, they leave filaments of their own energy on other people and things. This is the basis for the first exercise in shielding your children.

Shielding for a Child Exercise

Visualize your own energy flowing to your child and merging with his or her energy. As it flows through the cord that connects you, it becomes a bubble of white light surrounding him or her completely.

Say, as you send this energy, that this semipermeable boundary creates a sacred space around this child. State that this protective bubble prevents any and all unwanted beings, energies, and influences to reach your child, while it allows all the universal love and goodness to flow unimpeded through to him or her. Also state that your own filters will not permit any of your stress or negative energies to pass through to your child.

Call upon whatever deities or guides you work with and ask for their guidance and assistance in shielding and protecting your child.

Check to be sure that the bubble completely surrounds the child, with no holes. You should periodically check for any tears or leaks, especially if there has been any stress or unhappiness around either you or the child.

Egg of Protection Exercise

This is an exercise that can be learned as soon as a child knows what an egg is, can understand simple directions, and has begun to engage in imaginative play. It should be a great game of make-believe in order to keep it fun and creative for the child.

Have your child take a really good look at an egg. If it is a younger child, you may want to use a plastic or hard-boiled one, unless you feel like cleaning up a mess. Let your child thoroughly inspect it from all sides.

Now, tell her or him that you are going to play a game. Together, close your eyes and picture an egg surrounding the child. Ask them what colors it is and what else they see inside it. You may want to write down what they tell you.

Now, tell them that on the outside of this egg, they are going to make a beautiful white shell. Really get them to use their imagination and create a shell that goes all the way around them, on all sides. Let them know that they need to make sure there aren't any holes, so that the inside of the egg won't leak. Encourage them to see this shell as glowing or sparkling white.

An older child can add an outward-facing mirror, an additional shell of fire, or anything else that spurs their imagination and makes them feel safe.

While they are doing all this, use your own imaginative or telepathic abilities to watch what they create. If you see a hole, let them know. Tell them what a great job they are doing and how beautiful the shell looks. Ask them for permission before adding any of your own energies or seal up a tear in the shell.

Occasionally in everyday life, ask them how their egg is doing. Tell them how your egg is, so it becomes a game you play together. You may want to play the egg game again periodically, to check for holes and continue to develop their abilities in this area.

When protecting our living or working space, we can erect an Egg of Protection around a home, property, tent, office, or car. It is always a good idea to develop a loving and honoring relationship with the "Spirits of Your Place." Even when we go camping or backpacking, my husband and I always honor the Spirits of Place first and ask their welcome and protection for as long as we will be there. We leave a suitable offering when we arrive and when we leave.

At home, you can make it a normal family practice to thank the Spirits of Place at each meal or each time you enter your home. You may want to create a special altar for the spirits who contribute to your protection and the harmony of the home. Or you may simply include some symbol for them on your family altar.

We can also use the concept of amulets or talismans in protecting our homes. Many pagans use bottle spells or bury amulets around the house for protection and the maintenance of good health, harmony, and prosperity. Some people will bury one item in either a central location or around the perimeter at each of the directions, while others hang pouches and amulets inside the house.

Involving children in the creation of amulets, talismans, or altars for the house is an excellent project. It helps them to feel like an integral part of the family while it teaches them and empowers them. Simply by holding the belief that these methods will keep them safe, children will feel more confident and will attract safer situations.

Home Protection Amulet Exercise

Begin by creating a large disk of clay with your children. Write your names on it or simply write "Protection," and include a drawing of the house. You may choose to make up a simple chant for protection and write that on one side of the clay disk. Make it a simple, easy chant that your children will be able to recite with you when you charge the amulet. Something like this works well with young people:

Spirits of this Place, I pray,
Bring us protection, harmony, and play.
Guard us and our privacy,
Let in only happy energy.

Once the disk has been baked or air-dried, wrap it in a red or black cloth until you are ready to charge it with your family's energy and your chant.

Prepare your altar with black and/or white candles and either Dragon's Blood or essential oil of cedar, frankincense, rosemary, or sandalwood.

Count yourself and your children down into a light trance state. Thoroughly smudge, or purify in your usual manner, your entire home. Really clear it out and see it filled with white light.

Cast a Circle or call upon the spirits of the directions in your usual manner. Call in any helping or guardian spirits that your family members work with and ask their assistance in this rite.

Count down from ten to one again, into a slightly deeper trance state.

Bring out the clay disk and hold it in your hands. Have your family members hold hands around you. Each person on either side of you should place one hand on your arm nearest them. Guide everyone present to direct his or her attention and focus on the disk as you recite your protection chant.

Then, go around the circle and allow each person to mention any specific needs they have that they would like the amulet to assist with. These should be general or specific family protection, happiness, or success issues, and they should be very important. As ritual leader, you should be funneling these prayers into the disk.

Repeating your special chant or prayers, allow each person to anoint the disk with the Dragon's Blood or essential oil. Guide them to really feel the disk filling with this energy. Then wrap the disk in the red or black cloth and close the ritual, thanking all the spirits and deities that were called for assistance.

You may choose to bury the disk immediately after the rite or you may do it later on. Just be sure that each person who participated in the rite is present for the burial. Once the disk is fully buried, have everyone place their hands on the ground over the disk. Guide them to feel the energy of their prayers radiating out from the disk and surrounding your home. Once again, give thanks to the Earth Mother and all other helping spirits.

Spirit Guardians

Many children, especially those that watch any children's television, respond very well to cartoon or animated hero characters. They believe these beings are real in a way, particularly younger children. They can often relate to these characters. It also helps that these types of animated beings are not intimidating the way a large animal or deity may be. Often, these images can be good role models or teaching guides on their own.

Since our perception of our guides is a limited one, based on our beliefs and the restrictions of this reality, it is perfectly logical and worthwhile to use these characters as symbols for the guides and guardians of a child. This provides a framework within which the "real" guides can come through and interact with the child. Our guides will manifest to us in whatever way is easiest for our minds to comprehend, and they respond to whatever names we call them by.

Children can use any number of characters to chase away the bad things and to learn wonderful lessons in fun ways. Cookie Monster loves to eat everything, Thomas the Tank Engine carries us away, and the Lion King will protect us from anything. Talking animals and trees, singing wind and water, friendly dragons, and faeries are all age-appropriate images to assist in learning of our interconnections with All of Life.

Pathworking Exercise: the Child's Spirit Guides

For the infant and young toddler, you will need to call on your personal or familial spirit guardians or ancestors for protection. Call upon them in your usual manner, just as you normally would do for yourself. If you normally make offerings, do so now. Then ask these guides to watch over your child, guiding and protecting him or her. You can also ask them to help you contact the child's personal spirit guardians. For the very young child, this is a variation of the Pathworking given in Chapter 1.

> You may wish to use some of the dreaming or
> journeying techniques in this book to make contact
> with his spirit guardians and guides.

Even if you do not know who or what his guides
and guardians are, you can still call upon them to
help your child. After doing the Egg of Protection or
Shielding exercises, call upon "the spirit guardians of
my child _____." Ask them for their guidance and
assistance in shielding and protecting your child. Ask
them to watch over your child and to teach him or
her how to protect themselves as they grow.

One note for those connecting with the guides of
their children: be open to whatever may happen
during this Calling. You may see them. You may
receive vital information in guiding your child
through his or her life. On the other hand, if there
is a good deal of turmoil in your life or your
environment, be prepared for some questions and/or
demands that this be cleared up for the child's well
being. They may even offer some guidance in how
you may do this. A good rule of thumb when dealing
with spirits is: if you are not ready for any answers,
don't ask.

For older children, over the age of four, begin
by calling on their guides with them in the room.
Gradually work toward their participation in the call,
starting with some simple phrases. As children get
older, they can do the whole ritual on their own.

Pay attention to any animals that children have a
special affinity for. Even a baby may show distinct
preferences for certain animals. These may very
well be their animal allies, also known as totem or
power animals.

When these animals show up, create a simple altar
for images of them. An altar does not need to be the
traditional flat surface for holding special items. For a
child, it can take the form of room decorations, stuffed
animals, clothing, bedding, or amulets hung on the
doorknob. The idea is to bring that energy, in a

concrete form, into your child's presence. We are strengthening a bond and making a type of offering, or perhaps more of an honoring, of these spirit guides and guardians.

Older children can be taught to call on these animals during dreams and anytime they feel uncomfortable or threatened. This, like everything else, should be kept fun and light, as a make-believe game. Have them see the animal coming to their aid and "getting" the scary monsters under the bed or giving them the strength to speak up in class.

Nighttime Protection

This is better known as Pagan Nighttime Rituals. Most families have a nighttime ritual of bath-time, storytelling, and maybe a bedtime prayer. Pagan families can alter this traditional bedtime ritual to fit their own beliefs and needs. These rituals are important because children tend to feel more vulnerable at night.

They are often alone, in their own rooms, in the dark, when everyone else is sleeping. Their imaginations can run wild at times like this. If they are not prepared for interdimensional contact, they may be frightened by a visit from a departed loved one or the appearance of a Nature spirit.

At that point between sleep and awake, we are more open to Other realities. Children may be unnerved by a conscious awareness of Other worlds or the initial stages of astral travel. But, whether their fears are grounded in imagination, too much television, or some Other reality, we can help them feel more comfortable going to sleep.

The first thing we can do, as parents, is to educate both ourselves and our children on the difference between the media and reality. As parents, we should develop a degree of comfort with Other beings and Other realities and communicate that comfort to our children. We all benefit from joining our children in exercises and games, such as those in this book, that are specifically designed to increase a child's sense of safety and familiarity out-side the physical body.

We can choose nighttime stories that emphasize happiness and security. A number of wonderful books are available for pagan and other metaphysical children. Most of these are stories of the Earth and all Her beings; of love and protection and friendship. This is the best way to direct a child's mind toward more beneficial thoughts before falling asleep.

We can also help them feel more secure while they are asleep, aware of Other realities, or out of their bodies. We can let them know that everyone travels about during dreaming and that we are all very familiar with this type of journeying. We did very well without our bodies before we chose new bodies to live in and we remember all we need to easily once we are dreaming.

It is important for parents to learn to trust our children, even if we are exhausted or feel the child is overreacting. There may be nights when your children just do not feel prepared to handle being alone, especially after a nightmare. They may need you to check their beds for bugs or look under their beds and in closets for monsters. They may just need you to come when they call you in the middle of the night, simply for reassurance that if something actually did happen, you would be there for them.

You may need to be willing to sleep with your child or allow them into your own bed for comfort and security on particularly intense nights. In fact, many parents allow their children to sleep in the "family bed" for years, a common practice in many native cultures around the world.

Finally, we can tell them about the silver cord that connects us all to our bodies. And better yet, we can help them to experience this and become confident in its ability to bring them safely home. This next exercise is a great way to do this.

Silver Cord Game

With your child (or children), go outside on a nice day. Lie down and watch the sky. If this is not a possibility, sit in front of a window and play. Pretend that you are all rising up away from your bodies into the sky. Really get into it. Soar like birds, float with the clouds, pretend you are a kite, become One with the sunlight.

As you rise, remind everyone to look back and see the silver cord behind them, connecting them to their physical bodies on the ground. Suggest that this is exciting and fun. It is usually best not to mention negatives (like being frightened) unless someone brings it up. Describe the shining, strong silver cord and say that no matter where you go, you can always find your way back by following the cord. Tell them that it is unbreakable. It can be wound into knots and go as far as they can, but it will always bring them home.

Another wonderful tradition that will often incorporate protective energy is the nighttime ritual, whether it takes the form of a prayer, erecting a nighttime Circle, and/or calling in spirit guardians. Again, a parent will need to do this for very young children, gradually increasing their participation until they feel comfortable doing it for themselves.

Handling nightmares falls within this category of nighttime protection. A parent's first instinct is usually to immediately waken the child out of the nightmare. This is usually fine. However, some pagan parents may assume the recurring nightmares are the result of some form of psychic attack.

In truth this is rarely the case. It is far more likely that your child has past or present life issues to work through. They will continue to experience nightmares until the issues are cleared. It is not always in a person's best interests to prevent an uncomfortable situation or to avoid something troublesome, or even painful. This is part of the human experience and we all grow through these times.

There are things you can do to assist your child through the issues and the nightmare itself. You might try grounding excess energy while your child sleeps or working with shared dreaming to provide support and security during the dream. It may help for this child to talk about the dreams or to keep a journal. It is best to follow your intuition or spirit guidance in these situations.

I want to suggest again that you not hesitate to use the family bed when necessary. We all need to be close to those we love when we are going through a difficult time. Children need this closeness even more than adults, due to their relative lack of chakra filters and control over their own energy fields. This is similar to a child seeking protection by sitting in a parent's lap, as discussed in earlier chapters. However, while we sleep we tend to be more psychically open and vulnerable.

To insist that a child toughen up and sleep in his or her own bed when that child obviously needs energetic support can be damaging and may create even more fears and blocks. We would not insist that the same child cross a busy highway alone or stand by himself amidst fighting and violence. We would run to protect and assist that child.

To a child, nighttime fears and experiences are just as real as any physical, daytime experience. In fact, they can be more frightening because of the lack of light and physical comfort. My only point here is that we need not feel we are encouraging weakness or allowing manipulation if we permit our children into our beds when they need comfort or security.

One fun exercise is to devise your own nighttime prayers and lullabies. They are invocations for children and as such, should be kept simple. This process can encourage a feeling of protection and empowerment. Children love to rhyme, and rhymes tend to be more easily remembered. The following are some examples.

A Bedtime Prayer

Now I lay me down to bed
Great Spirit, bless my sleepy head
As I journey in my sleep
I know the Dragons, my soul will keep
Mother Earth and Father Sky
Watch over me here where I lie
Fairies, please carry my love to all
Relations and loved ones, I do call.

Lullaby

> The Goddess will watch you while you sleep
> She'll bless and protect you
> In Her arms She'll keep you
> Safe and warm with the moon and stars above
> The Goddess will watch you while you sleep.
>
> The Dream Lord will watch you while you sleep
> He'll bless and protect you
> Through His forest deep
> His Dreamlands will teach you
> Lessons you need
> The Dream Lord will watch you while you sleep.
>
> The Angels (Fairies) will watch you now and always
> They'll bless and protect you
> Both night and day
> Feel their wings surround you
> Their love all around you
> The Angels(Fairies) will watch you now and always.[1]

Another exercise that can be of tremendous benefit to parents and children alike is to do a nightly review of the day. This is a process that is better suited to the older child and it may help prevent some nightmares. You can do this through discussions together or by writing in a journal. It is a simple review of the day's events. What draws your attention? What do you feel is unfinished? What do you wish you had done differently? Did you live that day to its fullest? Did you tell those you love how much they mean to you? If you choose to, you may make plans for the next day based on this review.

---

1 "Ohana" lullaby sung at pagan festivals. The author is unknown, but is believed to be Laughing Starheart, who passed to the Summerlands in 1998.

Grounding Energy

The ability to ground energy is just as important as shielding. When we ground energy, we send unnecessary or unwanted energies into the Earth for release and purification. There are five main energy centers that are responsible for grounding: the root chakra, the chakras in the soles of both feet, and the chakras in the palm of each hand.

As I discussed in the Incarnation chapter, our energy progresses down the physical body and grounds us, through the root chakra, into this body and this reality. While energy constantly flows in and out of all our energy centers, our root chakra is the main grounding cord. This can be seen as a cord of energy, extending deep into the Earth. This cord naturally funnels off excess and undesirable energies.

We are also naturally grounded through the soles of our feet. These are minor chakras. However, they are very important in feeling anchored and connected to the strength and support of the Earth. They also will funnel off excess energy, although to a lesser degree than the root chakra.

There is a chakra point in the palm of each hand, as well as in the tips of each of our fingers. Although these are minor chakras, they are used continually. They can become very strong and sensitized, especially in the hands of healers. It is through these chakras that we send and receive sensory and emotional impressions of our world and other people. With regard to grounding energy, the palm chakras in particular are vital chakras to develop.

There are two basic reasons to ground energy. The first has already been touched upon here. We can, for a number of reasons, accumulate an excess of energy in our own auric fields. This energy can overload one's systems, resulting in anything from a spacey feeling and lack of focus to fainting. This buildup of energy can also prevent us from receiving beneficial energies because the flow through us has been blocked.

The second major reason to ground energy is to prevent the assimilation of other people's energies. When we pick up the energies of other people, without a way to pass these energies through us, we risk manifesting any mental, emotional, or physical ailments in our own selves. People will get a headache or feel anger that does not belong to them.

While some people may find this clear indication that metaphysical beliefs are real, it is not cool or funny to allow it to continue. There is no reason to get other people's issues. We are of no benefit to anyone if we begin to exhibit their symptoms. Quite often, the opposite is the case and everyone loses.

Grounding is generally so natural that even the youngest children (with some degree of language skills) can learn to do this. However, I believe there to be a correlation between one's astrological make-up and one's innate ability to ground energy. I would recommend that parents review their children's astrological charts with an expert to determine whether there is a need for additional practice in grounding.

Shower Time Exercise

This is a great exercise that can be used either as a simple meditation or as a more active meditation in the shower or in the rain.

> Count down as usual from ten to one. *This is a step that is not necessary, although it does help, especially in the beginning. It is important to develop the ability to use these exercises whenever and wherever you feel the need.*
>
> Visualize a shower of clear, white light over your head. Feel this light-water on your face and your hair. Let it flow over your entire body.
>
> Feel your tensions and worries dissolve in the water. As the water passes over your body, it washes away all unwanted or excess energies from your head down. See and feel the light fill you from your head down.
>
> Look down at the drain and see these unwanted energies spiral away. These may look like different colored water or symbols or images of people or events. Trust whatever you see and let it go.
>
> Continue to feel these energies drain from your body, as you are filled with this light. If any place on

your body seems tense or uncomfortable, direct the shower to that place until it is relaxed and clear.

Enjoy this feeling of light. See the light flow out of every pore of your body. It shines forth through your eyes and your hair and your hands and feet.

When you are ready, count back up from one to ten.

Hug the Earth Exercise

Children love this exercise almost as much as they love hugging trees, which can also help us ground energy. It is fun to lie down and try to hug the Earth, especially when a parent or sibling plays along.

Lie down on your stomach on the Earth. This may be on dirt or grass, as long as there is no man-made interference between you and the ground.

Stretch your arms out and hug the Earth. Press your hands in as you try to hug the whole Earth.

Now, feel any unwanted or excess energies gently seep out of your body into the Earth. As you hug Her, Mother Earth is taking away all these energies that you do not need. Feel them trickle out of your hands and the center of your body. Notice where you feel them drain from the most.

Continue to lie there and allow the Earth to pull out these energies. After a while, you will feel Earth energy flowing back up into your body. If you feel more comfortable, you may turn over and lie on your back at this point.

Allow the energy of the Earth to fill you with radiant light as the Earth returns your hug. Feel Her love for you and Her strength. Thank the Earth before you get up and go on with your day.

After using this exercise for a while, you and your children will be attuned to the Earth energy and you will be aware of where on your bodies the energies seem to build up. At this point, you can alter this exercise so that you can send these energies into the Earth at any time and in any place, without lying down.

Necklace of Lights Exercise

This exercise is designed to be used either alone or in conjunction with any type of grounding exercise. It restores energy flow while it balances the chakras. It begins with an exercise called the EarthStar Meditation.[1] Some of the wording for the chakra section may need to be changed for younger children. For example, a child who does not know what the solar plexus is should be able to understand "the middle of your belly."

EarthStar Meditation

To clear and balance one's personal energy field
Count yourself down from ten to one, as usual.

 See a ball of light at the center of the Earth. This is the embodiment of the Earth energy. See this energy flow up out of the Earth's core and into your body through the soles of your feet and the base of your spine. Feel this energy fill your entire body. Feel it pour out from the pores of your skin, your eyes, your hair, your navel. Feel it flow completely though you and out through the top of your head. Fully experience this flow.

 See a star at the center of the universe. This is the embodiment of the universal or Sky energy. See this energy flow down from the center of the star and into your body through the top of your head. Feel this energy fill your entire body. Feel it pour out from the pores of your skin, your eyes, your hair, your navel. Feel it flow completely though you and down into the Earth. Fully experience this flow.

---

1 From *Shamanic Guide to Death and Dying*, p. 70.

Experience both of these flows together for as long as you like, until you really feel them. See and feel your total energy space cleansed and purified by this light. Your body appears to be a long cord of white light.

Now, see a ball of violet light coming from the top of your head. It is like a purple bead on your cord of light. Feel and see this beautiful violet energy. Stay with this ball of light until you fully experience it.

At the center of your forehead is deep, dark blue ball of light; another bead on the necklace that is you. Feel and see this beautiful deep, dark blue energy. Stay with this ball of light until you fully experience it.

In the middle of your throat is a ball of bright blue energy. Feel and see this beautiful bright blue energy. Stay with this ball of light until you fully experience it.

In the center of your chest, right by your heart, is a beautiful ball of green energy. Feel and see this beautiful green energy. Stay with this ball of light until you fully experience it.

Move your attention down to the ball of golden energy at your solar plexus. Feel and see this beautiful golden yellow energy. Stay with this ball of light until you fully experience it.

In the middle of your abdomen, see a ball of vibrant orange energy. Feel and see this beautiful orange energy. Stay with this ball of light until you fully experience it.

At the base of your spine is a deep red ball of energy. Feel and see this beautiful red energy. Stay with this ball of light until you fully experience it.

See these balls of energy on the cord of white light that is your body, like the beads on a white necklace. Feel how it feels to be fully relaxed and balanced. Know that you can feel this way any time you want to, just by remembering the feeling of this necklace.

Above all, the best way to keep our children safe and balanced is to teach them, by example, how to live an honorable, respectful life. When we live our lives in this way, we are guided and protected by the spirits around us. In honoring this guidance and placing ourselves in the flow of universal energy, the abundance of the universe flows to us. All of our needs are taken care of and we live in a much freer and happier space, no matter what the circumstances around us.

We all choose our lives and our deaths before we re-enter this world. While we can certainly alter these plans as we go along, we don't always remember why we chose what we did, or even that we chose it. The process of incarnation, coupled with living in this reality, can have a tendency to block our memories of the time spent between lives.

There are certain events that we will experience, whether we chose them before incarnating or created them while we were here. We cannot protect our children from everything. And if we could, we would be depriving them of valuable growth opportunities. We can help them to handle these things in the best possible way by teaching them that every situation and every being we encounter is a potential teacher.

If we can teach our children how to use each experience and to grow from it, and if we can live this way ourselves, we offer them the tools they need to create truly happy lives. This is a lesson that goes beyond this one lifetime. It is a tremendous contribution to the evolution of their souls. What better gift to those who have chosen us as their parents for this lifetime?

5

Health and
Healing

This chapter is titled "Health and Healing" to highlight the differences between maintaining one's physical, emotional, mental, and spiritual health, and the process of healing imbalances. A large part of healing is the maintenance and support of the individual beyond any healing process. For any healing to be effective long-term, we cannot simply ignore our health once we feel better.

The healing sections of this chapter are not intended to function as training manuals. I do give an overview of alternative healing techniques, as well as some very basic physiology. If you plan to use these or other methods, I would strongly encourage you to investigate further. Please see the "Recommended Reading" section at the back of this book for more information.

Healing is not something to be taken lightly. Training and education are vital to your success as a healer, even if you are only using these abilities within your own family. I recommend learning about anatomy and physiology as you research your favorite alternative healing methods.

All parents, no matter what their spiritual path, find themselves becoming healers in their own families. This may be as simple as knowing when to take a temperature, and what to do if a child is running one, to handling severe accidents. As parents, we learn about antibiotics and pain medication and some medical procedures. It is a fact of life as a parent.

Fortunately, most pagan parents educate themselves on the realities of mainstream medical practices. At the same time, we seek out more natural and harmonious means to keep our families healthy as we attempt to treat what we can without drugs and undesirable procedures.

The medicine cabinet takes on a whole new meaning in a pagan home. Most medicine cabinets are filled with over-the-counter drugs for colds, pain, insomnia, rashes, etc. In pagan homes, there are often several "medicine" cabinets ranging from the variety of herbal teas in the kitchen to the homeopathics and flower remedies in the bathroom. Pagan families keep an assortment of healing stones, massage oils, meditation mats, audiocassettes, and aromatherapy gadgets in other rooms all over the house.

This use of alternative remedies carries over to the pagan first-aid kit. My mother jokes that, although I carry around a backpacker's first-aid pouch, she can't even get an Excedrin out of me. Although I do carry acetaminophen and ibuprofen, she has a point. My kit is filled with Rescue Remedy (a classic blend found in Bach Flower remedies), at least three homeopathic remedies, a snake-bite kit, an assortment of bandages and gauze, pads soaked in hydrogen peroxide, and a small first-aid/survival booklet that came with the pouch.

I grew up using homeopathic remedies and herbs. When I was a child, homeopathics were called tissue or cell salts and there were only about twelve of them available. Today health stores carry several brands providing both mixtures for different ailments and single remedies. Herbs are no longer limited to health-food stores. They can be found in many mainstream grocery stores and even in some bookstores.

With exceptions for certain conditions that require medical intervention, our son has only been treated with homeopathics, energy work, massage, diet, and other assorted natural methods. In addition, I research all conditions that he develops and all interventions that he requires, including vaccinations. I make certain that I have all the information I need to make informed choices about his treatment.

Except in extreme cases, this refusal to blindly follow the dictates of modern medicine is something the pagan community should be proud of. We think for ourselves and we tend to be avid self-educators. When it comes to the well-being of our children, we will not simply bow to accepted practices, particularly if those practices are questionable. In this way, pagan parents offer their children even more valuable tools to create better lives for themselves.

Throughout this book, I have described the impact of the shadow side on our children's well-being and on our own psychic and magical abilities. This also plays a role in maintaining one's health. Although children generally have far less submerged in the shadow side than do adults, it can still create health issues for them. While these primarily show up as emotional or behavioral situations, imbalance can cause problems on any level of being.

For children, keeping a daily journal, having consistent and honest discussions with parents, and doing various meditations are the best ways to encourage self-knowledge—and to discourage repression.

Healing Stones

There are scores of books available today on the various uses of stones and crystals. As a pagan, you may have come to your spiritual path through an interest in stones. Most pagans know at least a little about the meanings of some stones.

We work with stones in a wide variety of ways. Many of us wear jewelry with specific stones that feel right to us or carry the vibrations we wish to bring into our lives. Some of us, especially children, will carry a stone or two in our pockets. In pagan homes, stones can be found just about everywhere.

For healing, the best way to use the stones, unless you have been trained in specific methods, is to keep the stones on or near your body as much as possible, and to meditate with them. If you are working with a specific stone, you will need to keep it with you at all times for at least twenty-four hours; some people say seven to thirty days. This imbues the stone with your personal energy. It also permits an attunement to develop, synchronizing your energies with those of the stone, and allowing healing to begin.

When meditating with a stone, you can sit in silent meditation, opening to the stone and allowing any impressions or messages to flow into you. Some people find this frustrating and desire a more guided, active meditation. Alternatively, you can hold the stone during any meditation that you do. If you listen to an audiotape, hold the stone during the visualization. This is particularly effective if you practice shamanic journeying. I recommend the Elemental Attunement Exercise for anyone in the process of getting to know a specific stone or crystal.

There are some basic concepts to keep in mind when working with any type of crystal. The termination, or point, indicates the direction of energy flow through a crystal. This is true for any faceted stone. The angles and shape of the facets give direction to the energy. Some people believe that facets also increase the magnitude of the energy. Crystal or other stone balls send out a smoother energy flow in all directions. Finally, crystal clusters tend to radiate group energy. They can bring harmonious energy into a room or a home.

Many of the stones used in healing are also associated with the various chakras, generally based on color. These stones can be extremely beneficial when placed on the chakra or used during a meditation specific to that chakra. I will describe this in more detail in the section on energy work and colors.

No matter how we work with the stones, it is important to honor and respect them. Many pagans see them as the Stone People. We ask permission before using them and give thanks afterwards. Even if this is not your belief system, they should be treated with honor, as you would any ritual tool.

I have not included a section listing the common healing stones and their uses because of the considerable amount of space that would require. There are many books and charts available on the subject. There is also plenty of online information as well.

In addition, it is best to trust your instincts and choose what feels best, rather than what a book says you should be using.

When choosing a stone for a specific reason or person, it is a good idea to go into the store (or into the field) holding that purpose or person in mind. Send out a request for the ideal stone for that purpose and allow the stone to find you. You'll know this is happening when you suddenly feel drawn to a stone for no apparent reason. You walk around the store and keep coming back to that stone.

Sometimes, you will reach for a different stone and the one you need will end up in your hand. Children are wonderful at choosing the best stones for themselves and loved ones. It becomes a game for them. Most children under the age of ten can do this easily without interference from their analytical minds.

Clearing Stones

Stones, especially those purchased from a store, should be cleared before using them, because stones pick up energies from their surroundings and impressions from people who have handled them. If a stone had a previous "owner," it may retain some of that person's energies.

Even stones that you have had for a while should be cleared periodically. Some stones, like amber, must be cleared more frequently due to their tendency to absorb negativity. Other stones, like diamonds, are notoriously difficult to clear. To make it easier, I recommend frequent clearings.

When I was younger, the most popular way to clear stones was to bury them in salt or soak them in salt water. This is still beneficial for clearing stones. However, I have read studies that indicate certain crystals lose some of their piezo-electric properties when exposed to salt. Salt can also mar the surface of some of the softer stones, although generally this does not affect their abilities.

My favorite ways to clear and purify stones and crystals are: smudging with sacred herbs, burying them in earth for seven days, and using running water over them. The smudge ceremony is outlined in a later chapter. Burying them and running water over them allow the elements to purify your stones naturally. You might use the water from your sink, or submerge them for a time in a stream. When using any of these purification methods, visualize all the unwanted energies breaking up and leaving the stone as you carry out the action of clearing. Continue until you feel the stones are clear and ready to work with you.

Programming Stones

Once your stones are clear, you can begin to program them for the specific type of healing you desire. The simplest way to do this is to sit in meditation with your stones and send the intent into the stone. Hold it between both hands and feel the energy of your intent flowing through the stone, filling it. Ask the stone for its assistance in this matter and listen to any messages or thoughts you receive.

Homeopathy

I highly recommend homeopathic healing. I have used it since I was a child, and it has worked wonders for our son. The medicine cabinet in his bathroom is packed with homeopathic remedies, or what he likes to call "little balls." Karl loves to take the little balls, because they taste good and they are just fun. That certainly makes giving a child his medicine a lot easier on a parent.

Homeopathy is an involved discipline requiring years of study to practice it well. However, for the purposes of most parents, we can go about it in an amateur way without worrying about damaging ourselves or our families. It is true that you cannot overdose on homeopathics. I would caution you that some negative effects are possible. The only possible drawback is that the wrong remedy has the potential to create the symptoms it is intended to treat in an individual who does not already exhibit those symptoms. The truth is that this is a rare occurrence and usually the worst that will happen is nothing.

It is true that many homeopathic remedies can be costly. Most of those designed for infants can also create a considerable amount of plastic waste, something that many of us have ethical concerns about. However, with an initial outlay to build up an appropriate inventory and to obtain some simple supplies, even the parents of a newborn can treat their baby inexpensively and easily.

To treat an infant, all you need is the appropriate remedy, filtered water, and a glass (preferably dark-colored) bottle with a glass eye dropper. Those little balls dissolve very well in water. Also, since there is no scientifically measurable amount of the remedy in the "balls," you need not be concerned that you will dilute it out by dissolving it in a small bottle of water. Unless you are prepared to get deeply involved with homeopathic education, it is sufficient to dissolve four or five balls, or three tablets, of a remedy in approximately one ounce of water.

Before prescribing any remedy, homeopathic or otherwise, you should look for the cause of your child's discomfort. Often we reach for a pill, albeit a natural one, too quickly before exhausting the other possibilities. Unless the root cause is identified and cleared, you can expect the issue to arise again.

At the end of this section I have listed several homeopathic remedies and their general uses. Most homeopathic physicians will tell you that the big three for childhood are: *Aconite, Belladonna,* and *Chamomilla.*[1] I recommend that parents purchase a comprehensive homeopathic reference book that will help you to determine exactly which remedy is best for your child.

Often a remedy is specific to your child's symptoms, not merely to the condition at hand. For example, the colicky baby who feels better with a little abdominal pressure most likely needs *Colocynthis.* On the other hand, a baby in need of *Bryonia* for colic will be extremely irritable and cannot stand to be moved. Any pressure on the baby's abdomen will only result in more screaming.

For those of you who choose to have your children vaccinated, homeopathics are a wonderful way to restore balance, reduce the pain and inflammation of the injection, and prevent

---

1 Note: While Aconite and Belladonna are dangerous at full strength, the homeopathic remedies using these herbs contain such a small amount that it is not scientifically measurable, and are safe when used as directed. —E.A.J.

many of the adverse reactions that can occur. *Thuja* and *Ledum palustre* can ease much of the pain and worry of vaccinations.

A dose of *Thuja* (preferably 200x) immediately before the injection will prevent the fever and irritability that can follow an immunization. *Ledum* is used for all puncture wounds and can help with pain and swelling at the injection site. Give your child one dose of *Ledum* (12x or 6cc) just before the vaccination and another four hours later.

A favorite of ours is the homeopathic series for hiccups. It truly works wonders for everyone I have tried it on. Begin with one dose of *Aconite* and wait five minutes. If the person is still hiccuping, give one dose of *Arnica* and wait another five minutes. If there is still no relief, try one dose of *Ignatia* and wait five minutes. Follow this with one dose of *Magnesia phosporica* and wait five minutes. If the hiccups are still present, use *Lycopodium*.

Homeopathic Remedies for Common Complaints

Acne: *Calcarea sulphurica, Kali bromatum*

Burns: *Urtica urens*

Colic: *Bryonia, Chamomilla, Colocynthis, Magnesia phosphorica*

Colds: *Aconitum napellus (Aconite), Belladonna, Bryonia, Ferrum phosphoricum, Pulsatilla*

Constipation: *Alumina, Lycopodium, Graphites, Nux vomica*

Diarrhea: *Arsenicum album, Chamomilla, Colocynthis*

Ear Infection: *Aconitum napellus (Aconite), Belladonna, Chamomilla, Pulsatilla*

Fever: *Aconitum napellus (Aconite), Belladonna*

Headache: *Bryonia, Ferrum phosphoricum, Gelsemium, Natrum muriaticum, Iris* (migraine), *Lachesis* (migraine), *Lycopodium* (migraine on the right side of the head), *Silica* (migraine in the back of the head)

Insect bites/stings: *Apis mellifica, Ledum palustre, Urtica urens*

Injury/Shock: *Aconitum napellus (Aconite), Arnica montana*

Menstrual Cramps: *Apis mellifica, Belladonna, Chamomilla, Colocynthis, Magnesium phosporica*

Moodiness: *Chamomilla, Nux vomica*

Nausea and Vomiting: *Aconitum napellus (Aconite), Belladonna, Bryonia, Ipecacuanha*

Poison Oak/Sumac/ Ivy: *Urtica urens*

Teething: *Belladonna, Chamomilla, Silica*

Vaccinations: *Ledum palustre, Thuja*

Herbs

Herbs are some of the most common, and most ancient, remedies known to humans. Most pagans use herbs as much as possible. Herbal remedies have even made it into the mainstream, now that pharmaceutical companies have decided to certify and market them.

Many of our modern medicines are derived from the chemicals found in plants. Many people believe that herbs are as harmless as homeopathics. It is true that using the whole herb, rather than its derived or synthesized chemical component, is generally more harmonious to the human system. But, it is also true that herbs are medicines and can have powerful effects.

Some herbs can be dangerous to certain individuals. For example, goldenseal is a wonderful herb with a wide variety of uses. However, pregnant women and hypoglycemics should not use goldenseal in large doses, even though small amounts may help to relieve nausea during pregnancy. Goldenseal, used over a long period of time, will also diminish the absorption of vitamin B and destroy intestinal bacteria.

It is very important to research the herbs you intend to use, particularly if you are pregnant, breastfeeding, or prescribing for children. Herbs are one case where more is not necessarily better, especially when treating children. Herbs tend to work gently. As a result, you may not see an immediate effect. It is a good idea to start with small dosages for children, watching for any signs that the symptoms are improving, before increasing the dosage or switching to another herb. [Many herbal remedies are quite strong, but can work well for children when the dosage is reduced according to the child's weight or age. —E.A.J.]

Rescue Remedy (a classic blend found in Bach Flower remedies) is one of my favorite treatments, both for children and adults. We have used the cream for burns, cuts, rashes, insect bites, and injections. The flower remedy is good for just about anything that may cause fear, trauma, or stress. Rescue Remedy is ideal to use immediately after a vaccination. Give a couple of drops under the tongue, or mixed with water immediately after the injection and as needed for a few hours afterward. Gently rub a little of the cream onto the site of the injection to prevent pain and swelling.

Below I have listed some common childhood complaints and applicable herbal remedies. Keep in mind that echinacea should not be used indefinitely or it loses its effectiveness. At the most, you might use echinacea for eight days on and eight days off, or ten days at one time. Never give honey or tea with honey in it to a child under the age of one year. Honey has been associated with infant botulism, which can be fatal.

Some Herbal Remedies
for Common Complaints

Acne: Tea tree oil; Bach Flower Crabapple; alternate one week each of echinacea/goldenseal tincture, burdock tincture, and red clover tincture

Burns: cream, gel, or liquid of Aloe Vera, calendula, or comfrey root

Colic: Chamomile, fennel, ginger, peppermint teas. For bottle-fed babies, give one teaspoon of brewed tea three times daily in formula or water

Colds: Echinacea/goldenseal (capsule, tea, or tincture as directed); chamomile, sage, ginger teas; bath of chamomille, calendula, rosemary, and lavender

Constipation: oatmeal cooked in flaxseed tea; licorice tea or tincture; flaxseed oil

Diaper rash: Calendula cream; calendula or chamomille bath; evening primrose oil or lotion; mullein poultice

Diarrhea: Blackberry root syrup, powdered slippery elm bark

Ear Infection: Echinacea/goldenseal (capsule or tincture as directed); 1–2 drops warm mullein oil in the ear

Fever: Echinacea/goldenseal (capsule, tea, or tincture as directed); tea of lemon balm, chamomille flower, elder flower, peppermint leaf; peppermint or ginger tea when fever is associated with cold, flu, or stomachache

Headache: Chamomille, ginger, or peppermint tea; skullcap if the child is over six years of age; feverfew for migraines

Menstrual Cramps: Chamomille tea; hot ginger-tea compress; true cramp-bark (*Viburnum opulis*); chamomille and ginger tea bath

Nausea and Vomiting: Ginger, peppermint, or licorice root tea; raw honey; barley malt extract; brown rice water

Poison Oak/Sumac/Ivy: Calendula tincture; aloe vera gel; jewelweed juice (not garden-variety impatiens)

Teething: Clove oil on the gums; licorice root powder paste on the gums; chamomille tea

Vaccinations: Echinacea for three days afterward to prevent or ameliorate a low-grade fever, infection, or irritability

Bodywork

Bodywork is a general word that can mean anything from massage and shiatsu to acupuncture and cranial-sacral therapy. The various forms of bodywork can release repressed issues, keep the energy flowing through the body and maintain the health and vitality of all physical systems. For pagan parents, the most common benefit is pain and stress relief through simple massage.

I understand that this may be an uncomfortable technique to use, particularly with older children and anyone who is not comfortable with physical intimacy. However, it can be a wonderful tool for maintaining both health and an open connection to your children. As parents, we often unconsciously hold, stroke, and touch our children. This comforts them and allows the free flow of loving energy to pass through us into our children.

Many hospitals now offer classes on infant massage and there are several books available on pediatric massage. This therapeutic massage may include acupressure. There is a Chinese system of pediatric and infant massage called *tui na*. This is a special system of massage that is designed to treat pediatric complaints and diseases. We have used both *tui na* and therapeutic infant massage on our son with wonderful results.

Pagan parents can use their own intuitive massage, or be guided by their own spirit guides, in comforting their children and easing the discomfort of childhood illnesses. Even without a book or any training, parents tend to know instinctively what their children need. And the mere touch of loving hands can work wonders.

Begin by calming and centering yourself. If you can count your child down into a relaxed state of consciousness, this is even better. You might try some of the massage oils on the market that contain therapeutic essential oils. Ask for guidance in helping your child create a healthy body and mind. Allow your hands to take over as you send loving energy through them.

Acupressure is another technique that can also be taught to your children. Rather than asking for an aspirin or reaching for the Advil, a child with a minimal knowledge of this technique can apply pressure between the thumb and forefinger to cure a headache. The applications of acupressure and reflexology are far-reaching.

Diet

Many of the common complaints of childhood can be prevented through maintaining a proper diet and a moderate exercise program. Nutritional supplements and an occasional change in diet can make many of these conditions more easily managed. I will get into exercise in much more detail in the following section.

A chapter on diet could easily become at least an entire book on its own. Therefore, I will not write in very much detail regarding specific conditions that can easily be controlled through a change in diet. Suffice it to say that these conditions can be anything from diabetes and hypoglycemia to cancer and attention-deficit disorder.

Many of these conditions often mimic behavioral problems or biochemical imbalances. As a result, a parent might consider having specific tests done if their children show signs of ADD, extreme depression or moodiness, body tremors, and even psychosis. Speak with your physician or research the symptoms yourself. Special nutritional or blood analyses may indicate a nutritional cause for some conditions.

Even those conditions that may not officially have their roots in nutrition may be effectively handled with a change in diet. I would also recommend that any new mother who is exhibiting signs of postpartum depression look into the possibility of hypoglycemia. In many cases, diet can be much more important than drugs.

Most pagan parents are very well read when it comes to natural foods. We do our best to keep our families eating well, even if a good number of us also indulge in alcohol, desserts, and good coffee. For those of us that are diabetic or hypoglycemic, it is important to keep in mind that alcohol is a sugar too. Combining sugar or caffeine with simple carbohydrates or refined foods is an equation that can result in a good deal of suffering.

A well-rounded diet that is low in refined sugars, processed foods, preservatives, and pesticide-treated produce is a benefit to families for many reasons. Not only does it contribute to a healthy body that is more able to fight off disease, but it also allows us to maintain greater control over our emotions and our energies.

Food allergies, sugar highs, and reactions to preservatives have all been found to directly affect personality and emotional state. Some people even believe that they pick up negative vibrations from animal flesh, particularly if the animal experienced a difficult or painful life and death. Most people in modern society experience varying degrees of reaction to sugar and caffeine.

The path of a priest, priestess, shaman, druid, or whatever relies on the individual having complete control over his or her own emotions and behavior. We cannot expect our children to behave calmly and rationally, or to easily gain control in Circle, if we are feeding them nothing but hot dogs, soda, and chocolate cereal.

Exercise

According to the first-ever *Surgeon General's Report on Physical Activity and Health*, which was released in July 1996, almost fifty percent of Americans between the ages of twelve and twenty-one are not vigorously active on a regular basis. This lack of physical activity increases dramatically during adolescence. It would seem that far too many of our children, at least in the United States, are sitting around, probably watching television.

It is significant that more than sixty percent of American adults do not achieve the recommended amount of physical activity and twenty-five percent are not active at all. Our children learn from our example and most adults feel that they don't have enough time for themselves to work out, after answering the demands of work and family.

A study by the Centers for Disease Control found that although two-thirds of this adult population are trying to lose weight, most do not enjoy physical exercise. They perceive exercise as being time consuming, boring, and physically painful. On the other hand, physical activity is generally viewed as fun and enjoyable.

This is the key to getting our children to exercise. We need to find ways to make it fun for the whole family and set an example by becoming involved with them. As parents, we care about this for more reasons than simply wanting our children to look good. We care because the benefits of physical activity are substantial.

According to the surgeon general's report and the Centers for Disease Control studies, regular moderate activity can substantially reduce the risk of developing or dying from heart disease, diabetes, colon cancer, and high blood pressure. Moderate levels of exercise appear to reduce the symptoms of depression and anxiety, improve one's mood, and enhance one's ability to perform daily tasks throughout life. This also helps to keep health care costs down.

Regular moderate activity is the key. What this means is that we don't need to introduce our children to a competitive, training mindset to achieve these tremendous benefits. We can play, hike, or work around the house with them, as long we do it consistently. Certainly, the benefits increase with the duration, intensity, and frequency of exercise, but the average person can improve his or her health, future, and attitude just by having some fun away from the television set.

Pagan families can experience an additional benefit from moderate exercise. Not only do children have an abundance of energy that may interfere with meditation and ritual, but many adults retain the stresses and tensions of everyday life and work. This can make it difficult to achieve trance states or shut down the mind enough to obtain satisfactory results when working with divination or magic.

Exercise and play help us to release our tensions, and some of that extra energy that may interfere in our workings as pagans. Many of us find that we are more able to meditate and work effectively in ritual after some form of exercise, partially due to an increase in specific biochemicals called endorphins. Exercise, laughter, and orgasm are some of the best ways to consciously make the body produce endorphins.

Endorphins are biochemical painkillers with a chemical structure similar to morphine. When they are released, they bind to the opiate receptors in neurons, blocking our experience of pain, and increasing our experience of pleasure. They affect the flow of other biochemicals, which play a part in allowing the body to experience altered states.

Endorphins are largely responsible for "runner's high" and that great feeling we get from orgasms. They also have a similar effect as some of the sacred plants used by shamans and other ecstatics across the world. Many people feel as though they are automatically lifted into altered states once their production of endorphins is increased, most notably after exercise.

This can be another tool for pagan families to use to their advantage. Certainly with younger children, it is best to limit the time periods of ritual or meditation. However, these workings may be more productive when following a period of play or exercise.

Energy Work and Colors

As we know, from this book and others, the human energy field is integral to our existence. It permeates the physical body and interconnects us with the universal energy field: that which binds us to All of Life and all worlds. Many of us have heard the phrase "thought precedes action." This is a simplistic way of saying that everything that occurs in the physical realm is caused by events occurring in the purely energetic realms of existence.

What occurs within our energy bodies has a direct effect on the physical, and vice versa. Although physical events may have their precedent in the higher energetic realms, physical events are stored and carried by the spirit beyond death and often into the next incarnation. Working consciously with the energy of our families is an excellent way to clear old patterns and memories that may be causing current conditions. It is also probably the best method for creating long-term health.

Pagan families can use the exercises in this book for developing their abilities to feel and see auras. This is an important tool for healing as well. Disturbances in the auric field will show up in the physical. They may manifest as emotional or behavioral difficulties or physical problems, including accidents. If you are aware of these disturbances in the early stages, you can begin to work with them before they cause significant problems for your children.

These disturbances will often appear to be discolored or dis-figured auras. You may see a dark area or a color that is not quite clear or true. Sometimes, thoughtforms are visible within the energy field of a person. Or, if you are more shamanically inclined, you may perceive these as embedded spirits, insects, or animals. Working with the exercises in this book will provide you the opportunity to develop your own symbolism and ways of *seeing* accurately.

The easiest way to heal through using energy is to simply channel clear, loving energy to the individual in need. You can do this in a meditation or sit with your hands open toward the person and allow yourself to be a funnel for universal healing energy. Unless you are guided specifically, or well trained, it is best not to direct specific energy or colors to any definite area. Simply offer the energy and let the individual's higher self direct and use this energy as needed.

If you see disturbances in specific chakras, you may wish to channel the pure color that is associated with the healthy chakra. If the disturbances appear to be an excess of energy in that area, you may prefer to channel the opposite color for a balance. Keep in mind that any energy sent will be used according to the indi-vidual choice and best interest. We cannot harm or heal another without their participation or permission on some level of being. Belief plays a large part in both the participation and permission of a patient.

General Colors for Healthy Chakras
The seven major chakras and their associations are as follows:

Base (the base of the spine)
    Associated colors: red/black for grounding
    Associated body areas: spine, kidneys, adrenals

Sacral/Abdominal
    Associated color: orange
    Associated body areas: reproductive system, lymphatic
       system

Solar Plexus/Belly
  Associated color: yellow
  Associated body areas: pancreas, stomach, liver, gall bladder,
    nervous system

Heart
  Associated color: green/pink
  Associated body areas: heart, thymus, blood, vagus nerve,
    circulatory system

Throat
  Associated color: blue
  Associated body areas: throat, vocal chords, larynx, thyroid,
    lungs, bronchial tubes, alimentary canal

Forehead/Third Eye
  Associated color: indigo
  Associated body areas: lower brain, eyes, ears, nose, nervous
    system, pituitary gland

Crown
  Associated colors: violet/white
  Associated body areas: upper brain, pineal gland,
    hypothalamus

Breathing

Although the benefits of breath control were discussed in chapter 3, it is important enough to touch on here as well. Most biological parents have been though the Lamaze or Bradley childbirth classes. We know firsthand the importance of regulating the breath during childbirth. Unfortunately, most parents don't think to use this at other times.

The breathing exercises outlined earlier are recommended for anyone in emotional distress or pain. However, they can require a great deal of focus and concentration that may not be available when a child is hurt. Depending on the age of the child, another technique may be necessary.

Obviously, we cannot do much about the breathing of infants. They don't understand our directions and have not yet regained the necessary control over their physical bodies. Toddlers, on the other hand, respond very well to simple breathing techniques. I have been using "Blow Out the Candles" since our son was approximately two years old, to help him handle the pain of everything from diaper rash to cuts and bruises. Not only does it redirect his focus away from the pain, but it forces his body to relax, even just a little, allowing his endorphins to kick in and reducing both his fear and his experience of the pain. If there are times when you cannot redirect the child's attention from the pain, have her blow the "ouch" out rather than blow out the candles.

Our son loved to play birthday party as a toddler. Around the age of two, he developed a real fascination for blowing out candles. In fact, the Imbolc just after he turned two, he entertained everyone in our druid group by going around the cauldron during the ritual and blowing out all our candles. This seems to be a trend with children this age and again, we can use it to our advantage.

Teenagers may feel silly with these exercises and should be encouraged to use the breathing exercises in chapter 3. Alternatively, they may be taught a variation on the Lamaze breathing techniques for use after injuries.

Blow Out the Candles Exercise

In order to use this effectively in a crisis, you may want to practice it with your child when he is not hurt. Use it enough so that when you say "Blow Out the Candles," he will know immediately what you mean.

> Gain your child's attention in whatever nonthreatening way you feel is best after an injury or during a time of emotional distress.
>
> Say loudly (without yelling, if possible), "Blow Out the Candles!"
>
> Have your child follow your lead as you take a really deep breath and blow it out strongly. It is

important to really play this up with younger children. Make faces and silly noises as you suck in a deep . breath. Make sure you make noise as you blow out the hardest breath ever to put out all those imaginary candles.

Do not allow the child time to get refocused on the crisis. Immediately tell him that those candles are back and repeat both the deep breath and the exhalation.

Keep this up until the child either cannot maintain the focus or feels better.

Be a Bee Exercise

This is similar to Blow Out the Candles, but is recommended for children over the age of five. It is based on a pranayama technique called *Bhramari*, which translates as "a large bee."

After gaining the child's attention, tell her or him to Be a Bee. Again, practice will increase the effectiveness of this method in a crisis.

Breathe in deeply through your nose. Breathe out, also through your nose but exaggerate a nasal buzzing or humming sound, like that of a bee.

Repeat for a maximum of three minutes. If necessary, alternate with Breathing Exercise 1 from chapter 3.

Any techniques beyond this can be very involved and it would be a disservice for me to offer you additional specific techniques in this section. Your best course of action is to first develop your abilities, using the exercises in this book and then get some training in these methods. Alternatively, and mainly as an introduction, you may want to read a book that is specifically devoted to this topic.

6

The Family Connection

The family connection is a complex web of relationships that affects us on every level of being. Our first beliefs about the world and about ourselves are developed within the framework of home and family—whatever that may be to each of us individually. We first learn about love and trust and how to interact with other people through our early family relationships.

While these lessons continue and may change throughout our lives, those first beliefs about people and the world are carried with us, often in some deep part of the shadow side. We grow up and our point of view changes. In the process, we may forget these beliefs are there, yet they continue to affect our experience of reality.

The family connection may result in strong ties to the Great Spirit and personal spirit guides. It may foster a sense of self-confidence and the actualization of one's potential. This is certainly the ideal situation. On the other hand, one's experience of family may result in the loss of soul fragments and connections to power animals. It may prevent a close bond with Spirit, one's Self, and one's personal abilities.

While it may not always appear so to others, most parents do the best they can at any given time. This is not to say that everyone is an ideal parent at all times. Nor does it mean that everyone should be a parent, just because they physically can. The simple truth is, we all have our issues to handle and none of us are perfect. If there are problems in your family, or if you are experiencing something you would prefer not to, do not allow yourself to get bogged down in guilt or blame. This is an avoidance tactic and does not contribute to the healthy development of anyone.

It is our responsibility as parents to handle our own shadows. Before we had children, it was pretty much up to us if we wanted to remain stuck in our "stuff," but now our responsibility has greatly expanded. We can no longer tell someone to get out. We cannot simply leave the party and come home. Our behavior has a profound impact on the lives and psyches of our children—and we can't send them back.

This chapter is not about handling our own shadows or telling other parents what they should or should not do. My main point in beginning this chapter in this way is to set the stage for the web of relationships that is the family connection. I want it to be clear to readers that there need be no guilt if something in this book touches a chord within you. Guilt truly is a useless emotion, unless it is used as a motivator to effect change. Certainly, we all feel guilty at times but that alone does nothing for our children or our own spiritual development.

It should also be clear that we should steer clear of blame and judgment of other parents. However, there is a huge difference between judgment and discernment. When we judge, we impose our own beliefs and restrictions and fears on other people. We refuse to experience the energy that they embody and we limit ourselves in the process. In refusing to experience them, we also deny ourselves potentially valuable learning opportunities.

Discernment, on the other hand, is about choosing consciously from a wiser, more expanded place. We do not derogate, assigning a label of inferiority. We simply recognize that this is not an energy that we prefer to include in our lives at this time.

I have friends whose parenting tactics amaze me at times. My husband and I would never react in those ways or use those discipline methods with our son. However, we are not the parents in that family. We are not privy to all that goes on. Those children and parents chose each other for a reason. While we *discern* that this course of action is not for us, we do not *judge* and eliminate these people from our lives.

Nor do we attempt to tell these parents what to do. While we may suggest an alternate route, we recognize that what is best for us is not necessarily best—and may not work—for others. It then becomes a simple case of agreeing to disagree, supporting another's right to be different, and that is part of being pagan.

Unless there is blatant abuse going on, it is not our place to decide what is best for another family. There are probably readers who disagree with some of what I have written in this book. This is to be expected. We will not agree on every point. But as parents, we all agree that our children's best interests come first. If you are reading this book, you have proven that this is foremost on your mind. It is how you proceed from this point on that really counts. You cannot change the past, but you can work toward creating the best possible future.

Many people believe that psychic and shamanic or magical abilities are passed down through families. I believe we are genetically passing on these abilities to our children. Many researchers have found that the brain forms new connections between neurons during any kind of learning. Over time, these connections become more defined and change their strength, depending on the need for each. It is my opinion that we access our shamanic and psychic abilities through generally unused neural pathways.

The more we use these pathways, the stronger they become. With each generation, we produce more children with easier access to these abilities. Provided the family atmosphere is such that these abilities are not repressed and blocked, these children will grow up with greater abilities and deeper understanding of their interconnections with All That Is.

It is the family atmosphere that is the key to attaining the full potential of these genetic abilities. Studies have shown that while the overall program for determining neural connections is genetic, it is external stimuli, which are vital in determining what network connections are made. In many ways, experience causes our brains to continually rewire themselves. This is particularly true for small children. We are born with all the neurons we need. However, at birth our neural connections are relatively primitive. As we grow and learn, these connections develop into a useful network.

An alternate view of this passing on of abilities within families is reincarnation. Many indigenous cultures and pagan traditions believe that spirits have a tendency to return to this world along family lines. The Saami are believed to return to the Saami, particularly within the same family bloodlines.

Although there is a Naming ritual performed after the child is born in shamanic societies, the name is often received by the mother or shaman prior to childbirth. Commonly received during dreaming or journeying, it is frequently clear at that time whether this name is given to indicate the return of an ancestor. When a specific name is not received in this way, the name of a respected ancestor may be chosen for an infant in hopes of attracting that soul to reincarnate, or in an attempt to bring in the qualities possessed by that ancestor.

Whether you choose to believe this is all due to genetics or reincarnation or merely kindred spirits choosing to spend their time in this world together, the point is that these abilities exist. On a very basic level, we all feel connected to something greater than this physical body. Our early experiences, family atmosphere, and the beliefs we choose to follow as adults, contribute significantly to the actualization of this innate potential.

And that really is the main goal of this book: to provide assistance for those families who want their children to achieve their full potential, in all areas of life. Certainly, many of these exercises are designed to increase their spiritual and magical abilities. But, all of this merely contributes to their total sense of Self and well-being; to their feelings of being the creators of their lives and not the victims.

So, what does the pagan family do to contribute to all this? We treat our families as honored spirits and our homes as sacred space. We don't make it all right to take out our frustrations on those we love because they have to be there. We are as honest as possible without taking advantage and without causing harm.

Anyone who has participated in ritual, or worked any form of magic, knows that words and thoughts are power. What we say and think is real on some level of being. Our thoughts, including beliefs, precede the manifestation of events in this reality. Magical incantations, mantras, galdor, chants, whatever term you choose to use, they all have a direct impact on one's state of consciousness, experience of this reality, and on one's very being, in some cases.

Similarly, anyone who has experienced taunting or arguments can fully understand how hurtful words can be, even if there was no conscious intent to hurt. How others perceive us does impact our perceptions, as does the majority view of our reality. When you hear something about yourself enough times, particularly as a child or from someone you love and trust, you may very well start believing it.

The things we say are very often unconscious, as we respond automatically without thinking about the potential effects of our words. As parents, we would be amazed at what our words can do to our children. None of us would choose to harm a child, and yet, those words that we don't mean and don't think about can cause a tremendous amount of harm.

Questions like "What is wrong with you?" when a child has made a mistake or does something you would prefer they not do, will only make that child wonder if there is something wrong with her or him. When we tell a child they are bad for doing something we told them not to do, we reinforce the idea that the child, rather than the behavior, is bad. And the term "bad" is in many cases a judgment call.

My point here is that metaphysical parents understand the power of words and thoughts more than many other parents do, yet we often hear pagan parents using the same phrases without thinking. To be honest, I do it myself on occasion. I say this to encourage all of us, myself included, to be more aware and to speak to our children as respectfully as we would speak to the gods and the spirits in ceremony.

Parenting can sometimes be a very difficult path to walk. When we are experiencing particularly stressful times, it is difficult to give as much of ourselves as our children require. This is especially true of single parents and parents that have no support system.

Our children will psychically pick up on transition or death in the family. They intuitively *know* when we are stressed or depressed. Because they are children and rely on us for their security and stability, their reaction is frequently to need more physical contact and tolerance from us. Unfortunately, in times of stress, we may not have the energy available to give our children the support they need.

The bottom line is that we are the parents. For whatever reason, we chose to have these children, or to bring them into our homes. It is therefore, our responsibility to be there for them and to find it within ourselves to be significantly more understanding of their needs. We may need to consciously remind ourselves that they are children. Depending on their ages, they may not understand that we are moving to another country or that Mommy is away on business for a month or that Mommy and Daddy are having difficulty paying the bills. All they know is they feel our stress and sadness and they need us to comfort them.

This lifetime is limited and children grow up too fast. We cannot guarantee that we will all still be on this earth when we "get past the current problem or deadline." We cannot say for sure that our children will not have disappeared into their own defenses by the time we feel we have enough energy or happiness to give back to them.

For our own best interests and our children's well-being, we need to find ways to be there and make time for both of us. Even if a parent that works outside the home can spend only one hour each day giving full attention to a child, that can make a world of difference. Some type of physical exercise and meditative practice in some form regularly will help you handle your stress more effectively, and it will also make you a better parent.

There are many exercises that parents and children can do together. Our son loves to dance with me, even if only for one song. In the process, I lighten up and enjoy our time together while he gets my undivided attention in a fun way. We also do Yoga for Kids, work in the garden, and walk the dog together.

Busy parents may want to use audiotapes at bedtime for assistance in maintaining a spiritual practice. When there are simply not enough hours in a day, this is one of the best ways to fully relax the body while you center and balance the mind and spirit. My parents and I have routinely gone to sleep with audiotapes since I was a child. I particularly recommend the Monroe Institute audiotapes.

Anything we can do to release our own stress and stay connected to the Great Spirit will help us to be good parents. Children do not understand this reality as we do. They also live in the moment so much that telling them to go away or leave us alone can have a tremendous negative impact. It is often too late if we try to make up for it an hour or a day later. Certainly, we all lose control on occasion, but when we do it is far more important to make up for it by developing the ability not to react that way again than it is to say we are sorry and go out for ice cream. It is also important to be honest and explain our reasons to our children.

They benefit greatly from a truly honest relationship. They need to know that we are human and make mistakes. We need to find a way to communicate why we reacted as we did and to let them know we will not allow it to happen again, without blaming them for it. In doing so, we teach them, through word and action, that while there is no guilt in emotion, we can choose to handle our emotions differently.

The laws of karma apply here as well. When we walk an honorable path and treat others with respect and love, we will receive the same type of energy in return. Children who know without question that they are loved no matter what they do will give love. Those who are permitted to make mistakes and learn from them will very likely grow up to set examples for their friends and to have healthy families, continuing a healthier cycle. Self-knowledge is paramount in this process.

As pagan parents, we respect each member of the family, from the toddler on the time-out chair, to the goldfish, to the parents. We love and support unconditionally, even when the daughter of a strict feminist wants to be a cheerleader or the son of a Wiccan chooses to follow Zen Buddhism. As long as our family members are not putting themselves or others in harm's way, we support their right to choose for themselves.

The combination of discipline with love and gentleness is very powerful. As is true in most families, there are some things our son is not allowed to do in this house. Similarly, there are times when we need him to listen to us. We may yell or send him to the time-out chair. But, when the situation is over, it is over. We do not continue to bring it up. We do not nurse our hurt feelings or react to each new situation based on past experiences.

Our son knows he can always count on a hug, a kiss, and an "I love you" no matter what has transpired. It is clear to everyone that, while we may not always see eye to eye, we love him completely at all times. And while he may fight us on occasion, he trusts us implicitly. He knows without question that we will always be there to support him.

It is important for a child to know that his parents will go to bat for him and support his choices, within reason. My mother and I would have intense quarrels when I was young. I disagreed with a lot of what she did and she was not always so thrilled with my choices. However, I knew that she was always on my side and would fight for me, if necessary. Within reason and as long as I was honest with her, she would even lie for me. That kind of absolute trust does not bring with it any thought of manipulation—because of the honesty factor.

I obviously write from the perspective of one who is living the "traditional" family life. I have a husband and we are a monogamous, heterosexual couple with one biological child of our own. We discussed having an open relationship before we became parents, but neither of us found anything desirable outside our relationship. We are best friends and still very much in love and lust. This is but one type of family structure and it is not the type of family I was raised in.

Pagans embrace diversity in many ways. Alternative family structures are one of the ways we express our diversity. There are as many variations on the family as there are individual pagans; and all are accepted by the pagan community. However, all variations are not necessarily accepted by the majority culture. This is one reason why I strongly suggest that pagans in alternative families find a pagan support system.

Communal or polyamorous communities, although not common, are valid forms of the pagan family. These can offer the children a larger support system and, ideally, a greater amount of loving adults to rely on. However, they often have their own issues with stability and transience that should be addressed when children are involved.

Some married couples may choose alternative sexual lifestyles, either within or outside their marriage. This can be a more difficult situation for children than that of a polyamorous community, simply because of perceived differences and the generally-accepted beliefs regarding married couples. It is also frequently true that polyamorous communities are more open about their arrangements than these types of marriages.

Within these marriages, sexual experimentation or affairs are often hidden from the children, or one parent is more open than the other is. This can be very difficult for children to understand, particularly if they discover a hidden truth regarding their parents' sexuality. Again, honesty is very important, within reason.

As parents, we need to keep in mind that our children must live and grow in mainstream society. Unless they are home schooled from preschool through college, they will eventually need to interact with that social structure in their formative years. To be honest, total isolation during youth does not benefit them. Once we become parents, we can no longer avoid handling the issues raised by our life choices. And once we become parents, our life choices are no longer completely our own.

I have heard people say that they do not answer to their children for their choices. It is certainly true that, as adults, we can make whatever choices we desire. But, as parents, we need to weigh the consequences of our actions. We must consider how our actions will affect our children. And if we choose a lifestyle that is destined to create discomfort or pain for our children, we are honor-bound to be as supportive and open as we can with them.

We cannot always shield our children from pain, nor should we. These children chose to be born into a modern pagan family. Part of being a modern pagan is embracing the diversity of paths and people in our world. That alone is bound to cause them some difficult times. A parent that would go along with currently accepted social values simply to avoid discomfort does not teach their children about courage and integrity.

When we, as parents, live our lives as honest, respectful beings, we teach our children to live with honor. No matter what our sexual preference or lifestyle choices, we are their parents. We are responsible for loving and supporting them, and for doing all we can to encourage their development into physically and spiritually healthy individuals.

Nonparental adults in communal or polyamorous groups have special considerations when developing relationships with the children of other members. This also holds true to a lesser degree for members of covens, groves, or other spiritual/religious group. Children will bond to any adult that is considered to be a trusted part of the family. In a spiritual or religious context, this bond can be even stronger because of the inherent absolute trust.

If yours is a group that has seen a great deal of change or people coming in and out of the group, I would caution you to use restraint when your children are concerned. In truth, we should all be wary of the desire to instantly bond to someone new and invite them into our family. In groups such as these the children often end up feeling abandoned when it doesn't work out between the adults and a loved one leaves.

This is a possibility that should be openly discussed, both with newcomers to the group and with your children. It should also be periodically revisited, especially after someone has chosen to leave the group. Frequently, members have the best of intentions while they are in the group, and even when they choose to leave. No one wants to hurt a child, and many members will feel special bonds to the children. But things do not always work out this way and we need to be aware of that.

Whatever form of family you have, it is important to be open to questions and discussion with your children regarding your choices. Many of these groups or family structures are bound to raise questions, particularly once a child enters school. In any event, children are naturally curious. To refuse to discuss choices that directly affect their lives should be red flag to a parent. Perhaps there is some underlying issue that you do not want to have to face. Our children have every right to ask, and in most cases, to get honest forthright answers from their parents.

Now, let us move on to the things that families can do together to foster pagan spirituality. Beginning with the gradual introduction of our beliefs, as most of us must do in order to successfully tell a newcomer of our spirituality, let us begin with the simple and move upward. The total household atmosphere and the everyday activities of family members play a much more important role in fostering a child's innate spirituality than all the active teaching we can do.

Obviously, a part of this means including children in religious rituals, particularly our holiday rituals. Children, especially the younger ones, learn best when they are having fun. The seemingly superfluous activities that surround each of the eight main pagan holidays can be a powerful learning tool. House decorating, singing traditional or commercial songs, cooking, and making arts and crafts are all wonderfully interactive methods for introducing pagan ethics and beliefs to children. Also, many of the customs that are currently associated with Christianity have their origins deep in the ancient pagan cultures.

The Seasonal Festivals

One of the easiest ways to teach children about the seasons and the holidays is to create a family calendar. Simply through repetition and having something so personal to work with, children learn the relationships between the seasons and our holidays. They may also learn of the deities or other symbols that we associate with these holidays.

My husband and I love to have a special drink for each season. All this activity, with special foods and drinks, makes each season special and fun. Each special food or drink is traditional and/or symbolic of the deities, energies, or other special events of the holiday season. Perhaps some of these suggestions will spark your own creativity.

Winter Solstice (Alban Arthuan/Yule)

The shortest day of the year—many pagans celebrate the New Year at this time; some pagan traditions feel this is when the Veil between the Worlds is thinnest.

Activities: baking special cookies and cakes, decorating with evergreens and luminarias,[1] making door wreaths, decorating the Yule log, making bayberry candles, singing carols, decorating a Christmas/Yule tree and making your own ornaments.

Special drinks: eggnog, spiced red grape juice (served warm), or nonalcoholic beer.

Imbolc (Candlemas)

The first stirrings of life within the Earth; the heart of winter.

Activities: making the Corn Bride or Brigid Doll, decorating with wheat sheaves and early flowers, making and blessing

---

1 Luminarias are paper bags, filled with sand, in which a candle is lit. They glow on houses and stores throughout the Southwest during the winter, especially around Yule/Christmas.

candles; donating food or blankets, donating time at soup kitchens, baking Beive bread.[2]

Special drink: hot chocolate.

Spring Equinox (Alban Eiler, Eostre, Ostara)

Night and day are of equal length; balance and harmony.

Activities: decorating with pastels and Eostre bunny symbolism, coloring eggs, blessing seeds for planting, early gardening.

Special drink: ginger ale and white grape juice.

Bealtainne/Beltane

The first summer festival, celebrating fertility.

Activities: making Green Man masks, Maypole dancing, picnics, outdoor bonfires.

Special drink: Maywine for the kids—a punch made of white grape juice with strawberries and a sprig of woodruff (if you can find it).

Summer Solstice (Alban Heruin, Midsummer)

The shortest night of the year.

Activities: Solar Disc[3] or Beive ring,[4] faery offerings, camping.

Special drink: iced herb tea with honey.

Lughnasad (Lammas)

The first harvest.

Activities: baking breads, outdoor games, and sporting events.

Special drink: alcohol-free beer.

---

2   Beive is the Saami Sun goddess. In early February, the Saami bake a small loaf of bread in the form of a ring, usually made with reindeer blood and fat (although for our uses this is not necessary). This is then fixed outside, above the door as an offering to the Sun. On the holiday morning, the Sun is greeted with song.

3   The Solar Disc is a circular Sun symbol used by several traditions. It may be a Wheel of the Year: an eight-armed cross surrounded by a circle. Streamers are often tied to the solstice and equinox points. Alternatively, it may be any Sun symbol from a round disc covered with golden foil to a sunflower head.

4   At Midsummer, the Saami hang a brass ring above the door of the home or tent to catch and hold the warmth of Beive, the returning sun.

Autumn Equinox (Alban Elued, Mabon)

The last harvest, balance and harmony.

Activities: picking grapes, blessing and storing seeds, decorating with gourds and red chile ristras,5 making gourd rattles.

Special Ɵrink: red grape juice.

Samhuinn/Samhain

The apple harvest, preparation for winter; the Celtic feast of the dead.

Activities: apple picking, dunking for apples, making candy apples, hay rides, decorating for Halloween, trick-or-treating, making an ancestor altar.

Special Ɵrink: warm, spiced apple cider.

Mealtimes

Mealtimes can become quality time to sit down and talk with your family, unless of course, like many modern people, you eat in front of the television. The preparation of food is a sacred thing. In my family, we make a great game out of preparing foods together, particularly on the weekends. There is something for everyone to do and our son learns valuable lessons about safety and independence in the process.

To sit down for an entire meal without distraction and talk to one another is very special. We focus fully on one another and everyone is encouraged to join in the discussion. After telling the stories of the day, we can discuss more philosophical, political, or spiritual topics. With an upcoming holiday, we may go over the meanings of the holiday and what plans we are making.

Meals at many pagans' homes begin with a prayer of thanks. This is particularly true at our home when we are eating meat. Although we have been vegetarians at various times in our lives, we are currently omnivores. As we make offerings to our helping spirits or the faeries or the spirits of place, so do we feel it is important to offer back some energy to those who have given

---

5 In the Southwest, this is the chile harvest. Red chiles are strung into bunches for later use or for decoration.

their lives that we may eat. The following is one of our prayers that was first published in the Summer 1997 issue of *Circle Network News*.

> Great Spirit,
> We thank you for the gift of this food.
> We send blessings of peace, love, and release to all whose
> bodies and energies went into bringing us this
> nourishment.
> We honor you in our enjoyment and utilization of this meal.
> May it bring us health and joy,
> Reminding us of our interconnections with All That Is.
> As we receive, so do we give back
> And give thanks for this gift in the Cycle of Life.

The following is a good alternative prayer to use with younger children. It is short, simple, and to the point.

> Thank you, Great Spirit
> Thank you, chicken and peas and milk (or other food items)
> Thank you, Mother Earth
> We love this food.

There is also a value inherent in the simple act of cooking. To cook for another person is a sacred act. Through this act, we provide for their health and pleasure. We also imbue the food with our own energy as we prepare it. I strongly suggest that you not prepare food for your family during an argument or when you are carrying around destructive feelings. I know that this is not always possible, but you might want to step outside and ground out your tensions into the earth or smudge yourself before beginning to cook.

When you cook or prepare any food for your family, do it with love and that is what they will receive through the food. I make it a habit to charge food, utensils, and cookware with all the prayers I have for my family members while I am preparing anything, even a simple snack. In this way, an everyday meal becomes a powerful means to channel healing and love to our families.

Charging Food Exercise

This exercise can be used to charge anything from cookware to soda cans to crystals

> Taking deep breaths, count yourself down from ten to one, into a light trance state.
> Hold your hands out over the food or around the food container.
> Feel and see loving, healing energy streaming through your hands into the food.
> If you have any specific prayers or blessings, direct these through your hands and see them imbue the food with their energy.

Children love to participate in special family activities, whether these are holiday celebrations, soccer games, or camping trips. Developing your own unique activities is a great way to have fun while connecting with your children. It can also provide an easy way to bring your spirituality into everyday activities, thereby reinforcing the idea that everything is a sacred act.

I would encourage each family to find something they all enjoy that reflects the personality and spiritual path of their family. In addition, try to make each activity a spiritual one, whether you bring an awareness of the God and Goddess into it or simply do it with honor and respect for all concerned. Arts and crafts projects are the most common of these spiritually fun family activities.

Many families will create holiday decorations together and use them year after year. My mother still has some of the decorations that we made when I was very young. These items become almost like family heirlooms and each time we see them we are reminded of that family connection. Decorative eggs for the Spring Equinox are something else that everyone can look forward to all year long.

Drumming and any kind of music-making are activities that everyone can get involved in. All children love to drum, hum through a kazoo, or play guitar. Our son got his first drum before he was born and he was banging away at it by the time he was six months old. By the ripe old age of three, he had his own little doumbek to play at home and at drumming circles.

It is important to allow this to flow naturally and allow the child to play whatever instrument calls to her or him. Most people respond to drums. They are the rhythms of Mother Earth and seem to call to most of us. However, some people prefer guitars or harps or saxophones. And some people prefer song and storytelling without musical accompaniment. While our son is quite the little drummer, he also plays a mean guitar, rattle, and kazoo.

These instruments do not need to cost a great deal. In fact, the making of instruments can become another fun family activity. A coffee can with rubber stretched over the opening or different size plastic storage dishes make great beginners drums. And who among us has never played the rubber band and tissue box guitar? There are an infinite number of ways for your family to construct rattles, horns, harps, and cymbals, all with materials you have around the house or outside in the yard.

In truth, the family connection includes everything contained in this book and more. Our every act as parents affects our children, whether we choose to see that or not. How we live our lives impacts our children on many levels. The role of parent demands a tremendous responsibility that may very well also involve becoming more mature and less self-centered individuals. We all do the best we can at any given time, but perhaps we can all take another good look at our selves and our family dynamics to see how we can do more or do it better.

Parents do not necessarily gain the respect of their children, simply because they are parents. As our children grow up and become more aware of our actions, they may very well lose respect for us. In most cases, this is typical teenage rebellion and we just need to get through it. But in some cases, our children have a point that is worth investigating.

The main questions we might ask ourselves periodically as parents are: Am I honestly following the Rede, "An it harm none, do what ye will" (whether you are Wiccan or not)? Am I taking the time I need for myself? If I were my child, how would I feel about my parent? Am I being a buddy or a parent? Am I being fair or dictatorial? Do I want my child to grow up to be like me in all ways? Am I doing anything that I would not feel comfortable honestly and completely telling friends and family about? And finally, if my child were to get involved with someone like me, how would that make me feel?

7

Children and the Community

Community has been defined as any group living in the same area or having interests, work, etc., in common; and the general public. Many of us participate in more than one community at any given period in our lives. We have our local or neighborhood communities, our work communities, and the communities defined by any clubs or special interest organizations we may belong to. Children are usually an integral part of most of our communities, but they also have their own groups, exclusive of adults. These generally include such "communities" as sports teams, neighborhood friends, and other special interest groups.

While most pagans also participate in multiple communities, their identities are often quite different, depending on the community. This is certainly true to some degree for all people, but pagans have the added component of their religions. The majority of us are closet pagans, at least in some of our communities, and unfortunately, our spiritual communities often do not coincide with our neighborhood or work communities.

This can make things difficult for both pagan parents and their children. Within a community, our children learn the behaviors that are acceptable to that society. They also begin to learn who they are through the mirrors of their community members. Parents are responsible for teaching and guiding their children through the complex web of relationships and acceptable behaviors specific to that group.

While each community has its own particular flavor and ethical values, the mainstream community tends to be very different from the pagan community. While we may wish for the ideal world where we can all live together in diversity and harmony, pagan parents and children walk a tightrope of social values. It can sometimes be a challenge for a young pagan to avoid bleed-through of social values from one community into another.

We want our children to feel comfortable with the human body and with both intimacy and sexuality. They are certain to encounter a majority of humans who are afraid of sexuality and nudity. Many of these people carry similar fears regarding simple intimacy and "alternative" sexual preferences.

We hope that our children will honor themselves as well as each other and the Earth. We dream of them walking this lifetime in spiritual connection with All of Life, but this is another area where our children are likely to encounter truly saddening and frightening variations in belief.

The behaviors and ethics of pagan communities will obviously differ to some degree from those of the mainstream. It is important that pagan parents recognize this as we are supporting the development of healthy, balanced identities in our children. We may need to make it clear to younger children that running around the neighborhood naked is not a good idea, nor is it always safe. The subject of pagan and mainstream identities will be discussed in greater detail in the chapter on "Honesty versus Secrecy."

Any community is not truly a *community* unless it fulfills specific needs for all its members. A community exists to bring people together to meet common goals. We need not all be pals in a community, but we do need to know that if we need help we are not alone. Community members pull together when someone is injured or has lost a loved one or is in need of an operation they cannot afford.

Pagan community members have contributed to court cases for other pagans wrongly accused of a variety of things, mainly related to their alternative religion. Pagans have banded together to clean up parks and riverbanks and to speak out against discrimination or harassment. We have come together magically to support someone through a difficult emotional time, to send prayers and energy to help someone pass an important test or get into a certain college, and to aid the police in stopping a serial criminal.

Communities need to be there when there is no crisis as well. It is with our communities that we share our thoughts and feelings. These are the people who are there when a baby is born, a child reaches adulthood, or a wedding takes place. They are our babysitters, our rides to events, and the people we go out to the pubs with. We share the good times and the bad with these people and we all grow through the experience.

This is the essence of community. The strength of our communities is vital to our survival and well-being. A strong community becomes a type of extended family for many people. This is an essential need for our children, who are the future of our communities and of our world. Children need a community to help them feel connected and a part of something.

Even in mainstream culture, it is a fact that the modern family is going through some very difficult changes. Many people do not live near their extended families. Many do not even have contact with everyone in their nuclear families. When the contact is present, it is often strained by a lack of honest communication as well as other factors.

For pagans, there can be an even greater need for a spiritual family. Many pagans have either not informed their biological families of their spirituality or they were rejected by family because of their choice of religion. They are left without the one institution that is supposed to always be supportive and love you unconditionally: the family. As a result, more and more pagans are looking to their spiritual communities to fill the roles of family.

Pagan Communities

Many of us will seek out pagan community for our children. Whether we are new to paganism or have been solitary for years, we want our children to be able to interact with a community that is welcoming and supportive of our beliefs. We don't want our children to grow up always needing to be careful what they tell to whom. Whether one is Druid, Wiccan, or Santero, we want our children to feel safe in being open about their spiritual beliefs.

As parents and guardians, we recognize that children need the company of their peers. They need to be able to play with others of their own age. They need to be able to talk about life and develop their own identities and get into trouble—all with other children. This is another major reason why pagan parents often decide to become involved with some type of pagan community.

As a child raised pagan at the beginning of the New Age movement, I always wished for friends my own age at metaphysical gatherings and seminars. Although I was included in everything my mother did, and I was accepted by the new leaders of the movement, it was very clear that I was the only child. Rarely did we encounter other children and this was difficult for me at times.

As a result, it has been very important for me to seek out other pagan families and communities that might provide our son with peers and friends within a spiritually safe space. I find this to be the case with most pagan parents I meet. Many individuals that once resisted involvement in a group will actively search for one when they have children.

. Since children will develop energetic bonds to trusted adults, we need to be aware of the group dynamics in any community. Covens and Groves can become a child's family. We spend a considerable amount of time together. These are the people that attend and perform Namings and adulthood ceremonies. We share all the festivals with them and we are both emotionally and energetically open to them in Circle.

Although I discussed this in "The Family Connection" chapter, it is important enough to touch on again. These people are not always blood relatives. Therefore, more than most blood relatives, they can simply walk away from the group. This can leave the children in these groups feeling abandoned. In groups with a high degree of transition, children can suffer soul loss and energy damage.

My intention here is not to recommend against involvement with these intense types of groups. My husband and I have worked with covens and we are solidly involved with a druidic grove. My point is simply this: be aware and exercise restraint and wisdom when involving your children with a new "family."

When a group breaks up or a special member leaves, treat it as a type of death. Recognize that there will be grief that needs to be expressed. This grief will often be accompanied by a variety of other emotions, just as in a physical death. There may be anger, feelings of abandonment or guilt, deep sorrow, loneliness, and a multitude of other feelings that need to be freely experienced in a safe space.

On the other hand, these types of communities can provide a necessary extended family and support to parents and children alike, even if they do not include other pagan children, as long as the children are honored and treated with respect within the group. These are the communities that teach our children, through word and action, that they are important and valued members of that community.

This is a tremendous benefit to the pagan child involved with any pagan community. Too often in modern society, children are "just kids" and as such are treated as annoyances, restrictions, or as unintelligent second-class citizens. We ignore them and pacify them with television, food, and video games.

Children are rarely included in decision making or creating community. However, they receive a great deal of the blame when they begin to get into trouble and act out of their soul loss and energetic blocks. They are labeled as "at-risk" or bad kids and we often blame their parents, who are frequently lacking any real community support or involvement, for their actions.

This is not the reality in pagan communities. Certainly, our children get into trouble, but we handle it differently. We all remember doing much of what they do ourselves. Some of us still do it, whatever it may be, but most of us treat it as a process of growth rather than as a sign that we have bad kids who need excessive discipline and punishment. Discipline is balanced with love and encouragement. Most children that I know who have been raised pagan, within some form of pagan community since before school age, are considerably more respectful and responsible than other children.

Festival Communities

More than any other group, with the exception of the Dead-heads, the neopagan movement has spawned a series of extended "family" communities based around the various festivals held across the country. While many pagans do restrict themselves to regional gatherings, there are a large number who travel from coast to coast. These are often pagan speakers and vendors who generally travel individually but hook up with the rest of their magical family at communal house gatherings or campsites.

Children of festival families are treated as our own. While children are usually given a greater degree of freedom at festivals, largely because these are safer spaces, everyone in the community keeps an eye on them. A child cannot get hurt or lost at a pagan festival without everyone in the general area coming to his or her rescue.

Furthermore, anyone who dares to harm a child in any way at a pagan festival will answer to everyone else, whether we know the child or not. There is zero tolerance for this type of behavior at pagan festivals. Even if an individual is merely suspected of harm to a child, they can count on being watched very carefully.

Most festivals have some form of childcare or kid's track of workshops and games designed specifically for younger pagans. Not only does this allow parents to attend workshops and interact with other adults, but it also provides a safe space for children of varying pagan paths to play together and make friends without having to hide their spiritual beliefs.

In recent years, the children's and teen's tracks of workshops have become very popular at many festivals. These serve several purposes. First and most obvious, they provide a forum for our children to learn about other paths from known and respected practitioners. This encourages them to explore and define their own spirituality. It also frequently gives them the opportunity to meet with well-known pagans, such as authors, elders, or other leaders in the community.

Perhaps more importantly, these events empower our children. Children are not simply expected to go off to play so that the adults in the community can do their thing. They are encouraged to learn and do what the adults are doing, without having to attend "adult" classes. Many children, especially teens, do not feel the adult classes are always applicable. Furthermore, they don't want to always have to do things with mom or dad.

In many cases, children are encouraged to share what they have learned, often through creating and offering their own rituals to the community. This can go a long way to developing community interaction and leadership skills, as well as supporting the healthy development of ego and self-confidence. It also provides our children with a format within which they can express themselves as they see fit and not merely from within the framework of family or tradition.

Festivals are the times when all pagans can freely and openly express themselves. These are the safe spaces where we feel comfortable just being whomever we feel we are or whomever we choose to be at the time, one reason many pagans attend such events. Pagan parents must keep in mind that their children will be exposed to all this wondrous diversity at a pagan gathering, particularly at the outdoor festivals.

Alternatives are the reality of many pagan festivals. Of course, the nudity is not generally in evidence at the indoor festivals, but the variation is still very evident. While this is freeing and spiritual to most, it can be intimidating or even frightening to many, especially if it is one's first pagan festival.

Those parents that are not comfortable with nudity, sexuality, body piercings, tattoos, men in skirts, or a wide variety of wild outfits would be well advised to avoid the outdoor festivals and be cautious about hotel conferences. These parents might prefer to find a metaphysical or pagan community in covens, meditation groups, Groves, or even churches, such as the Unitarian Universalist church.

Many of those who were not raised in a pagan family grew up with the indoctrinated beliefs that are prevalent in mainstream society. Even if we have chosen to consciously reject these beliefs, they are often still present and can act to color our reactions and our perceptions. This is often the case among pagans attending their first festivals.

Sexuality is possibly one of the most emotionally charged subjects in modern society. These feelings do not automatically change once one realizes that he or she is pagan. Pagan individuals and events can bring all of our sexual and body image fears, hang-ups, and judgments to the foreground.

At any type of pagan gathering, large or small, you are likely to come face to face with people of varying sexual preferences. As a result, new pagans are constantly offered the opportunity to handle any indoctrinated beliefs, or lingering judgments, they may have regarding certain sexual preferences. I have yet to meet a pagan who does not support another's right to sexual preference and lifestyle choices.

Pagans are notoriously accepting of the personal expressions of others. So, whether you choose to go naked, robed, or proudly display body piercings and tattoos, we support your right to choose and freely express yourself, provided you do not harm anyone and are responsible for your actions. Many pagans believe that they are not only expressing their freedom from limiting and unhealthy societal morals by being naked, but they deeply feel that this brings them closer to Nature, their spirituality, and their deities.

Some pagans feel that being skyclad in their rites and celebrations is asked for or required of them by their gods. Others have the exact opposite beliefs: that their gods will be offended if ritual participants are not appropriately clothed. And of course, most pagans are somewhere in the middle of these two belief systems.

I am not going to say that there are no judgments on both sides of the nudity issue. I will say that one of the beautiful things about pagans is that it is almost against our religions to dictate the attitudes, beliefs, or behaviors or other pagans. We have had enough of that from the majority culture. We will not do it to our pagan brothers and sisters. I would only hope that, as pagan parents, whether you choose to experience these events or not, you would encourage your own family to continue the important pagan tradition of supporting each other in the right to choose.

The festival ideal is that you may do as you wish, provided you harm no one. The reality is that separate sections have been created within some of the larger festivals for things like quiet camping or clothing required. The childcare area, if present, is almost always a clothing-required space. This has come as the result of our differing beliefs and feelings regarding the various freedoms at pagan events.

Not all pagan paths require, or even permit, nudity in ritual. Not all agree on the monogamy/polyamoury issue. And not all agree on the wearing of ritual garb outside of ritual. But while we all do support the choices of other pagans, not all of us feel comfortable in that space and not all of us want our children exposed to all that can mean.

It is our responsibility, as parents, to decide what we feel is beneficial and appropriate for our children. If you were not raised pagan, I would recommend that you spend some time considering this before deciding to head off to the summer festivals. If your children are old enough, you may want to include them in a discussion about these subjects and find out how they feel.

Many children these days have body image issues. As they reach puberty, these issues are compounded by all that chaotic energy and rampaging hormones. Sexuality and appearance become extremely important. Therefore, it is normal for a child, whose family is new to all of this, to initially feel uncomfortable at an outdoor festival.

These children should not be pressured to conform to any standard of behavior or dress at a festival. We do not dictate behavior and emotion to our children. We empower them to think for themselves with wisdom. It is best to allow them to decide for themselves what is comfortable. However, if you have limitations for children under a certain age, it is very important that you make those restrictions clear to your children up front. Things can feel very loose and free at a festival. Children need to know if there are boundaries and they need to be very clear what those boundaries are.

Festival communities can provide a necessary support system for children, in the absence of an extended pagan-friendly family or a coven, grove, temple, etc. This is particularly true when the family returns to the same festival year after year. A type of social structure will evolve among the children during a festival that can be similar to a school or neighborhood community.

All the usual dynamics are present in these festival communities, from sexual tensions and dating to competition and trouble making. However, there is the additional element of spirituality. These children will often make long-term and long-distance friends at festivals, largely because they share what is often perceived to be a mainstream social stigma. They all belong to the same underground or minority society and this brings them together for a common purpose.

The festival community also brings together people of all ages groups for a common purpose. This environment has even greater potential than do groves, covens, etc., in creating a bond between the generations. Elders are very much a part of the festival community. They are honored and respected in many ways. This is an important attitude for our children to develop. By contrast, attitudes regarding the elderly in modern, mainstream society are frightening and saddening.

Pagan children are exposed to a community where elders are valued for their perspective, power, and life experience. Both generations have the opportunity to interact and to learn from each other, empowering both the young and the old. Our elders are able to share their knowledge and experience, while gaining a feeling of inclusion and respect. In return, our children learn about life and spirituality from those who have been around for a very long time. The Old Ways are passed on, giving everyone a feeling of continuity and connectedness.

School Communities

For most children, the primary community of importance is that of school and school friends. As parents, we affect the school community in a myriad of ways. The very first and most potent way is our decision of what school our children will attend. For most parents, this is mainly a choice of public versus private school. However for a growing number of parents, home schooling is becoming a valid and preferred choice.

I would caution any parents considering this that home schooling is not the ideal situation for all families. It is highly recommended that you speak with others that are home schooling and educate yourself on the home schooling laws in your particular state or country. Socialization is a concern for many parents and this is something that needs to be addressed if your children do not have opportunities to interact with another community of their peers.

Home schooling is an attractive alternative for many pagan families because it eliminates the issue of honesty versus secrecy in this community. It also allows us to teach our children in the manner we believe to be best and to incorporate more of our spirituality into the teaching process. And of course, safety is another important concern that we have considerably more control over when our children are home schooled.

When making this type of decision, it is very important to keep in mind the long-term effects and whether our children are being isolated from the world or not. If there is an available community within which your children can socialize and interact with a diverse group of people, then perhaps home schooling is a beneficial alternative to mainstream schooling. However, unless a child is raised in an area of the world where the eventuality of professional or social interactions with a modern society is slim, we do them a disservice by isolating them when they are young.

If we, as parents, can wisely walk a strong and sensitive path within our communities, we truly honor each other and ourselves. We learn from each experience and, ideally, bring that new understanding into our homes and our relationships with our families. We then become the type of parent that most of us would like to be. Our children may still argue with us, but they will certainly respect us as honest, strong, spiritual beings who love them very much. If we are truly blessed, our children will choose to walk a similarly honorable path.

8

Handling the Tough Questions

When we talk of parenting, we must think about answering the questions that inevitably arise from our children. Most of these questions are tough because we are not really sure of the answers ourselves, or we retain limiting beliefs about the answers. How does a parent discuss sex with a child when he or she is not fully comfortable with nudity, sex, or intimacy? How do we answer questions about what happens when someone dies when we aren't really sure and are afraid of death ourselves? And how do we guide them through their relationships when we still have difficulty with ours?

The first course of action is to recognize that each parent is human. We are all still growing and learning. It is our responsibility to educate ourselves as best we can, but we can only work with what we have available to us at any given time. The answers a parent gives at one time may change as they learn more and gain more experience. It is okay to say that we do not know. Better to be honest with our children than to lie to them by pretending to be more than we are.

The answers to these questions will vary according to the child's age, family tradition, and the parent's personal beliefs. My overview of the general pagan and metaphysical beliefs about most of these issues here will certainly miss some questions. It would take an entire book to fully answer the really big questions, and even then we could not possibly come up with every difficult issue that may be raised in real life.

I can only suggest that you trust your intuition and be as honest as possible without inflicting harm. If you do not know the answer, let the child know that you will find out for them—and then do so. Be sure to frame your responses according to the child's age and comprehension or emotional level. Be supportive and understanding of their responses and make it clear that you are there if they need you.

What happens when you die? Where do you go?

Pagans recognize the cycles of life in all things. We celebrate the seasonal cycles and honor the death and rebirth in our world. All pagans believe that the spirit continues after death. Some of us believe in a form of reincarnation and some of us do not, but we all believe in the possibility of contact with the departed after death; that life and love continue without a physical body. We also believe that spirit guides or deities are with us once we leave this body, to guide us safely Home.

Many of us believe that our free soul, or astral body, travels about during sleep. During this time, we have access to other dimensions and other beings. We may very well carry on relationships with departed loved ones while our physical bodies sleep. This is probably the best way to explain this to young children.

Toddlers are just not ready for an in-depth discussion of the spirit versus the body. They may be able understand that a loved one's body has died but that this person still lives in the Dreamtime. In a way, they have just moved to live in another place, without their body. We can still see them, especially when we are dreaming.

In my book *Shamanic Guide to Death and Dying*, I discussed the spiritual effects of the death of the physical body. Earlier in this book, I described how a child's energy enters through the crown chakra and integrates through the root chakra, grounding this being into the physical. At death, the opposite occurs. The lower energy centers begin to break up first. They release from the physical body and pass over through the top of the head. If your child is interested enough to get into this kind of detail, You may want to read one of the books that are devoted solely to this subject (Recommended Reading, p. 241).

Will you ever die? Will I die? What would you do if I died?

It is best to be as honest as possible when faced with this question. The truth is that all of our physical bodies will die eventually. The important point is that we have all died before and will probably die again, if you choose to believe in other lives. The Otherworlds are not unfamiliar territory. We merely lose access to those memories in this reality due to limitations of mind and body.

Many children under the age of five appear to have a casual attitude about death. It is so much like sleep that they cannot fully comprehend that loved ones will not return. At this age, children who play games where someone is killed are not callous products of our violent society. They are just not old enough to realize that physical death means that the body is gone forever. Be aware that discussions of reincarnation at this age may result in the child's assumption that the physical body will come back to life.

During the elementary school years, children come to recognize death as a permanent condition. They also learn to fear it as more than a separation from friends and family. In our modern society, children fear that they will simply end or that they will go someplace frightening or have a painful death.

We never want to lie to a child. We particularly do not want to promise something we cannot guarantee that we will be able to follow through. Imagine how your child would feel at your funeral, after you had promised never to die. How easy might it be for this child to completely trust in another person again?

As for what you would do when asked if your child will die and what you would do if he or she does, be "as honest as possible without causing harm." Harm in this case may be telling a child that your life would be over; that you would be utterly devastated and would never recover should they pass over. Not only does this place a tremendous amount of responsibility on the child, responsibility that is not within their conscious control, but it does not reinforce any assertion you may make that life and love continue after physical death.

What happens if I kill myself?

The answers to this question will largely depend on exactly what the child means by "what happens." Few modern pagans believe that a soul is relegated to an eternity of suffering for taking one's own life. On the other hand, if the child is asking what you would do in this situation, you must answer accordingly.

If the child wants to know what happens to the soul after a suicide, it is important to find out why. This child may merely be interested. However, we cannot ignore the possibility that the child is either looking for attention or is honestly considering taking his or her own life. In any case, explain the spiritual effects as you understand them and be aware of any other warning signs from this child or others in your family. A child may ask because they have heard a friend, sibling or other family member speaking about suicide.

In my shamanic travels, I have not observed that those who have committed suicide go to any form of Hell, other than perhaps a Hell of their own creation, depending on their beliefs. For a time after death, we experience reality based on the beliefs we held in the previous incarnation. Someone may indeed create a Hell or other difficult situation if their beliefs are strong enough. For the most part, these people meet up with guides and go through the same process as any other departed spirit.

The cold, hard truth is that suicide does not eliminate one's problems. It may postpone them until the next life, but you just have to handle it all over again. It may also be difficult for a spirit to fully release from this reality if there is unfinished business or if the spirit feels they have made a mistake in taking their own life.

The child that asks what you would do if he or she committed suicide is also begging for attention and help. It is not worth the risk to assume that this child is merely looking for attention. To ignore this could mean missing or denying vital warning signs. It could also send an attention-seeking child into a real depression or rebellion that could result in death. If this is a possibility in your home, call a suicide hotline or speak with your doctor or counselor immediately.

Do animals have spirits?

The answer to this is an absolute yes. Few people today, pagan or not, would disagree. It has been my experience that animals experience similar death processes to humans. They reincarnate and they tend to forget other lives while they inhabit a body. They may be spiritual guides for their people, on both sides of the Veil, and they may have their own spirit guides who show up after death.

Some people may argue that animals are only part of a group soul. I would have to disagree, based on my experience and the experience of other deathwalkers I have known. In a way, we are all part of a group soul. We are all interconnected at some level of being. This does not preclude the existence of an individual soul and its personal development.

Where do babies come from?

This should probably be handled from a purely physical point-of-view first. Every young person who is nearing the age when they are physically capable of getting pregnant or impregnating a woman should know the basics of anatomy and conception. Most pagans agree that our children should also be educated in contraceptive methods. If a sexually uneducated child becomes pregnant or impregnates someone else, then the parents have failed in their jobs.

On the market today are a number of good books for all ages that deal with these topics. The age and comprehension level of the child should dictate an appropriate conversation. Many pagan children have seen plenty of naked bodies. This is natural and healthy, within the pagan belief systems. These children are well aware that there are differences between the male and female bodies. This generally makes descriptions a little easier.

We need not fear that our descriptions will lead to sex or pregnancy. Kids will experiment whether we talk to them or not. Curiosity is natural and healthy, within reason. We are not better parents if we cling blindly to the dream that our children are innocent, asexual cherubs. Just as we demand all the facts in order to make the best decisions for ourselves and our families, we owe it to our children to provide them with the tools necessary to make their own intelligent, informed decisions.

As pagans, we tend to be much more open and natural with our sexuality than nonpagan parents. We recognize that our children are often sexual beings at a much younger age than the usual age of consent. While few of us encourage our children to become sexually active at any age, we realize that this possibility exists. We do them a disservice if we close off all communication related to this and pretend that it won't happen until they are legally adults.

It is important that our children feel comfortable enough to come to us if they need to talk about sex or possible pregnancy. We need to be able to handle this with maturity. Since many neopagans were not raised pagan, they will need to work with their own shadows and feelings regarding sex. It is not a subject that is easily avoided in pagan communities. Our children and our society will benefit greatly if they can grow up without the multitude of hang-ups and fears surrounding sexuality that the previous generations did.

As far as where babies come from on a spiritual level, this will depend on your personal beliefs. You may want to discuss reincarnation or concurrent lives with your children. You may want to use this as an introduction to the cycles of life and what happens after death. As always, keep in mind the age and comprehension level of the child.

Can I have a baby?

As we all know, there is a big difference between *can* and *should* when it comes to having and raising children. From a pagan perspective, we are manifestations of the God and Goddess. Sexuality and procreation are sacred gifts. However, they are gifts that must be enjoyed with honor, respect, and intelligence. Anything less minimizes the blessings and does nothing to benefit our total soul growth.

If your children are still living with you, this is not a decision that they make alone. It will impact the entire family. This is something that parents may want to discuss without the children before they reach puberty. Everyone needs to know what you are and are not willing to tolerate. You need to be clear on your reactions and decisions if a child should come home and say, "I am/My girlfriend is pregnant."

This is also something that should be discussed along with contraception if you suspect that a child may be sexually active. Unless it is a personal decision, most pagans support abortion rights. While some may decide this is not right for them, they will almost always support the right of another to choose. If you are personally opposed to this for everyone, you may want to examine your beliefs and where they came from. This may be a carry-over from a more restrictive religion.

Whatever your decision, keep in mind that your child may decide on a different course of action for him/herself. This is something else that should allow open communication so that our children feel comfortable coming to us with these issues. We do not want them to feel alone or backed into a corner. Children having children must be a family decision (if at all possible), with full family support if the pregnancy is not terminated.

My boyfriend/girlfriend wants me to have sex. What should I do?

This is a question that goes beyond the mere act of sex in a relationship. It encompasses the self-esteem, self-confidence, and personal strength of a child. Each of these areas will need support no matter what the decision is.

The child may or may not want to become sexually active. This question does indicate a feeling of being pressured. The child may fear that the fate of this relationship may depend on sex. Sex given in this way does not honor the God and Goddess, the relationship, or one's Self. Pagans may appear at face value to place a high emphasis on sex and, to be honest, many do, but no one who follows an Earth-based religion or spiritual path would respect a pressured or forced sexual encounter.

Since sexuality is viewed as sacred (and fun) to pagans, it is important that it be done right. Consenting adults may do as they please, but it is important that our children grow up without fears and issues surrounding their sexuality. These issues often lead to body image problems, lower self-esteem and confidence, and the attraction of unhealthy relationships throughout one's life.

Your reactions to this may vary according to the actual and emotional age of the child. Sexuality involves much more than one's physical body. At its highest and most beautiful, sex can activate all of the energy centers of both people, clearing the aura, and bringing both energy systems into complete harmony at the highest levels of self.

Unfortunately, sex can also create unhealthy energetic bonds and cause auric damage, depending on the situation. This, plus the multitude of physical conditions a person may contract through sexual intimacy, are valid reasons for education and a good deal of thought before making any decisions.

Without unnecessarily limiting beliefs, judge for yourself what is behind the question. Is the child afraid of losing his or her partner? Does he or she want to become active but is nervous or afraid for some reason? And most importantly, is this child ready to handle being sexually active?

What if I told you I was homosexual/bisexual?

In most cases, this is not a big issue in pagan families. Alternate sexual lifestyles are as accepted as any other lifestyle that may be common among pagans. However, parents may have surprising reactions, whether they were raised pagan or not.

Sometimes, parents will fear for the difficulties that may lie ahead for a homosexual or bisexual child. While the desire to protect children from the hardships of life is admirable, we cannot protect them from their own learning experiences. In addition, our reactions and expectations of difficulty may contribute to our children's beliefs and fears, making things even more difficult for them.

Occasionally a parent may be supportive yet feel sad for themselves at having no grandchildren. Keep in mind that homosexuality and bisexuality do not preclude the possibility of children. Sexual preference does not necessarily prevent people from adopting, if they should choose to. There are also plenty of homosexual and bisexual people with their own biological children. It should also be noted here that heterosexuality does not guarantee grandchildren. As parents, our main concern must be with the health and happiness of our children.

While many people may not want to admit it, even to themselves, deep within their subconscious there remain lingering beliefs and fears about alternate sexuality. It may be perfectly fine for other people, and you may have several homosexual or bisexual friends, but to have it within your own family is not acceptable. You may even be very supportive of your child, but there is a nagging discomfort or uneasiness about it.

Repressing these feelings is not healthy for anyone, and your child may pick up on them psychically, particularly if the two of you are close. It is important to be honest about them, while supporting your child. It is also important to work to clear these limiting beliefs so that you can unconditionally love and support your child in all of his or her choices.

You might also remember that this is not a choice, any more than one chooses to be heterosexual. It is not something that can be cured or cleared or changed. Individuals may deny their sexual preference their entire lives to make other people happy, but this does not mean they are heterosexual. It also does not mean that our children are happy.

Why are you homosexual/bisexual?

This is probably more difficult than the previous question. If your child is asking this, there is a good possibility that to the outside world, you were once heterosexual. You may have been married to the child's other parent.

If your child has never known you to be heterosexual, it is likely that there is no feeling of betrayal or resentment involved in the question. A child certainly recognizes when his or her family differs from the majority. A child may need to know the realities of sexual preference and is it best they hear it from you to get an accurate understanding.

There is always the possibility that this question is the result of taunting from peers and other members of the community. If you are openly homosexual or bisexual, just as if you are openly pagan, it is your responsibility as a parent to present the best possible face of this lifestyle. You need to be willing to discuss it, not because it is anyone's business, but because most people who have not experienced it can not really understand it. And ignorance is often dangerous.

If you are willing to discuss this, within reason, with your child's friends and their parents or with teachers, you have the potential to do a lot of good. Not only do you make things easier on your children, but you also pave the way for others who may be too afraid to "come out" right away. You set an example as an honest, respectable member of the community. You show through word and example that there is nothing to hide, no reason to duck your head and feel ashamed. In living this life, you become an ideal role model for your children.

Where is my Mommy/Daddy? Why doesn't he or she live with us? Why are you getting a divorce?

When answering this type of question, it is vital to make the point that the child is in no way responsible for the absence of a parent or the break-up of a marriage. Even if the marriage dissolved as the result of a difficult or sick child, it was the inability of one or both parents to cope that created the problem and led to the break up. It was not the fault of the child.

As pagans, we don't hold the belief that a relationship must last until "death do us part." Traditional handfastings (at least the first one) are for one year and one day. Then, the couple may decide whether to extend the relationship or say a friendly farewell.

Many pagans do not practice a monogamous lifestyle. Even if those involved are polyamorous, the breakup of any relationship can be very difficult. Whether a parent has one or more lovers, children will bond both to their own parents and also to any other consistent adult in the family. When that person is gone from the relationship, the children may effectively lose a parental figure.

While most of us do hope that a relationship, particularly one with children, will last forever, sometimes it is just not realistic. People grow and change. Ideally, the couple spent enough time together to be certain of the match before entering into a legal marriage contract. Whatever the reasons, it is our responsibility as pagans to be respectful of our relationships while we are in them, and to be honorable about the other person when it is over.

We respect our children by telling them the truth, within reason and without bashing the other parent. Children do not need to know the gory details, if there are any. They do have a right to know the generalities and whether or not the separation may be temporary or is definitely permanent. They have the right to expect a discussion as to the whereabouts of an absent parent and why they can only see a parent at certain times.

Why are we pagan? How do I explain our religion/spirituality to my friends?

This differs from the next two "why can't I . . ." questions in that it is often asked by children who were most likely not raised pagan from infancy and are trying to understand it. They want to be able to share with friends but are not sure how to go about it without risk. This child is probably comfortable with the family's chosen path.

There is another side to this question. Those raised pagan and surrounded by a pagan family and/or community may not be aware that paganism is not the path of the majority. They may not be aware that everyone doesn't feel and believe the same things.

The first question here is highly individual. Any answers are very personal and will vary according to the person. I can only say to be honest and speak from your heart. If you have explored other paths, let your child know. Be open to his or her own potential need for exploration, as well. Telling them your truth, from the heart, will say more than all the books in the world possibly could.

While explaining why you have chosen a particular path, be wary of belittling other religions. Certainly there are pros and cons to all religions. All followers of a religion are not the same. There are misguided and destructive followers of paganism just as there are fearful, hate-filled followers of any religion. In following a spirituality or religion that we feel is "better," we do not serve that energy or those spirits by denigrating the paths of others.

As for explaining the family path to friends, take time for some creative, flexible thought before deciding on a strategy. How you go about doing this will largely depend on the individual you want to share this with. I have had some friends who were so open-minded that we quickly and easily progressed from the more acceptable New Agey topics. On the other hand, I lost some good friends in grammar school and high school as a result of being too open.

These days, paganism is much more accepted and is quickly moving into the mainstream. We have some friends who invite their children's friends to holiday rituals and pagan gatherings. This has generally worked out very well for them. While they never hide who they are, they are not always completely open about their religion initially or at school. There is a difference between being in-your-face blatant and simply being who you are. The former often indicates a need for attention.

Unfortunately, not everyone is accepting of other paths. While the children may have no issue with a pagan friend, their parents may be another story. A young friend of ours found a wonderful boyfriend when she went away to college. She has always been very open about her religion. They had planned to share a house off-campus when his parents found out that she is pagan. The parents threatened to take away his car and his college tuition if he continued seeing her. Sadly, this situation is a real possibility for pagan children, even today.

As pagan parents, we must decide how we want this issue handled. I have devoted chapter 11 entirely to the question of honesty vs. secrecy. We need to decide how "out" we are willing to be in our communities before getting our children involved in our religion or spirituality. There may come a time when we are not ready to be open but our children refuse to keep it a secret.

Can you or I cast a spell on someone for love/revenge/good grades?

I would hope that as a parent, the answer to this would be very clearly "No." This is another case of *can* versus *should*. Followers of Earth-based religions do not interfere in the free will of another. We do not send out destructive or controlling energy because we know it will return to us.

However, it is not always an easy task to explain this to a child who feels invincible and knows, with the melodrama of youth, that they will certainly die if they do not get what they feel so strongly about. This is one reason why we must stress balance and responsibility when raising children in spiritual-magical paths. While it is true that magic is really just about creating change in one's reality, we don't want to use ritual magic or spells as an excuse for growth or as something to hide behind.

I took a telephone call the other day from a young man who has recently chosen the Wiccan path. He has been into it for about six months and has "read almost all the books." He told me that he knows you are not supposed to interfere in another person's life, but he wanted to know what he should do about this person he was interested in. He wanted to cast a love spell and wanted someone to tell him that it was okay to do so.

In the course of this conversation, it became clear this was a case of hiding behind magic and wanting something so much that ethics were an annoyance. While it is basically true that we cannot control another without his or her permission on some level, pagans do not interfere with someone else's free will. There are a number of reasons for this.

As pagans, we understand that we receive the same type of energy we put out. This extends from spell work to thoughts, and from gossip to actions. You will experience the type of world you create. Therefore, if you would not want someone else to include you in such a spell, don't do it. This should carry over to all our actions. Treat others as you would be treated is pretty good advice, no matter where it comes from.

The other major reason to avoid these kinds of spells is the end result. Not only may they backfire, but you need to be very skilled, very clear, and very specific before engaging in any form of magic. You may get what you ask for and find it is either not specifically what you really wanted, or it is not what you expected.

Ask a child that is interested in a love spell how she or he would feel if they were magically bound to someone who turned out to be a very self-centered or nasty person. An individual generally feels the need for a love spell for two reasons. Either they desire a person who is clearly not interested or they are afraid to get to know the person and ask him or her out. In the first case, it is best to move on and find someone who is interested while working on any personal esteem issues that may be contributing. In the second case, you need to handle your fear first and work within this reality. You might ask the love interest out for coffee, or just start a conversation and see where it goes. This is real life and magic should not be used to try to avoid it.

As far as a spell for good grades goes, it would be most beneficial to cast one on yourself. I used several techniques when in school for learning and grades. On occasion, I would telepathically receive the answer from a spirit guide, or even the teacher. However, we accomplish nothing if our grades are not our own. We need to learn and retain this information or abilities for future success. What worked best for me from grammar school through graduate school were spells or techniques to improve my own memory and access to stored information, concentration, the ability to quickly and easily absorb and process what I was learning; anything that helped me learn and remember better.

Am I a witch/druid/shaman/etc.?

The answer to this will very likely depend on your point of view, as to who is and who is not any of these things. For some people, you are automatically a witch if your family follows that path or you have decided that you are. However, many paths require a period of training or other criteria to attain the title of Druid or Shaman or Vitki.

For example in the Order of Bards, Ovates, and Druids (OBOD), we all follow a druidic path and certainly consider ourselves druids. Within OBOD tradition, we are not all Druids, meaning we have not all completed the necessary training for admittance into the Druid Grade. In our seed-group, we may call our children Baby Bards, but are they really? It is a matter of perspective but many of them are not even old enough to speak yet, let alone "Bard out." Our children are children and until they choose to follow the druidic path, they are not druids.

This chapter will certainly not answer all of your family's tough questions. It is a good overview of some of the more common ones. While my answers may not be right for your family, it is my hope that they will give you a place to begin when deciding what to say. Often we need to get clear on our own beliefs and feelings first. After that, the answers that are right for us seem to flow easily.

As parents, we need to avoid the temptation or expectation that we will be perfect and all-knowing individuals. We are who and what we are, and having children does not often change that significantly. What we can do is to strive toward being the best individuals and role models we can. We can admit that we are human and are still learning. Most importantly, we can always be there with unconditional love and support for our children.

9

Spirituality

Spirituality and religion are separated in this book, not because I find them to be mutually exclusive, but rather to clearly show that one may follow a spiritual path without belonging to a religion. Spirituality, as far as this book is concerned, is that innate sense of one's connection to All of Life. On the other hand, religion, in this book, includes those rituals and beliefs that comprise a religious path.

Many pagans find that they do not fit within any of the self-described religions, although they may be intensely spiritual. If you prefer, you may view it (at least within these pages) as the difference between honoring our connections to all beings and the ways in which we work with or worship those beings, particularly deities.

We enter this reality as purely spiritual beings, working to integrate our spiritual energies into a purely physical realm. Very young children remain spiritual beings unless their families or societies give them reason to block this experience. The young are naturally spiritual and tend toward being respectful.

The total household atmosphere and the everyday activities of family members are the main influences that foster a child's innate spirituality. If the family is respectful toward other people and the natural world, it is likely that the child will behave in similar ways. Of course, daycare and other relationships will affect any child's behavior. Children emulate those they trust and respect.

Our son has always had tremendous respect for all of life, although he does not always understand that his actions can cause harm. This is common among young children. At about three and a half, he decided the sowbugs were his friends. He literally loved one to death, not realizing that playing with them could cause them harm.

Our son does pick up behaviors from children around him, either at daycare or with friends. He has learned to play guns and swords and lightsabers. He pretends to die and kill people. While we try to limit this, we recognize that this is modern reality. It is normal and we cannot insulate him from it forever. Nor should we, since it is a facet of our society that he must accept and learn to handle on his own.

What we can do, as pagan parents, is to foster respectful spiritual values at home. As I said earlier, we pray over meals, particularly when eating meat. We hold to the eight holidays and will often honor the full or new moon phases. We include our son in all rituals and encourage his participation in smudging and other ceremonies when he shows interest.

We thank the garden spirits and spirits of the land when we harvest from our garden or pick sage for smudge. When I plant the garden, our son helps me bless the seeds and the soil. He learns about human interaction with wildlife from the raptor research and education organization that I work with, as well as from my own wildlife rehabilitation work. He is well aware, even at his age, that our educational and rehab birds can no longer fly free, mainly because of interactions with humans.

To many pagans, spirituality means those innate and intuitive connections with the natural world. Even those pagans who have never slept under the stars in the wilderness feel their connections with "All Our Relations." It is important that these feelings and experiences become more than mental exercises, to be honored indoors at the appropriate holidays.

Try to get outside with your family. Not only is this beneficial on a physical and psychological level, but with a goal of connecting to the spirits of the land, it can become a truly magical experience. Even if you can only get to an outdoor playground or find a tree on a city street, the spirits of nature are there. They may be sleeping, waiting for a pagan to wake them from their protective sleep, but they are there. It is within our power to create sacred sites, even if only for ourselves.

I was fortunate to have grown up where I did. There was a sacred valley, filled with power and spirits, that accepted me as one of its own. I would retreat to this place for comfort and guidance. It was where I headed when I was upset or overwhelmed. When we moved away for a time, it was where I cried and said goodbye. As I returned home that day, I felt a strong need to run as fast as I could. As I reached our door, rain began to pour down. I felt that the valley and the woodland spirits that had become my family were also saying goodbye. To this day, I return to that valley on a shamanic level for peace and guidance.

However, I have not always been so fortunate as to live in a wilderness area. Nor have I always had the time or means to be able to travel to a state or national park. Even in the absence of an obvious wilderness, the spirits of the wild have found me. In two of our apartments, we had a tree outside a window. These trees became my daily lifeline to the natural world. In Connecticut, we found a small city park, filled with beer bottles and old condoms. After some time spent meditating and sending out energy blessings, this park came alive with spirit energy. We even began to see evidence of wild animal activity as the squirrels, deer, and birds moved back in.

Even when I was locked in a laboratory, occasionally for more than sixteen hours each day, my office plants helped me to center and balance. At least once each day, I would sit and silently meditate on the plants. The chemists working for me called it my "veg out" time. This time spent communing with the spirits and filling my self and my work space with sacred energy worked wonders for my well being as well as my productivity and my ability to be a good scientist and manager.

Here in the city, although we have access to wilderness areas, we know all the trees on the street. The sagebrush and ricegrass on the highway where we walk our dog are our friends. We need only to tune in and the spirit world awakens from its hibernation, eager to interact with those who would acknowledge and honor its existence.

Nature Spirit Attunement Exercise

All children respond well to attuning to Nature spirits. This exercise is designed specifically to connect with the spirits of the natural world. Use this to practice attuning to trees, metals, stones, crystals, lakes, etc. Vary it as you choose, to incorporate all kinds of different experiences, including things we may not view as natural, such as bicycles and computers.

> Begin by having the child feel and inspect whatever it is he or she will be "entering" during the meditation. Then have them get comfortable, either sitting or lying down. If possible, have them hold the object during meditation.
>
> Count your child down from ten to one or guide him or her to enter a light trance in your usual way.
>
> Guide them to see the object before them, big as a house or bigger. Have the child inspect the outside of the object. Teach them to be respectful. Instruct them to ask permission to enter the object. Tell them to trust whatever comes up for them and if permission is denied, try another object or wait until the child is better prepared. It may be beneficial to have the child tell you what they experience as it occurs. You can either record this with a tape recorder or write it down so details are not lost. This is also a great way for the child to develop their own ability to retain information obtained in Other realities.
>
> If permission is granted, guide them to enter the object through a door in the side of the object. Ask them what they see inside. Ask what the temperature

is, the light level, how the walls feel. Ask if there are any sounds or smells that they are aware of. Get all of their senses involved in the experience.

Next, have them explore the object, giving you a narrative as they move along. Ask them if they encounter any beings within the object.

When they have explored most of the object or seem ready to come out, guide the child back to the door they entered in. Have them stop before leaving and give thanks to any one or any thing they have encountered. Instruct them to ask if there are any last messages for them before they return to everyday reality. Give them some time to receive these.

Guide the child back out through the door. As he or she leaves, have them stop at the door and, taking a last look at the object, instruct them to leave an offering and thank the spirit of the object for this experience.

Count him back up from one to ten as usual, or in the same format you counted him down.

This respect and gratitude is an important facet of pagan spirituality. The more respectful we are, the more teaching and support we will receive from the Other Worlds. Our greatest power flows through us from the universe. It does not belong to us and it cannot be depleted, as long as we are in alignment with Spirit.

When we interact with the spirits, gods, and goddesses, we enter into a give-and-take relationship with them. We do not deny our own innate divinity and become the servants of these beings, nor do we expect them to become our slaves. We make offerings and give prayers and rituals of thanks to honor the gifts we receive on a daily basis. In this way, we continue the energetic cycle of blessings and beneficial energy.

This is a similar concept to that of treating other physical beings as we would be treated. We would not, under normal conditions, continue to assist and give to a person who offered us no thanks or respect back, particularly if that person was abusive. We should not expect the spirits and the gods to continue to give selflessly. Even if they would do so, we would dishonor both them and ourselves by living this kind of life.

I mentioned the prayer we offer during meals in an earlier chapter. This may remind you of the Christian grace, but its meanings and origins are much deeper and more ancient than this. In honoring these beings with a prayer before eating, we celebrate each meal as a ceremonial meal. We release any unwanted energies from our food and imbue it with blessed and sacred energies.

Indigenous peoples honored the spirits of the animals they needed to kill for food and other essential items. They respected the fact that these "relations" filled a vital place for us in the cycle of life. These animals were our brothers and sisters as well as our teachers and guides. We all shared the need for food and sustenance in the planetary life cycle. It was understood and accepted that we may also become a meal for one of them someday. Even if we did not, our ashes would become one with the ashes of all our relations and continue to create life on this planet.

In modern society, many people have adopted the belief that animals are lower forms of life deserving of little to no respect. Many people feel that animals were put on this Earth for us to use and discard as we choose. They are not sentient beings; they are commodities.

This is not a common pagan belief. The majority of pagans will at least offer lip-service to an opposing viewpoint. I have had many teachers who were in animal form, both in this reality and in Others. I have been told by some of my animal allies that they are aspects of me and that we are One. Many of you have had these same feelings or experiences.

Whether we view these beings as potential species for our own reincarnation, as the manifestations of our spirit guides, or simply as other children of Mother Earth, they deserve our respect. Those who walk their Earth journey with respect for All of Life will receive respect and power from the natural world.

The only way our children will grow up in this way is if we hold that energy within the family and act accordingly.

It is this respect for other beings, no matter what species, including the tree and stone people, that leads to respect and honor among our own species. I perceive a lack of connection with our world and respect for self and others to be at the center of most of the crime issues in modern society.

Wild Plant Walks

Periodically, I take our son on sage-picking walks to replenish our smudge supply. This is a great way to introduce the concept of give and take with young children. It is also a wonderful method for teaching the basics of plant or herb identification and to foster a connection with the land.

The sage-picking expedition that follows is an example that can be varied greatly, depending on your needs at the time. You may choose to go on identification walks with your children first. This way they can get an idea of what the plants are and the environment in which they live. Play amateur naturalist with your children as you both learn about the plants, animals, geology, and water cycles in your area.

There is one strong caution I would give any parents who may be considering taking young children on medicinal or edible plant walks. Do not allow a child to put anything in his or her mouth until both of you are absolutely certain what it is. It is a very good idea to educate yourself on the poisonous plants in your area and learn how to identify them. Then teach your children which ones to avoid. A good rule of thumb is: if in doubt, don't touch it.

Unless you are an expert at mushroom identification, never taste or eat a wild mushroom and caution your children about the dangers of this. Mushrooms contain an incredibly large number of complex chemical compounds. Many varieties of mushrooms are harmless, but some are hallucinogenic or dangerously toxic.

If you are picking plants that you plan to ingest in any form, it is also advisable to avoid areas close to highways. These plants will absorb any petroleum products that leak onto the ground as well as the airborne exhaust of passing vehicles.

Many species of edible or medicinal plant life bear strong similarities to poisonous species. Ingestion of many of these other species can be debilitating, even fatal. Unless you really know your identification well, I would recommend avoiding any of the similar species in the wild. I made it a point not to put any wild plant in my mouth around our son until he was old enough to understand that some plants can hurt him, and old enough to know that this is not the time to argue with a "No."

Now my son is old enough to begin to learn about these things. From our everyday walks, he can pick out a sagebrush by sight and knows to rub the leaves to be sure of the smell. He also knows that we do not remove parts of plants for fun or on a whim. A sage-picking trip is a serious (although fun) event.

Sage Picking Expedition

We begin by choosing a place where we have not picked recently. Although over a dozen species of sage are common to New Mexico, it is important to recognize the potential effects of overharvesting one area. We let the other places "rest" for a while. We gather up our water bottle, a paper bag for collection, and any offerings we may want to leave in return for the sage.

A paper bag is preferable to a plastic bag for drying plants, although it doesn't really matter what you collect them in. Plastic bags retain the moisture of plants, preventing drying and increasing the possibility of mold growth. You may also wish to hang plants to dry. In the desert Southwest, water is about as valuable as gold in most areas. Many times we feel that this is the best offering we can give to the plants and we usually carry an extra water bottle. Other offerings may be sacred herbs, corn, a crystal, or simply a blessing and sending of loving energy.

Once we get to the area we are going to harvest, we take some time to be quiet and center. We ask permission from the Spirits of Place and wait for an answer. If we get an uneasy or doubtful feeling, we try another spot or go home. We find the oldest bush in the area and leave our offering. This may be a bush that is obviously larger and older, but it may be just a feeling that we have. Then we each take a small piece of sage and put it in our mouths. As we chew on the sage, we go wherever we are led for harvesting.

We pick only as much as we need, being sure not to take too much from one bush. Then we move on until we either *feel* a clear signal that we have taken enough or we have the amount we believe is enough. We leave an offering at each bush we harvest from, along with a prayer of thanks.

When we are finished, we return to the oldest bush and give thanks for the gifts of this sage. We promise to use it in a sacred manner and to always honor the spirits of the land. Then we come home and keep our promises.

Some form of purification and cleansing is part of most spiritual paths. We may purify our selves, our homes, the sacred space of Circles or other ritual space, or just about anything we wish to make free of unwanted energies and beings. Two methods of purification are easy for children to learn and participate in.

The smudge ceremony is something with which even a toddler can assist. Children should always be supervised around matches and anything that is burning. However, this is a simple yet profound ritual that really evokes a sense of reverence and gratitude. It is a ritual and as such could easily have been included in the following chapter. I have chosen to place it here for two reasons.

One reason is its innate spiritual feel. Many people feel it is more of a moving meditation than a true ritual, although for some it is akin to casting a Circle and calling directions. With conditioning, the lighting of the smudge alone can be a trance-induction method. Rather than being a full ritual in itself, it is frequently a form of ritual preparation.

The other reason is that it is a borrowed element of native cultures. Most world cultures use some form of purification or consecration by fire, often burning herbs. The sage-cedar-sweet-grass-copal smudge ceremony is typically indigenous to the Americas, even though many scholars believe it is a recent development. Most neopagans do not follow traditional, indigenous American religions, although many of us incorporate some of their spiritual elements into our own paths. Therefore, while smudging may be included in some neopagan spiritual paths, it is not really a part of most of these religions.

With a basic understanding of the ceremony, it is a simple thing to come up with ways for children to participate. Our son began when he was a little over a year old. Although he could stand, he was a bit unsteady on his feet, so he sat and held his arms out (just like Mommy and Daddy) while we wafted the smoke around him. As he showed more interest, I often carried him with me when I smudged our home.

By two years old, he actively participated in any way he could. By the age of three, he was allowed to carry a smudge stick around the house with supervision. At three and a half, he created his own smudge fan. He walks around the area to be smudged with me and imitates every move I make. When we are finished, he thanks the Great Spirit and the Spirits of Place.

The smudge ceremony and drum purification ceremony, as I first described them in *Shamanic Guide to Death and Dying* (pp. 71–73), follow for your information. Feel free to experiment and discover what works best for you and your family. Older children can take a more active role. When I was approximately five years old, I was allowed to carry the incense or smudge for my mother. Eventually, I was old enough to light it with supervision, and by the time I reached junior high school, I could burn candles and incense alone in my room.

The Smudge Ceremony

You will need: a source of purifying smoke: smudge sticks or loose herbs such as sagebrush (*Artemisia* spp.), sweetgrass, or incenses such as sandalwood and myrrh; matches or a lighter; a candle will give you a continuing flame, helpful especially for smudge sticks, for which it may be difficult to maintain smoking; a heat-resistant container or incense burner; optional: a feather or fan.

Take a moment to center yourself. It may help to count yourself down from ten to one, remembering to breathe deeply from your diaphragm.

Light your smudge with respect. Invite the smoke of the sacred herbs to purify your energy and this space.

Using your feather or fan to move the smoke, or carrying the smudge stick with you, offer the sacred smoke to the six directions: North, East, South, West, Earth, and Sky; and to the Great Spirit in the center, which permeates all things. Offer blessings of respect and gratitude to each of these.

Beginning at the navel, bathe yourself in the sacred and purifying smoke. Move the smoke up to your heart area, then over your head, along your back, down to your feet, and back up to your navel.

As the smoke moves along your body, feel yourself centering deeply. Breathe deeply of the smoke. See your worries and tensions dissolve in the warmth as they are carried up and away by the smoke. Ask the smoke of the sacred herbs once again to purify your energy, to clear you of all limitations, and to help you become a clear and protected channel for healing energy.

Offer the smoke once more to each of the six directions and the Creator. Give thanks to them for their presence in your life. Thank the smoke of these

sacred herbs for their assistance in purifying your
energy and preparing you to meet with your
loved one.

Some individuals and groups believe that once a
smudge is burning, it should be left to burn itself out.
The truth of this will depend on your beliefs and
experience. In my experience, allowing something to
burn for extended periods of time is not always possible or preferable. In my journeying and work with
these sacred plants, I have been taught that whether I
extinguish the flame or leave it to burn itself out is not
important, provided my every action is made in
respect and honor.

Another purification method that is wonderful to actively
involve children in is the drum purification ceremony. Children
tend to find this one lots of fun. While this assists them in maintaining an interest, it is important that they do not get carried
away with the fun and lose the spiritual connection and sense of
reverence. They can follow your lead with a rattle, small drum, or
even by clapping their hands. It is the attitude and energy we create that is most important. Therefore, a homemade film canister
rattle or a touristy rubber and cardboard drum will do just fine.

Drum Purification Ceremony

Take several deep breaths and center yourself. Begin
to beat the drum. In determining the speed of the beat,
go with what feels right to you at the time. It is
generally recommended that this be faster than a
heartbeat.

Continue to beat the drum until you feel yourself
center deeply and enter the trance state.

Holding the drum up and out from your body, offer
its sound to each of the four directions. Then offer it
to the Sky and the Earth. Then to the center again, to
offer it to the Creator.

Continue to drum at the pace that resonates best for you along your entire body, stopping at each chakra for a few moments. Allow the sound and energy of the drum to harmonize your energy systems and clear unwanted vibrations. Hold the drum at each chakra, or any area that feels the need, drumming until you feel this area come into balance with the rest of your system.

Hold the drum out to center once more as an offering of thanks to the Creator. Beat four times more quickly and then end with one strong beat.

When I think of spirituality, the main thing that comes to my mind is the web that connects us with All of Life. This includes interdimensional beings and those life forms that modern science may or may not recognize as being sentient, or even alive. Of course, much of this is the result of how I was raised, and the fact that my husband and I follow a druidic-shamanic path.

Within this type of belief system, our every action becomes sacred, or it should. We recognize that everything we choose to do reflects our spirituality and our deepest Selves. Our spirituality is inherent in our treatment of other people and the natural world. This is something that we want to pass on to our children. Certainly we do so by example through how we live our lives.

Elemental Attunement

As children explore and become more connected to this world, they naturally fall in love with the Earth and all Her creatures. How many of us could not (or still cannot) resist a mud puddle, a flower, or a beautiful rock? I first began my rock collection when I was seven years old and it continues to grow today. In modern society, the key seems to be keeping our children in

---

1   The preceding two paragraphs and much of this section on growing things were first published in an article titled, "Attuning to Earth," in the Summer 1998 issue of *Circle Network News*.

love with the Earth and encouraging their natural respect for all things.

One way to do this is to teach them the various ways to attune to the Earth. For children, this is usually quite natural. Physical activities and games are often the best way for children to stay in tune. Due to their attention and energy levels, depending on the age of the child, we try to keep the meditations and passive visualizations to a minimum. Once we are connected on a spiritual and physical level, respect follows naturally.[1]

Family Calendar

Celebrating the eight seasonal holidays is a wonderful way to maintain a spiritual practice and attunement throughout the year. It brings a measure of discipline when life events might otherwise threaten to postpone or eliminate spirituality and religion from our lives. Honoring these special days serves to realign us with our spirituality and the natural world.

> A teaching calendar can be invaluable with young children, particularly preschoolers. Ideally, this should be made on a large, brightly colored piece of board or fabric that is large enough to allow for the changing days and seasons. If they are old enough, involve your children in the creation of this calendar. The calendar our son and I made when he was two years old may inspire your own creativity.
>
> We chose a brilliant blue fabric for the background and decorated it with iron-on fabric trains and animals that he picked out at the store. The days of the week were permanently marked, decorated with significant symbols and one side of a square of Velcro sewn on each day. I made cards for each season. These were laminated and the other side of the Velcro was attached to the back of each. I laminated a small photo of my son and placed Velcro on its back. Each morning, he moves his photo to the next day and at

the solstices and equinoxes, just after ritual, we change the season.

In this way, pagan children not only learn the days, months, and seasons that they will need to know for school, but they can also learn about the cycles of nature and the pagan holidays. If you choose, you can include any number of things, such as the gods and goddesses associated with the names of the days and months, the names of the holidays you celebrate and any holiday symbolism you like.

Association Web Game

For each element, creating an association web can be a fun method to discover additional ways to encourage your children's connection with Nature. It can be a written exercise or played as a game with as many players as you choose.

The main goal is to give the child, or children, one word, in this case, an element. They are then responsible for writing or calling out anything that comes to mind when they hear the name of the element. If they are not writing you may want to record their answers. With more than one player, answers will spark new associations in each of the players' minds and may create some interesting (and long-lived) games.

I would suggest that you pay attention to any unusual answers or anything that is related to past events. These are often keys to deeper meanings or possibly difficult situations that the child may be ready to deal with. In any event, most of the associations they come up with will give you ideas for new games or exercises that will deepen their awareness of the elements and increase their abilities to work with each element.

Earth

I wrote earlier that our son helps out with the garden. Attuning to the Earth through growing things is a fun and educational method for teaching children about any number of things, from physical science to interactions with faeries and plant devas. Not only does this allow us to get our hands dirty and witness the miracle of life, but through growing things we recognize the cycles of life and learn to be stewards of our Earth. This is a great process for children. They get a real sense of accomplishment and confidence in caring for "their" plants.

Every child can grow a small plant from a bean. Most of us did this in elementary school. Keep the bean moist in a wet paper towel or sponge until it sprouts. Once the sprout begins to grow, plant it in some potting soil. Make sure it gets sun and water and it will be just fine.

You may also want to teach children to grow plants from seed. This generally takes no longer than sprouting beans, and depending on the seed, your child can produce a flower or vegetable for additional wonder. When space was an issue and we had no yard of our own, I grew tomatoes and peppers in big containers. While they did not get as big as store-bought vegetables, it was wonderful to have ones we grew and loved. Strawberry and blueberry plants are also easy to grow indoors and delight everyone.

Growing Things Exercise

If you do have the space, give your children a corner of your garden or yard for their own gardens. Our son thoroughly enjoys helping me plant and water his garden. The first year he was just two years old and we planted sunflowers, cantaloupes, chile peppers, and peas. He was amazed by the entire process and learned some patience along the way. During his anti-vegetable period, he would even eat the peas out of the pod, just because they were his peas and the pods were so cool!

Depending on the age of the child, blessings and rituals for the planting and harvesting of the garden add to the sacredness and respect that children gain from the experience. Be sure to give thanks for each flower and all the food that you receive from the Earth. Explain the interconnections involved in life on Earth and how none of us exist independent of other life.

Very young children have an innate connection to life and energy. Even a child who is not yet walking will be attracted to the sight of a parent holding out open hands over a seedling and speaking simple blessings. Most children will instinctively mimic this act. As your children's language and comprehension skills advance, they will most likely want to speak the blessings themselves.

Older children, particularly those that were not raised in this way from birth, may feel silly or uncomfortable doing this. It is best not to pressure them to do so. Merely continue as you normally would, neither hiding your actions nor expecting the child to participate. When they are ready to participate, they will, although they may begin to do so in secret. And if they do not join us, we allow them their freedom to choose.

Rocks

Now what about those rock collections? I still have one, and I'll bet many of you do too. Mine has grown from a general collection of simple igneous, metamorphic, and sedimentary stones to a widely varied tool kit of crystals and stones for all types of self-development and healing. My husband and I have visited rockhound sites to dig for our own stones and we still keep my grandfather's maps of favorite rock-hunting sites. Our son loves to discover cool new rocks on hikes into the desert and mountains.

Rocks are a great way to connect, not only with the Earth element, but also with Otherworlds. Many rocks serve as gateways to other realities, as well as storing ancient wisdom and memories. If your child has an interest in rocks, I would suggest encouraging that. The Nature Spirit Attunement Exercise in this chapter is an excellent way to connect with the spirits of the stones and access the wisdom stored within each.

Air

Air can be an elusive element, unless a weather system is present that creates wind. It is also one that may require related objects for a child to really work well with. Until a child is comfortable with amorphous or philosophical ideas, she may need to focus more on the effects of air and wind, or the animals and things that rely on air or wind.

For the baby and toddler, dandelion fuzz can be the tool for their very first natural magic. Dandelions grow in almost all areas and most of us are familiar with making wishes while blowing the fuzz from them at the end of their season. This is very similar to the wish-spells associated with blowing out birthday candles. Just as in any form of magic, belief and emotion are vital to the success of a dandelion fuzz wish and with very young children, a parent may need to initially provide this.

Dandelion Fuzz Wishes Game

>Before going outside to find a dandelion in fuzz, decide on the wish you will be making. Then go outside with that wish in your minds and ask to be led to the dandelion that wants to help you make that wish come true.

>Ask before picking the dandelion of your choice. When permission is given, pick it with a prayer of thanks. If your child is able, have her or him say thank you along with you as you pick the flower.

>Hold the dandelion's stem and have the child hold it gently with you. An older child can hold the plant

alone. Repeat the wish out loud. If your child is old enough, tell them to imagine the wish growing really big in their head. Then blow the wish out into the dandelion fuzz and watch as it is carried off into the air.

Tell your child that the wish is now part of the fuzz and the air will carry it to the Great Spirit or God and Goddess.

Older children may prefer to work with weather. Children over the age of ten may perceive the game of Dandelion Fuzz Wishes as being childish. Honoring and attuning to wind-driven weather systems is a powerful way of aligning with the element of Air, as well as increasing a feeling of interconnection and respect for Nature. This exercise is also one way to redirect the focus of any child who may be afraid of storms.

Becoming the Storm Exercise

This exercise can easily be altered to assist you with becoming a bird or a kite or anything else you choose.

As soon as the wind begins to pick up, and as long as it is safe, sit with your children by a window and watch the wind move in. Guide everyone to take a deep breath and feel the wind. If possible, you may prefer to open the window a bit to help your children feel it.

Thank the wind and the weather for their presence and for the benefits they bring. Ask that they share their essence with you and speak to your Spirits.

Guide your children to continue taking deep breaths and to imagine becoming the wind and its power. Encourage them to include all five of their physical senses as they become the storm. Suggest that they listen to the voice of the storm and hear anything it may say to them.

Maintain this as long as you wish or until your children begin to come back to their bodies and get

fidgety. Bring them back slowly and gently by guiding
them to feel their bodies, the chairs they are sitting on,
the temperature of the room, etc.

Discuss your experiences or record them in your
personal journals.

Air can be also seen as the breath, or the kiss, of the Great
Spirit. Children can easily visualize being kissed or touched by
this Divinity each time they feel even a slight breeze. Teaching
this to children can remind them, as they go about their everyday activities, that they are safe and loved by the gods. The
breathing exercises in chapter 3 are also highly recommended
for connecting to the power and influence of Air as Breath.

Fire

Most of us attune to Fire instinctively in the summer. Tempera-
tures are warmer, we lie out in the sun, and we may become
more physically active. Summer is usually a school-age child's
favorite time of year, unless they are in a year-round school. And
the Sun is the best way to work with Fire for young children.

Using the Becoming the Storm exercise on the previous page,
anyone can become the sun or a bonfire or a candle flame with a
few alterations to the specifics of the exercise. This is an ideal
exercise to do anytime you are spending some quiet time outside
in the sunshine. It is perfect for anyone laying out to get a sun-
tan, as is the next exercise.

Your Inner Sun Exercise

Count your child down from ten to one, reminding
him or her periodically to take deep breaths.

Guide the child to see a golden star, or a small sun,
in the center of the body. Describe it in great detail,
using imagery that involves as many of the senses as
possible.

Guide the child to see and feel this golden star
in his or her center expand and glow brightly. Its

radiance extends out beyond the body in a protective egg of light.

Suggest to the child that their inner sun will keep them safe and healthy and that they can use it in any way they chooses. Tell them that whenever they need help making a decision, all they need do is look to their inner sun. It will give them all the answers they need by glowing brighter or dimmer.

Give them some time to fully experience their inner sun before counting them back up from one to ten.

Discuss the experience or allow the child to write it in a personal journal.

Water

Water is another easy element for a child to attune to, and working with it can often be combined with Earth attunement exercises. When we water our gardens, we thank the water and charge it with beneficial energies. The Become the Storm exercise is also excellent to use during rainstorms, to attune to the water as well as the wind in a storm. The Nature Spirit Attunement exercise is recommended for attuning to the spirits of lakes, rivers, or any body of water, even a house fountain.

For children, water attunement serves another very important purpose. It helps one to connect with emotion. In many modern societies, emotion is something to keep hidden from all but our closest friends. An understanding of one's feelings and the ability to experience them is often seen as a weakness, rather than as the strength it really is. Unfortunately, this belief is particularly ingrained into our young boys.

Emotion is one important aspect of the Water element. As such, it should be given the respect and attention that it deserves. Pagan children benefit in many ways from working with this element and from the example of strong, yet sensitive, pagan men and women. Far too often in our society, people cannot even give a name to their feelings, let alone accept and honor them. This creates blocks in their energy field and can contribute to soul fragmentation.

One simple way to teach self-knowledge is scrying. While many pagans use the scrying bowl or mirror for divination, it works in much the same way to put children in touch with their emotions and inner selves. A bowl, preferably black, filled with water serves as a focal point, external to one's self. This allows us to be objective in what we see, releasing the analytical mind that would normally interfere with these matters.

Scrying for Self-Knowledge

Set aside a bowl to be used only for this purpose. It is preferable for each family member to have his or her own bowl for scrying. It is preferred that the interior of the bowl be black, but this is not necessary.

Scrying with the Younger Child Exercise
This section is recommended for children under the age of ten. The amount of guidance will depend on the disposition and age of the individual child.

> Fill the bowl halfway full of water and place it on a table in front of the children. Guide them to pass first their left hands, then their right hands over the surface of the water. Ask that the spirit of the water allow them to see what they need in the bowl. If they are able to speak, have them repeat after you as you ask for the assistance of the spirit of the water.
>
> Guide them to take deep breaths. For children over five, count them down from ten to one in to a relaxed state of being.
>
> Ask them to picture themselves, or the situation at hand, in the water, as if it were a mirror. If there is a specific emotion they need help handling, focus on the events that create that emotion for them.

Ask them what they see. Encourage them to tell you the story they see or to describe in as much detail as possible how they look or feel in the bowl. Depending on the issue at hand, you may also want to encourage them to describe how they are affecting the other people in the picture and how that makes them feel.

Ask for them, or have them repeat after you, a request for guidance in recognizing these emotions when they experiences them. Then ask if there is anything else they need to see at this time and give them time to experience anything that may come up.

When you both are satisfied that the most benefit was achieved in this session, give thanks to the spirit of the water and to the children. Dispose of the water together, either in a garden or as an offering to the spirits of your home.

Scrying with the Older Child Exercise

Older children will require minimal guidance and may prefer to do this on their own.

Fill the bowl at least halfway with water. Pass first your left hand, then your right hand over the surface of the water, aligning your energy with that of the water. Ask that the spirit of the water allow you to honestly and gently see your Self in the bowl. If there is a certain situation or emotion you need to deal with, ask for specific guidance in seeing this clearly.

Give yourself time to see whatever shows up. If you see only symbols, ask that they be made more clear, or give yourself additional time to allow the meanings to flow into your conscious mind. Know that you can focus on specific elements of the image by simply relaxing and allowing yourself to become more open. What you are looking at in this exercise is your own inner self and you control your access to it.

If you need guidance in making a decision or handling something differently in the future, ask for it. Your spirit guides and the spirit of the water will hear you.

Ask if there is anything else you need to see at this time and give yourself time to experience whatever may come up.

When you are satisfied that the greatest benefit was achieved in this session, give thanks to the spirit of the water and to your Self. Dispose of the water with respect and thanks, either in a garden or as an offering to the spirits of your home.

Since most pagans are followers of Earth- or Goddess-based religions, Earth stewardship can be a vital expression of their spirituality. For some this is achieved simply, through honoring the spirits of the land in prayer and meditation. Others feel they are called to get more actively involved through alternative lifestyle choices, career choices, or involvement with activist organizations.

Most pagan parents tend to support these choices if their children feel drawn to them. It certainly benefits your children if you are also involved with caring for the Earth in some way. The health and survival of humans and many other species depends on our ability to live in harmony and attunement with our world. We desperately need to develop less harmful power sources and more constructive ways of dealing with our global and individual differences.

But just as importantly, these are also lifestyle choices that will allow our children to incorporate their spirituality with other aspects of their lives. While this is possible in almost any situation, some lifestyle choices are inherently more spiritual and healthy than others. If a child feels drawn to a choice that allows a concrete means of honoring the Earth and the God and Goddess, they deserve all the support we can give them.

One of the best goals we can hope to achieve, as pagan parents, is to teach our children that our every action, our every thought has power. Therefore, it is vital that we live our lives as though each act is a spiritual and sacred one. When we call upon the Spiritkeepers of the directions, our spirit guides, or the gods, we pray, "May our every action honor You." In this way spirituality is not some separate aspect of life, to be solely encased within a religious framework. It becomes life itself and we learn to walk each day as the spiritual beings that we are.

10

Religion

Religion is generally defined as the belief in and worship of a deity or deities. It also includes the faith, beliefs, and system of worship or service to those deities. As noted before, religion and spirituality are not necessarily mutually exclusive. I separated them for reasons of clarity and order in this book, as well as for those reasons described in the previous chapter.

The pagan relationship to the gods and goddesses is a complex one that varies not only with the individual, but also with the path or tradition. Although children may be raised in one path, they may feel a strong connection or attraction to deities of other pantheons. This is generally accepted in pagan homes, no matter which path the family follows.

The main exception is that of a pagan-reared child who feels strongly drawn to the God and religion of the Christians, although the more orthodox forms of other mainstream religions can also cause some concern. This may cause some discomfort and upset in a pagan family.

The divisive issues between pagans and Christians are well known. Many pagans resent the intolerant and often violent history of Christianity. The belief that theirs is the only true path, coupled with the refusal to acknowledge the existence of any other gods, is a constant annoyance to many pagans. Furthermore, many of us do not appreciate the missionary attitude that leads many Christians to attempt to convert us and save our souls.

There is no real point in discussing this issue here, except as it relates to the raising of children within a pagan tradition. This is another situation where we, as parents, must examine our own reactions if a child decides that he or she is a Christian. Before discriminating or forbidding it, ask yourself why you are reacting in this way. Does your behavior benefit your child and will it prevent this interest? Are you adopting the same kind of belief and attitude that leads Christians to become missionaries? How would you (or did you) feel if your parent refused to allow you to pursue your pagan interests?

Many families will allow their child to explore Christianity (or any other religion), while insisting that they continue to celebrate and honor the Old Gods along with the rest of the family. If a child does not want to participate, she or he is usually not forced to, but there is always an insistence on respect for the ways of one's family. This is often accompanied by the family's willingness to respect the child's preferences. Some families will even encourage this exploration of other paths, including Christianity.

Although some children may continue to be drawn to the mystical side of Christianity or other mainstream religions, it does appear that few pagan children continue along this type of path for long. The vast majority of children that were raised pagan are not willing to accept a belief system that denigrates all others and would sentence their families to eternal damnation merely for holding differing beliefs. Once they have gained an experiential understanding of the limitations and intolerance of such a path, they generally move on in their search.

Through supporting, or at least allowing, their search, we demonstrate our unconditional love for our children. We also reduce the risk that they will resent us for impeding an honest spiritual search. We do not want to become those intolerant people we warn our children about.

There is another benefit to allowing this search. If a child is becoming involved with Christianity, or any religion, for reasons of rebellion or revenge, we eliminate the desired effects of their rebellion. By not allowing ourselves to be pulled into a drama, we may effectively defuse the situation. When we forbid or punish in situations like this, we only drive them further away.

However, this does not often become an issue until children are much older, possibly not until they are adults. Therefore, we may turn our attention to the various aspects of raising children within the pagan religions. Since there are plenty of books out on the eight most common pagan holidays, some of which are even specifically for pagan families, I will not get into this aspect in any more depth than I did in chapter 6.

Certainly, our rituals are the most obvious aspects of our religion. These are also the most complex and we will discuss these in a later chapter, but there are other ways that we work with and honor the deities and spirits that are an integral part of any pagan's life. These generally include altars and the various spiritual and magical tools we use.

Altars

All pagans have some form of altar, whether it is a talisman hung innocently on a doorknob, a few crystals on a shelf, or a separate altar room. Altars may take the form of a few well-chosen objects on a desk at work or they may be altars-in-a-box, hidden under living room tables. Whatever form they take, an altar is a focal point as well as a means of connecting with one's honored spirits.

The main goal of an altar is to become an honoring place for that which is special to the individual or group. There are innumerable altars to family in homes that are not recognized as such. A piano or mantel with photos of family members is a form of altar. A pagan family can create altars and assist their children in creating their own first altars by simply being creative and flexible.

Just as we were willing to recognize the possibility of Elmo as a spirit guide, we must remain open to our children's innate creativity and personal symbolism at a given time. A child's altar may be a special place for favorite rocks, a garden shrine, or a beloved tree. Children tend to need less "stuff" on their altars. Their altars are often much more freeform than that of an adult. To a child raised pagan, the natural world is one big altar.

While this is true for most pagans, we can be instrumental in teaching our children the value of more formal altars. In doing so, we can guide them in creating a special space for those energies they feel most attuned to and which they want to bring into their lives. The best way to start is to work with your child and decide on a spot for the altar to be.

Give the child the choice of several places in your home, or in the child's room. It is important to know whether or not the child wants the altar to be private. If so, the inside of a closet or a hidden corner of a bedroom is probably the best choice. When I was a young teenager, my altar took up the middle shelf of a bookcase in my room. I kept a large cloth over the bookcase, hiding my altar from obvious view. Not only did this keep it safe from prying eyes, but it also preserved the special energy of that small space.

I would also suggest having a family discussion ahead of time regarding altars and the privacy and respect they are due. Without an agreement among the family that these altars are sacred and are not to be disturbed by siblings for any reason, you are just setting your family up for fights and hurt feelings. If there are pets in the house, this should be kept in mind when planning the location of an altar. Dogs can easily knock over a floor altar and a cat wanting food or attention at 3 A.M. may walk across a tabletop altar on purpose.

The next step is to sit down with each child individually and discuss the type of altar they want. Do they want an altar cloth and if so, what color? Is there a specific animal or rock or deity that the child feels connected to, and how can you best represent that in an age-appropriate way?

The very young child may have difficulty with the language, or even with analyzing spirituality in this way. It is most effective to go about this as a game. A child over the age of two can normally let you know where he wants his special table set up. You may want to take him to a metaphysical shop or a fabric store and see if he is drawn to anything in particular. You can also do this at home by collecting his favorite things and deciding together which should be included.

Since children can be attracted to anything that catches their eye at the time, you may want to remind them each time of their altar and ask if they want this item for their altar. Pick each item up and carry it with you. When you are finished looking, show him or her all the things once more and determine which are really special enough to bring home.

For the older child, this discussion is probably unnecessary unless the entire family is very new to paganism. A teenager who has been raised pagan is generally well aware of altars and their uses. For the very young child, you may prefer to create small altars for them in the beginning.

Our son created his first formal altar when he was a little over three years old. Out of the blue, he decided that he wanted his very own altar in his room. We searched in the garage for something to use as a base and came up with Daddy's old small ironing board. He set it down just under his window. I showed him the remaining blue cloth from his calendar and he decided that was perfect for him.

Then he ran all over the house collecting his rocks and his candles. He asked for the tiny faery sculpture I keep on a bookshelf and set it right next to his hatching dragon sculpture. He decided that his baby tree should stay in the living room but he wanted his little Earth flag on the side of the altar. These days, his altar takes up the top of his bookshelf, under the same window in his room.

He is so happy and proud of his altar that he tells everyone who comes to our house about it. Everyone has to go see it, even the nonpagans that I work with. They may not understand it, but he is so ecstatic about it, they just have to be happy for him.

Our son has several altars in his room, many of them I started when he was still an infant. He has changed some; others he has chosen to leave as I originally created them. On his bedposts, he keeps a dragon pendant that I gave him, along with two other amulets that were made by a dear friend and given to him when he was a baby. On his doorknob, he keeps a plastic mala that he chose when some Buddhist monks visited our area, and a medicine pouch with all his favorite stones.

This may seem very simple, but for a child it is not at all simple. Each of these items has a special and specific place. During a period of nightmares, when he did not decide to come sleep with us, our son would often hold his dragon pendant through the night. I would find it in his hands when I checked on him or responded to cries. He still often wears his necklaces from time to time. None of this is simple. On the contrary, it is very important to him that these things be where he can access them when he feels the need.

Another form of a bedside altar often involves stuffed animals or dolls. Bedtime is frequently when children need to feel the safest. Stuffed animals and dolls can become their friends and protectors. As such, they require honored spaces, just as an adult would honor power animals or deities on a more formal altar. In fact, stuffed animals or dolls are very often the focal point for the energy of a specific guide. A parent may wear a Thor's hammer or have a carved eagle on an altar. A child may gain the same energies and benefits from a stuffed lion or a warrior doll.

For a young child, this is an altar. When I was growing up, my altars varied according to my age and what was going on in my life at the time. By the time I reached school age, I had my favorite rocks lined up in a definite way in very specific places around my room. My stuffed animals had their own places on my bed. As I got older, my altars became more sophisticated.

In addition to a personal altar, a family altar is a wonderful way to get everyone involved and cocreate something for your home and family. As is true with personal altars, these can be as blatant or as inconspicuous as you choose. The goal is to bring in harmonious and beneficial energies, while honoring the guides and guardians of your home and family.

Each room in our house has its own altar, although some are more obvious than others. Somewhere in each room you will find a combination of rocks, shells, and/or feathers. In one room, a faery sculpture stands watch over an ivy plant and some rocks. In another, a crystal bowl of stones is topped off with the Ponderosa pine cones we collected on a family outing when our son thought pine cones were the coolest things on Earth.

A family altar should be something that does not need to be off-limits to any member of the family, at least once your children are over the everything-in-the-mouth stage. When they are still young, this may preclude the use of anything breakable, or anything that holds an emotional significance to you. Children should certainly be taught that altars are not play areas and the objects on them are not toys, but if they feel they are not allowed to touch, the altar becomes the parents' property, thereby losing its connection to the children.

If you do choose to establish a family altar that will remain up all the time, it may be a good idea to change it slightly according to the season and upcoming holiday. Children of any age love to use the colors, plants, and symbols of the season in play and decoration. It is also important not to force the altar to remain stagnant. Allow it to change and grow with your family.

Your family altar will become a microcosm of your family's spiritual and religious life. As such, it should reflect where you are at any given time. When a child outgrows Big Bird as a spirit guide, that symbol should be replaced with something more applicable and appropriate. When a child reaches their dedication or adulthood rites, add something to the family altar to recognize this special event.

Magical Tools

Although we do have a pagan clergy, such as high priests, high priestesses, shamans, and archdruids, most pagans are priests and priestesses in their own right. Solitary pagans perform all of their rituals alone. Even those of us who belong to some type of pagan group perform many rituals on our own. As a result, pagans probably possess more ritual and spiritual items as individuals than any other religious group.

These are the tools that our children will be exposed to at young ages and trained in the use of as they grow older. The tools you use will vary according to the path you follow. The various uses of certain tools also depend on one's stage in the training of that path. For example, many pagans use drums for recreation these days. Among those following a shamanic path, many can use the drum to facilitate shamanic trance states. However, only those in advanced shamanic training learn to use the drum for divination, healing, invocation, and other magics.

In light of this, I will only discuss those tools that are commonly used by the general pagan community. These are items that most pagan children will be exposed to at an early age and include the drum or rattle, the wand or knife, the chalice, incense and smudge, candles, and oils.

Creating Magical Tools

As is true with anything, creation tends to become more sophisticated with the age of the child. For this reason, we try to keep the tools and their creation simpler for younger children. While some families view magical tools as too serious to be played at by children, most families agree that play is the first step in learning and gaining familiarity.

A child certainly does not need a sharp knife or a crystal chalice. However, a child's blunt knife or toy wand and a plastic cup can bring the same special significance to ritual for a child as the real thing does for an adult. It also increases a child's ability to participate, thereby increasing their interest.

In some families and some magical traditions, ritual tools are part of the training process. The creation of tools may be a prerequisite for various initiations. In these cases, the creation of magical and ritual tools is serious business and there will be definite guidelines to follow. In this book, I will not attempt to outline all of the traditions, tools, techniques, and tests that might accompany this facet of a specific training system.

Fire Tools/Candles

Incense, smudge, and candles have an almost universal importance to spirituality and religion. However, each of these items requires parental supervision until the child is old enough to be entrusted with the responsibility of fire use. I was in junior high school before I was allowed to burn candles, in glass holders, alone in my room. There are plenty of children who cannot be trusted alone with burning candles even at that age.

Fire is an element that must be respected and treated with caution. All children should be taught the dangers inherent in the use of fire. Children rarely think about potential consequences of their actions and can easily forget or attempt to hide a burning candle. House or brush fires are often the unfortunate result of a lack of education.

Children around the age of two seem to prefer to blow out all the candles rather than play with them. Around three, they become fascinated with them. In their bids for independence and attempt to mimic the adults around them, older toddlers develop a real interest in lighting, blowing out, and relighting candles. By the age of eight, many young children find it an exciting adventure to play with matches and candles. They need to learn to stay away from any fire and that the candles are not part of a game. Candles are a serious part of a ritual.

Children can assist in making candles and they gain a great sense of satisfaction from this. You might consider allowing them a small amount of wax to create their own candle, in whatever colors and design they choose, in return for helping you. This is also a way to teach the value of reciprocation: the need to balance energy and continue the flow when someone does something for you. Most craft stores sell wax granules that make this an easy project to share with children. With these granules and a small bowl, pot, or glass, you can create beautiful candles of any design or color combination you desire.

The innate wonder and magic of a child's mind makes candle magic truly powerful for them. It makes sense to children that when we write our wishes on a candle and burn it, the magic is released. After all, we make real wishes with each birthday cake. Obviously, this will require varying degrees of parental supervision, but this can be one of the first simple spells you teach your children.

Candlemaking Exercise

Choose an appropriate color for candles together and write or carve key words or symbols into the side of the candle. You may want to also anoint the candle with a special oil. Then charge it with whatever you want to manifest and let it burn all the way down. Bury any remaining wax and let the Earth assist with the spell. The following are some of the most common candle colors and their major associations. See also the associations with the chakra colors given in chapter 5.

White: similar to a clear crystal in that it can embody any energies.

Black: protection, grounding, banishing

Red: physical vitality, sexual energy (particularly male), life energy

Rose or Pink: romantic love, emotional healing, comfort, self-love

Orange: sexual energy (especially female), decision-making, energy, vitality, fertility

Yellow: manifestation on the physical plane, self-confidence

Blue: healing, seeking vision, divination, dreamwork, peace, communication

Green: balance, harmony, general healing, money, success

Purple: clairvoyance, astral travel, meditation, protection

Gold: the God, the Sun, general healing

Silver: the Goddess, the Moon, psychic development

Oils

Oils are used by pagans in many different ways. Some people use them simply for fragrance, preferring the essential oil to synthetic, chemical-laden commercial perfumes. Others use them for ritual and magic, calling on the properties of the plant the oil was made from. While children should be taught not to drink even essential oils, these are generally safe for children to use and make.

You also may prefer to reserve the making of oils as part of an older child's training. This gives children something to aspire to and allows older children and teens a more advanced stage to participate in. A progression of steps in any teaching system increases healthy competition with oneself and a genuine feeling of pride and achievement.

Essential Oil Exercise

> To make a simple essential oil, use approximately one cup of light vegetable oil. Place it in a clean glass jar. Gather approximately one-quarter to one-third of a cup of the plants you need and soak them in the oil for three days, in a dark place with the jar capped. Using unbleached cheesecloth to filter out the plant parts, pour the oil into a second clean glass jar. Repeat the process three times or until you achieve the degree of scent you desire. This can be a fun exercise in patience for children, but young children should be supervised when using glass containers.

Drums

The drum and rattle are widely used for trance induction and to facilitate shamanic journeying. Followers of many paths will use drums in ritual to ease meditations and to raise energy. The drum, in particular, is used for healing, divination, and the invocation of spirits. Furthermore, modern researchers have found that the study of music has a definite and beneficial impact on a child's reading and math skills.

Most children love to play with drums and rattles. A tin can covered with rubber on both open ends and a film canister filled with sand are two very inexpensive, very simple instruments that can introduce a child to the use of rhythm in magic. Many parents who are also drummers have found that introducing children to drums and/or rattles at a young age encourages them to develop respect, not only for the drum itself but also for other drummers in a circle. We have found that it helps children to maintain their connections to universal energy as they grow up. Furthermore, when used correctly, drumming can facilitate the healthy release of emotions.

I use the drum regularly for the release of tension, anger, or even sadness. Our son is learning to play his drum rather than hit or throw things when he is angry or upset. The goal is not to force any particular rhythm, but rather to allow the energy of the emotion to flow through you. Allow the drum to speak for you. The drum grounds and releases this energy as it purifies both your personal energy field and the space around you. This is beneficial for all children, but may be particularly useful during puberty when emotions are rampant and the child may not always be able to easily talk about his or her feelings.

If you choose to purchase drums for your children, you might begin with small, simple drums for very young children. As they grow and learn to respect the drum, they will gain the ability to properly care for a larger or more expensive drum. While it is true that a child who started on a covered plastic bowl will need a more sophisticated instrument as she or he grows up and their ability increases, it is not necessarily true that this instrument must be an expensive or commercially made one.

Through encouraging children to experiment and create their own objects, we prepare them for life in many ways. We support the healthy development of their self-confidence and ability to problem-solve. We teach them very basic scientific methods as we bolster their abilities to combine intuition and creativity with physical manifestation and analytical thinking. This facilitates the development of true and complete intelligence.

Consecrating Magical Tools

The consecration and use of magical tools is what sets them apart from everyday items. These are tools that were crafted for a specific purpose and that have been ritually dedicated to that purpose. This is something that children generally find very easy to understand. This makes these objects special. Children recognize that these tools are not toys and, therefore, require additional care.

As is true with any ritual involving children, we design it to be as simple and short as possible while retaining the necessary power. It is also very important that these rituals involve some sort of physical action for the children; something to get them interested and fully involved. Below I have outlined a simple and generally nondenominational consecration ritual that is intended to be used as a guide. It is my hope that this will spark your own creativity and that of your children as you design an appropriate ritual for your own family.

Tool Consecration Ritual

An older child should be encouraged to perform this ritual alone, if they choose. However, he or she should be supervised through their first ritual for guidance and support. Guide a younger child as appropriate without interfering or attempting to do everything for him.

> Have an anointing oil or a bowl of sage ready on the altar.
>
> Begin with the smudging ceremony to purify your self and your child, the altar, the tool to be consecrated, and the surrounding space.
>
> Create sacred space or cast the Circle in your usual manner.
>
> Call upon the spirits of the directions, the helping spirits of the child, and any deities the child or family works with. Ask that these beings guide and assist the child in this rite. Request their blessings and their acceptance of this special tool.

Taking up the anointing oil, hold it between both hands and offer it first to the gods and the spirits. Then anoint the tool with a small amount of the oil, saying as you do so that you are anointing this tool; you bless it and prepare it for consecration by the gods.

If you are using sage, and sage may be preferable when consecrating a drum, hold the bowl up to the gods and spirits first. Then sprinkle a small amount over the tool, saying as you do so that you bless and purify this tool in preparation for consecration by the gods. Spread the sage around to anoint the entire surface of a drumhead. Then return the sage to the bowl.

Take up the tool and hold it with both hands. Beginning at your root chakra, bring the tool up through all your chakras, tuning it to your personal energy.

Hold the tool up to the gods and the spirits. Speak from the heart, but be sure to make it clear that you have created/chosen this as your working tool. Ask the blessings of the spirits and the gods for all that you do with this tool. Ask that universal energy may flow freely through you and that you may be divinely inspired when working with this tool. Promise to treat it with respect as a working partner and to use it only for the highest good of all.

For a younger child, it is best to end the ritual at this point. An older child may prefer to stay in Circle and perform a meditation or simply sit in silence, attuning to the newly consecrated tool and receiving any messages that may come through.

Make sure that the child keeps the tool near them, at least at night, for the next few weeks. This will reinforce the bond between child and tool and will further harmonize the tool with the child's personal energy.

Honoring the Spirits

The Spirits in this section include any nonphysical beings that you work with in your path. They may take the form of ancestors, gods and goddesses, faery, power animals, or any interdimensional helping spirits. Certainly, the ways in which we work with and honor these beings will vary according to the type of being, your personal preference, and your tradition, but there are common ways that most pagans honor their spirits and that is what I will focus on here.

Offerings are probably the most powerful and the most common means of honoring the spirits. This method crosses all cultural boundaries and is as ancient as humankind's awareness of these spirits. Offerings can be as simple or as elaborate as you choose. An offering need not be a bribe or a plea, as many mainstream people think. It is a continuation of the flow of mutually beneficial energy that honors those who give to us.

Since ancient times, our ancestors have offered corn or sacred herbs in thanks for the blessings of the Earth. In ritual, we may also offer a sprinkling of wine, mead, or vodka. We may light candles as an offering and a blessing. It is also quite common for the first and best portions of a meal to be set aside and given to the spirits of the family or place. And many people still leave out a bowl of milk for the faeries. This is not silly, it is an equal exchange of energy in return for the protection, guidance, and love we receive on a daily basis throughout our lives. It also opens us to the continual flow of this energy.

While many pagans still engage in these customary forms of offerings, modern pagans have become more innovative in their offerings. We offer water to plants in drought or desert areas. We collect food and old clothes for donation to the homeless or other needy people. We volunteer our time at many different organizations. We stop to help stray or injured animals. We work toward peace, tolerance, and harmony with our world and all peoples. And we offer back pure, unconditional energy in our every action. Simply living one's life in a sacred and honest manner is an offering of the highest kind.

These are concrete ways in which children can get involved in offering something back for the blessings they have received. These types of offerings teach a child that she or he can make a difference in their world and that everyone wins if they just try. These offerings are also an opportunity for a child to experience many people and situations that they might not ordinarily see, except through the media. These are rare occasions for growth on many levels of being.

The Give-Away Ceremony

One of the ways that my family makes use of these types of offerings is through the Give-Away. We give-away anything from old clothes, to food, to volunteer time. Volunteer time can take many forms. Anything that gives something back to the planet or the community is ideal, from time spent reading to challenged children or serving meals at soup kitchens, to planting trees or assisting at a respite center.

The actual physical give-away can be seen as a type of medicine. It is a part of our selves and our energy that we freely release and offer to others for their own pleasure and benefit. In this way, the energy is free to move throughout the community and the planet bringing balance, happiness, and abundance to all. This process is a means for us to accept our role in the great Web of Life and to integrate the understanding that we will be taken care of, as long as we remain in that flow.

In modern society we can get so focused on ourselves and our own problems that our communities suffer. In looking out for Number One, we may lose sight of the needs of others, including those of our ecosystems. The Give-Away is a ritual recognition that all our needs are related. The process of Give-Away takes us outside of ourselves and allows a more expanded, less personal view of our situations.

Once we have collected or determined what it is we will give-away, we bring that into the Solstice ritual. If we are donating time, we bring the image and intent into the ceremony. If there are specific deities related to our donations, they are invoked at the beginning of the ritual. Then, in the middle of the ritual, we consecrate the donations (including image and intent). We bless them all with the highest good for all involved, that everyone who contacts these gifts may be blessed. We ask that these gifts restore balance and be accepted as thanks for all we have received so that the cycle of blessings may continue.

The most important thing about the give-away is that it does not simply end with the end of the ritual. We have to handle the practical aspects of how to carry out the giving of our offerings. We actually follow through and complete what we have intended. This is an excellent lesson for children in keeping promises and following through on actions.[1]

Honoring Through Creativity

We also honor the spirits through the use of altars, artwork, and jewelry. We discussed altars earlier. In addition, artwork and writing can be extremely beneficial for children. Opening up to one's own inner self and to one's helping spirits through creativity of any form is a tremendous honoring. Children should be encouraged to draw, paint, write, create music, or be creative in their own ways.

You may be quite surprised by their creations when children are working directly with the spirits. I have never been a great artist in terms of painting and drawing, but beginning around the age of ten, I have created some truly inspired drawings of deities and power animals simply through allowing them to work through me. Most of the time, I slipped into trance and was not aware that I was opening to anyone, but the drawings that resulted could never have been created by my overly analytical self.

This is also how I write, and I strongly encourage children to write poetry or stories or rituals if they have any desire to do so. Often I will edit my story or chapter and wonder who really wrote it. This method of allowing spirit to work through one can be very similar to the scrying method given earlier. The main

---

1 Much of this section on the give-away is reprinted exactly as it first appeared in an article in the *InnerConnection*, Litha 1998 issue.

idea is to find which method works best for each child, and then support them in developing that ability.

Children love to play with clay or modeling compound. If drawing and writing don't seem to be doing it for your child, get out the clay and allow them to sculpt along with you. Put on some music and light some incense. Then just let your imaginations run wild without any critique of your creations.

As children grow up, they will be more able to understand the creation of statues of the spirits that work with them. However, as children get older and assimilate into school and society, they tend to become more analytical, often blocking the free flow of that creativity. Parents of older children, particularly of children not raised pagan from a very young age, have special considerations when encouraging this. You may need to develop some specific attitudes and a good deal of patience in order to assist your child in reestablishing that link to her innate creativity.

If this is your situation, you might start out very simply by simply creating symbols. Another form of sculpture that anyone can do is to create figures from found objects. This encourages the child to recognize potential in the world around them, including old junk. It also rarely manifests as a realistic animal or being.

This type of sculpture is highly symbolic. It can take any form the child desires, provided it speaks to this child in some way. In one sense this is great therapy. In another sense, it can allow a child's intuitive doors to open just enough for the spirits to begin to work with her or him.

Begin by gathering things like glue, string, wire, clay, or anything else that may possibly be needed to hold your found objects together or serve as a base for them. Then go out on a "Junk Walk." If you are taking young children with you, they should be supervised to prevent injury. Children will certainly love this type of walk, but it is recommended more for older children and teenagers.

Junk Walk Exercise

Take a bag with you and pick up whatever discarded items capture your attention. It is important to do this with honor and use common sense. Do not do this on private property without the permission of the owner. Do not take something that may belong to another person and absolutely do not remove any part of a living thing. You may choose to do this in your own backyard or in a park. You may also walk along the road or the beach. If you live in the West, Open Space areas are perfect for these walks.

Trust that you will pick up whatever you need and then some. If there is a specific spirit or issue that you would like to focus on, sit in silent meditation with the child before going out on the walk. Both of you should focus on that and hold it in your minds as you walk.

When you return from your walk, dump everything you've collected out onto the floor or a large working table. Take a short break, if you wish, and then move directly into your creation. Feel free to experiment. Dismantle anything that doesn't feel right and start over. Keep in mind that someone else may have been guided to pick up something for you. It is permissible to ask to use objects that another person brought home, but if they feels strongly that the object is theirs, do not push.

It may help to work with some light music on, speaking as little as possible. However, if the talking flows easily and does not focus solely on the creation at hand, it may be just the thing to keep the analytical mind occupied while the spirit and body-mind create.

Depending on the child, this may flow immediately or it may take some time for them to allow themselves to be creative. Make whatever comes up okay and eventually they may feel comfortable enough to try again. Even if they do not want to try this exercise again, they will benefit greatly from your lack of nonjudgmentalness and unconditional love.

Many people today feel turned off by the very idea of a religion. Most of these individuals are reacting to negative experiences with some of the older and more stagnant organized religions that attempt to control followers, and they reject the importance placed on politics rather than honest spiritual beliefs. This can color their view of religion itself.

It is important that our children understand that religion does not have to be like that. Religion in its highest form is simply honoring and working with our helping spirits. While we may prefer to call this spirituality, that line is not so finely drawn.

Our children may not have a specific label for their religion or spirituality, but that is not important. Many pagans tend to resist labels because they consider them to be limiting. If our children learn to walk in honor and respect for all life and to strive toward self-knowledge, they may label themselves "pumpkinheads" if they choose. What matters is how this affects them and their lives. If our children grow up happy and healthy, then our "religion" has served its purpose.

11

Honesty vs. Secrecy

Honesty is one of the most vital characteristics of a healthy family. Without honesty, there is no trust. Without honesty, there is no confidence in self or others. However, within pagan families, honesty outside the immediate family, particularly regarding spirituality, can be an extremely sensitive issue. It is a sad fact that there are many pagans who cannot even be fully honest about their spiritual belief within their immediate families.

As wonderful as it was to have been raised outside mainstream religion, there was a downside for me, and for every other child raised as I was. I learned the importance of secrecy at a very young age and began to live a double life. Even now that the New Age movement has become big business, and paganism is on the rise, we are still not readily accepted by the dominant society.

Children growing up in metaphysical homes today still deal with the same conflicts, although often to a lesser degree. There is tremendous pressure on children to conform in order to make friends and avoid taunting. Children also have less available options for escape than adults do. They cannot move to a new area, change jobs, or socialize superficially with one group while having real friends in another area, particularly at school. This raises the question of whether to be totally honest or to pretend conformity to some degree. It is a question faced daily by anyone on the fringes of the majority. Children often have an instinctual desire to be honest with people, particularly friends. Oddly enough, children who were not raised pagan are often more likely to be open about the pagan exploration of their family than are children who were raised pagan from birth. It is an exciting new development that they naturally want to share with others.

However, in order to function in society, complete honesty and openness are not always possible. We all play a variety of roles throughout our lives. Each role is tailored to the situation at hand and may be exclusive of our other roles. Furthermore, many of our public roles may be in direct conflict with our more private roles.

The difficulty arises when roles that are meant to share openly with another person become necessarily restricted. For example, the role of friend should be relatively open. Children growing up with metaphysical beliefs will often not share this side of themselves with mainstream friends for fear of rejection and ridicule. This puts the relationship at a disadvantage from the beginning. As a result, pagan children have even more roles to play and more reason to keep these roles completely separate.

As toddlers, children are beginning to learn how to behave in society. As they explore and question their world, they are also being programmed to view it as the adults around them do. Older children will frequently feel the need to conform in some ways just to fit in and make friends.

A large part of this public role is deciding what should be encompassed within that role. For most followers of mainstream religions, this is not even a question that comes to mind. Unless the individual is extremely devout, religion is often not a part of their public persona. They neither hide it nor broadcast it. It is like skin color, hair color, or anything else that is an integral part of who we are without needing to think about it.

This is the ideal perception for pagan families to develop. Then the major focus of discussions can be on things like whether or not to correct assumptions regarding your religion, how to handle direct questions, and when the public persona should give way to the private friend and family persona.

Having some form of pagan community to associate with is the ideal way to handle these issues with children of all ages. Within the community, your children should be able to hang out and make friends with other children their age who are following the same or similar spiritual paths. There is also the opportunity for interaction with older pagan children who may serve as role models.

These communities often become a subculture within the larger community where we live and work. Among these people, our children do not need to be careful about what they say and to whom. A community may develop out of a Grove or coven, even a study or meditation group. These communities generally follow the same path, but will certainly stress acceptance of diversity.

Another type of pagan community is the festival community. These may or may not be extensions of a local community. Festivals, especially the outdoor gatherings, are a unique experience. They frequently become a sort of world within a world, where everyone is pagan and accepting of pagan values and traditions. People share their thoughts, feelings, and practices.

Among the festival communities, children are honored and respected. There are often special events for children, such as games, rituals, and workshops. There may also be workshops or discussion groups on pagan parenting. At larger gatherings, there are often organized get-togethers for older children and teenagers.

Within these groups, the children decide on their own speakers, fire circles, and discussions. This is particularly true of the teen-only groups. Often, these discussions focus on issues that particularly affect children of that age, including the questions of sexuality and openness regarding their spirituality.

I strongly support these types of discussion groups, whether at festivals or elsewhere. It gives children an opportunity to see firsthand that they are not alone in their feelings and experiences. They are free to share with peers who understand and they can often exchange ideas on how to handle what may come up. In learning to act with integrity, children need to think for themselves and gather information so that they may make informed decisions. However, decisions regarding this type of honesty must also be discussed with the family, if these decisions have the potential to affect others in the family.

Unfortunately, not every pagan family has access to a pagan community, or for some reason they are unable to interact with the local community. A feeling of isolation can be very difficult on both parents and children in the absence of some form of support system. This situation calls for a great deal more family creativity and closeness. It requires open communication and support within the family.

When my parents were children this was not an issue. These things were not discussed outside the home. When I was a child in the 1960s, the silence had been broken. Many people flaunted alternate beliefs and activities. However, anyone that explored alternative lifestyles was generally thought of as foolish, or worse, by the vast majority of mainstream people. This perception made life very difficult for children like me.

Although we have much to thank the New Age movement for, pagan paths are still misunderstood and feared by many. Things have changed, but not so much that children no longer need to think first before telling someone about their Solstice celebration. I know from my own experience how difficult it is to be without a pagan community.

This fosters a bond between family members that is very special. As parents of pagan children without a supportive community, you have it a bit more difficult. Not only must you handle your own feelings of loneliness but you also must create a very supportive family atmosphere. It is up to you to guide your children through, whether you choose to be open about your spirituality or not.

Being open about a pagan path can be very liberating for an adult who is not afraid for their job, home, or standing in the community. After years of living a double life, it has been a sometimes tense but mainly freeing feeling to be open today about who I am. However when we decided to have a child, this issue required a great deal of thought that will continue until our son is out on his own.

A parent does need to consider what is best for his or her child. Our actions have a definite impact on our children. Once we accept the responsibility to be parents, we are parents, no matter what role we are living at the moment. Even if we are not interacting with our children, or are miles away, how we live our lives affects how our children view the world. It also has more power to affect their behavior than many of us want to believe.

However, it is a fact that simply having to think about this issue will often bring up related issues that a parent may have repressed. It is important that the parents handle their own issues before making any decisions for their children. Unresolved issues have a way of controlling us without our knowledge.

This is part of what shamans call the shadow side. It is discussed throughout this book and I went into great detail regarding the shadow and its effects on an individual in my book *Shamanic Guide to Death and Dying*. The shadow side is that place where we hide away all of those things we do not want the world to see. It also contains those memories, beliefs, and fears that we don't want to have to face, or do not want to admit are a part of our inner selves.

These shadow aspects only gain more power over us when they are submerged in the unconscious. We are no longer aware of them, yet they continue to influence our lives, leaving us feeling like victims or out of control. They create a filter through which we make decisions and experience the world. Consequently, any decisions we make as parents with unresolved issues in those areas may not be the wisest or the most beneficial decisions we could make.

For example, I have known pagan parents who were terrified that someone outside the pagan community would discover they were pagan. They avoided meeting other pagans in public and some even kept their religion a secret from their children. These children were very hurt and confused when they reached an age where their parents felt they could keep the secret and told them the truth. Those children who were aware of the family religion grew up with deep feelings of embarrassment and fear.

I have also known pagan parents who decided that they needed to be totally open about their religion and expected the same of their children. These were occasionally people who had decided for various reasons to be blatantly pagan in all situations, sometimes simply for shock value. Some of these children were even berated or punished for not wearing certain jewelry to school or for not being fully open with a teacher.

These are certainly two extremes. For most parents, the best decisions lie somewhere in the middle, but I offer these examples to illustrate how we can unconsciously project our own issues onto our children. Rather than accepting their individuality and their right to choose for themselves within reason, we may have expectations of them that are based solely on our own shadow "stuff." We need to continually examine our own motives for our actions.

I cannot say what choices are the best for anyone else's family. Each family must find their own way and make the best decisions they can at the time. Keep in mind that these decisions may change with time and that is perfectly normal. The decision to be open about an alternative spirituality may depend on a number of factors, including region, neighborhood, jobs, and many more.

Whatever we decide, it is important not to bash other religions, or belittle others for their close-mindedness or fear. If our children are to avoid the destructive paths taken by many of those who would discriminate against pagans, they must be wiser and more centered in their own higher selves. The cycles of violence and oppression do not end by the minority, who may be gaining ground, indulging in the same behaviors as their oppressors.

Our children need to know that these people act as they do because they do not know any better. They are afraid and ignorant. They are reacting through thousands of years of indoctrinated dogma and their lack of ability to think for themselves. If we are to create a happier, healthier reality, we need to set the example.

In making these types of decisions for our families, it is important to fully think them through and get clear on all the factors involved. As parents, we feel the need to protect our children. As a result, we may desire to protect them from issues that we know have the potential to cause them pain. But in doing so, we may become overly protective, insulating them too much from real life issues that they will have to face sooner or later.

In an earlier chapter, I described my young friend who lost her lover at college as the result of his parents' reaction to her spirituality. Sad as this is, it is a possibility for anyone dating outside a specific religion, mainstream or not.

This young woman's parents expressed what most parents feel when something like this happens to our children. "It would have been easier if she broke her arm instead of her heart. As a parent we hurt as bad as they do and it is tough to say 'these things happen and it won't hurt as bad in time.' That sucks as an explanation." Indeed, it does. It is even more difficult when a child is hurt because someone fears their religion or skin color or anything else that does not necessarily define who one is.

As difficult as it may be, we parents need to be strong and control our often-overwhelming need to protect. Unless we are prepared to change our religion or spiritual beliefs to conform to mainstream society, we must prepare our children to handle this before they are out on their own. We do not benefit them by hiding this reality. Nor do we support them by believing that they will always encounter difficult situations. There are many people who are very openly pagan and have little or no problems with neighbors or strangers.

It is interesting to note that most young people are far more accepting of pagan paths than their parents, as illustrated by the situation with my young friend in college. While their impressions are often colored by media representations of pagan paths, in recent years the media has been inclined to glamorize pagan practices unrealistically. As a result, many young people think it is cool or exciting that a friend or a friend's family member is pagan. This still calls for educating young people, but our children are getting a head start by the increasingly beneficial perceptions of certain pagan paths.

The best way we can prepare our children is to talk to them about all the possibilities. We should avoid bringing up extreme examples unless they are a reality in our lives. It is no different than discussing the possible consequences of unprotected sex or drug abuse. We have honest discussions and lead by example. We do not demand perfection of ourselves or of our children. Life is a learning experience for all of us.

Beginning in the toddler years, it can be useful to engage the help of older siblings, friends, or other young relatives. The young child who tags along after an older child will naturally imitate the words and actions of the older child. Older siblings, in particular, become like gods to the young child. I know one boy who followed his older sister everywhere. If she said, "let's play a game and pretend," he was right there acting the part. When she said, "keep this a secret," his lips were sealed.

Enlisting the aid of other children in these discussions is a definite option for many parents, whether you prefer secrecy, openness, or something in between. Children of any age also tend to view parents and most adults as authority figures. Even in a good parent-child relationship, children may feel more comfortable hearing the facts of life from a sibling or friend. Suggestions or directives about how the family is going to handle certain situations may be more easily accepted and followed if another, preferably older and respected, child is included in the discussion.

An older relative or friend can speak to the child on his or her level. This older child may be able to relate applicable personal experience. If handled well, this has the potential to make the discussion more than a parent-child talk. While family is very important to a child, peers have tremendous power to affect their decisions and behavior. Rather than resenting this, in many situations we can use it for the greatest benefit of all concerned.

Rather than limit this to a one-time talk, it is much more effective if time is set aside for family discussions on a regular basis. It is your responsibility as the parent to keep your finger on the pulse of your family, in a sense. It is very important that you develop a feel for how often these talks need to happen and how deep they should be. They should be regular enough that emotions do not build to a difficult point, but not so often that your family feels suffocated.

If you have the time to get together for nightly dinners, these daily conversations can be as casual or as serious as they need to be, without allowing them to become arguments. In this way, the small things that tend to build can be discussed and handled quickly. If something comes up at dinner or in other casual conversation more than once, or if there is a lingering emotional charge, this should be dealt with in a separate discussion.

Keeping the serious discussions separate is a very important point. While we do not want to make anyone uncomfortable by putting them on the spot, there must be a time without distraction for family sharing. Not only does this strengthen family bonds and pave the way for greater trust within the family, but it also provides a definite forum for the handling of issues affecting family members. It also allows for the group energy of the family to be focused on the resolution of these issues as well as on the unconditional support of each family member.

Obviously, these discussions will not be limited to the issues of this chapter. However, when faced with these types of issues, it is even more important that our children feel the support and strength of the family. They need to know that they are not alone and that they can share their feelings, fears, and successes with someone who honestly cares. This can make all the difference in the world to a child who cannot share their spirituality with anyone outside the family.

With that in mind, you can eliminate the need for a set time and formal discussion by maintaining your own openness with each of your children. By living your life and responding to your children as the parent you would want to have in your life, you open the lines of communication, encouraging the trust of your children. Children who know that they are a parent's top priority and that they will be able to talk openly whenever it is necessary feel much more confident and secure.

Bedtime is a perfect time to share and talk. When it is quiet and we are trying to sleep, our minds tend to go over the events of the day. Difficult events can end up in a kind of loop, preventing sleep. Journal keeping is a great way to work through these issues, but it is not for every child, and it is obviously not an option for the very young.

After the bedtime story, or whatever the ritual is in your house, consider spending some additional time with your child after the lights go out, just to be together and talk if anything comes up. If you have more than one child with similar bedtimes, you may want to alternate nights with each child.

When I was young, my mother worked a considerable number of hours as a single mother and needed her down time when I went to bed. I began to share with one particular stuffed animal, who was my confidant for many years. Even today, I hold special feelings for that little stuffed lamb, which is no longer with us. As a mother myself, without the restrictions that my mother had, I want to be able to be a confidant if our son needs to share, so, after my husband reads him his bedtime story, I lie down with him for a little while.

Sometimes we just hang out and giggle, but he often talks to me about things that are on his mind. These are frequently things that have either disturbed him or concepts and ideas that he has not yet fully grasped, like the differences between us and angels or faeries. All of these things are treated with the utmost respect and seriousness, and he is then able to fall easily to sleep.

In the dark, at bedtime, small things may become big monsters, working up our emotions and preventing restful sleep. Big issues become even more imposing and can appear impossible to overcome. The many unique issues facing pagan children can often be effectively defused, or at least diminished, through this very simple bedtime sharing. All you need to do is to be there without pressing for anything. Allow any conversation to flow forth spontaneously and accept that quite often your child may simply need the closeness of your loving energy.

The Legality of Religion and Spirituality

If you read any pagan magazines or newsletters, you are aware that plenty of pagans have encountered problems with ignorant communities and legal actions, ranging from police at the door to custody battles. We do need to be aware of, and prepared for, these possibilities, but most pagans who have educated their neighbors and communities about their religion, without hiding it, have not encountered these types of situations.

This is a generalization and the potential for police or other legal involvement will largely depend on your area and your practices. However, those pagans that are bringing pagan businesses into certain neighborhoods, or are involved in divorce and custody battles, need to know their rights. These are most often the pagans who end up in court over their beliefs.

It is far more likely that we will be the ones deciding whether or not to fight publicly for the protection of our rights. This may manifest as anything from getting our religious holidays off at our child's school to fighting to keep the Ten Commandments from being posted in public places, although there have been more extreme cases. The sad truth is that many people in the majority culture do not recognize our practices as valid religions. And even those that do may feel that our religions should be outlawed.

In fact, Article 18 of the United Nations Universal Declaration on Human Rights[1] states that, "Everyone has the right to freedom of thought, conscience and religion. This right includes freedom to change his religion or belief, and freedom, either alone or in community with others and in public or private, to manifest his religion or belief in teaching, practice, worship and observance."

In America, we can look to the First and Fourteenth Amendments to the United States Constitution. Most of us realize that Wicca is a formally recognized religion, and therefore protected as such under Constitutional law. The first real lawsuit to set this important precedent was Dettmer vs. Landon, in 1985. In this case, the District Court of Virginia ruled that Witchcraft is a

---

1   Foundation for Religious Freedom w bsite.

legitimate religion and falls within a recognizable religious category. In 1986, J. Butzner upheld this decision in Federal Appeals court.

But what about those of us that are not Wiccan? While many people think of pagan as Wiccan, this is not necessarily the case. Pagans are druids, shamans, Santero, Voudoun, Asatru, vitki, and many more disciplines, including a huge number of "unlabeled" pagans. Do we have the same rights?

In addition to those rights guaranteed by the United Nations, Americans have the freedom of religious belief, as well as the right to freedom of speech and peaceful assembly. To be protected, as a religious belief under United States federal law, it must be sincerely held and perceived by the individual as religious. Canadians have the right to freedom of thought, belief, opinion, and expression, as well as the right to peaceful assembly and association, according to Article II of the Canadian Charter of Rights and Freedoms. Many other countries have similar rights. It would be beneficial for you to look into the rights guaranteed to you by the United Nations and the particular country in which you reside.

What we do in our own homes (within reason) is further protected by the United States Constitution. The First Amendment guarantees all citizens the right to be secure against unreasonable searches and seizures. This means that no one can search your home, person, or vehicle without probable cause, supported by "oath or affirmation," and a warrant.

It is true that many states and cities have enacted more stringent laws regarding what you can do where. To assemble for any purpose in a public place may require a permit. These laws will vary from state to state and it is your responsibility to know when the rules change. It is also true, at least according to the U.S. Constitution, Amendment Fourteen, that no state can enact a law abridging or violating these guaranteed privileges and immunities. However, it is in everyone's best interests to get informed and know exactly what your rights are in any given place.

There are some issues that we pagans may disagree with but still are held accountable for if we are caught. The possession of feathers is one of these. While many pagans wold never kill for an animal's fur or plumage, most of us have no idea where the feathers in a smudge fan or dreamcatcher really came from.

As followers of Earth-honoring spiritualities, we need to recognize that there are many people, pagans and indigenous peoples included, that will hunt to sell these feathers. In light of this, we only honor ourselves, our deities, and our animal allies, by finding out what animal the feathers or fur came from and how they were obtained. Sad as it may be, the laws regarding possession of feathers and body parts of certain animals are in place to protect the species of concern. Law enforcement officials do not know whether you picked that feather up off the ground or killed the bird to obtain it.

Unless you have specific permits, you are not permitted to have any part of an endangered or threatened animal. You are also not legally allowed to possess the feathers of most wild birds. Certainly, people may have collections of feathers they have found on the ground, but if you are buying feathers, please find out where they came from. Those of us that house and rehabilitate wild birds have so many feathers during molting season that they usually get thrown out. I won't pretend that many pagans will simply obey the laws and not keep or purchase any questionable feathers. So, if you are going to obtain them, please make sure they are molted feathers.

The possession of what mainstream society may term "weapons" is another contentious issue with many pagans. It is illegal in many places to carry a weapon, particularly a concealed weapon. Our athames, swords, and other knives are all considered weapons by the uninformed, and therefore potentially dangerous. The possession of these ritual items may result in a ticket or other legal action, particularly if we should choose to carry them into a public place.

This is a difficult topic. Many pagan gatherings, especially hotel conferences, have their own rules in place to avoid liabilities and the groups don't want to risk not being permitted to return to the hotel for another event. This is simply a fact of life in the modern world. Wishing it away won't do you much good.

Furthermore, there are plenty of dangerous or unstable people that really should not be carrying any form of weapon into a public place, and many of these would pretend to be pagan if it would allow them to legally possess such items.

Knives and swords are an integral part of many pagan paths. They are sacred ritual tools. As our children grow up, they are taught to properly respect and work with these items. I would only recommend that you also teach your children about the laws pertaining to their use and possession so they might make informed choices.

Some pagans have gotten themselves into a fair amount of legal trouble by carrying knives out in the open or by being utterly blatant about hiding them. Most of those I have been aware of received a summons for far more than simple possession of a weapon. As pagans, we need to be aware of our own behavior and the possible projection of our own fears of oppression. I have known pagans to react with overt hostility or excessive defensiveness simply because they were stopped or questioned by a police officer. It was generally their behavior that led to further inquiries and eventual legal action.

I do not mean to place all the blame on pagans. To be honest, I have had my share of difficulties with the police and other "authority" figures. But for the most part it is true that we receive the kind of energy that we send out. If we treat the police as beings, just like us, who are seeking happiness, joy, and meaning in life, we can treat them with the respect they deserve as humans. This type of attitude has gotten me out of some close calls. If nothing else, it can prevent a bad situation from getting worse and shows that we pagans are not a bunch of rude, out-of control fools.

Drugs and alcohol can be a very touchy subject for some pagans. It is another issue that we need to be very careful about while examining our own motives for certain actions. Pagans tend to be very adamant about our freedom, and can be rather anarchist in our philosophies. We don't generally like authority or hierarchy, and prefer to live in a circle of equals with everyone being self-responsible. As a result, we may object to legal restrictions on drugs and serving alcohol to minors.

We may also object to any laws restricting sexuality. Sexuality is one of the gifts of the Goddess and many pagans feel they honor the union of God and Goddess by engaging in varied sexual encounters. There are pagans who encourage or allow sexual contact between minor children. There are even those that allow this between minor children and adults. This is another controversial topic among pagan communities.

While we are far less afraid and confused about sexuality than the culture of the majority, we do not want our children to get hurt or contract a sexually transmitted disease. We do not want them to have to experience an unwanted pregnancy and all that can accompany such a circumstance. It is a parent's responsibility to decide where the boundaries are for their minor children. It is also our responsibility to educate our children about sexuality and what is associated with it.

While some of us may claim that these things are part of our religion, few neopagan religions require the use of sex, alcohol, or drugs. As far as I know, none require that minor children either ingest these substances or participate in sexual encounters. We need to be aware, when we loudly proclaim that the laws are interfering with our religious freedoms, that there is a difference between what we want and what is actually part of our religions.

We are all striving for respect and acceptance. We do that by choosing our fights wisely, particularly when we have children. Choosing to flaunt legal restrictions and risking ending up in jail might be more wisely reserved for truly important fights if there is no one to care for our children in our absence. Even if our children can stay with family, we need to consider our actions. We do want our children to learn to stand up for their beliefs and their rights. We want them to see us as strong individuals who do so with honor and conviction. But, we do not want to be perceived as parents that fought over absolutely everything and put their family's well being at risk over relatively unimportant issues.

The focus of this chapter is an unfortunate fact of life for pagan families. While no one can give you an easy way around it or tell you absolutely how to handle its effects in your family, you need to know that you are not alone either. Obviously your children have you, and I have discussed ways for you to use that fact in everyone's best interest. However, pagan parents also need to know that there are many of us out there, experiencing many of the same issues.

If you do not have a support system, or are a single parent, I strongly recommend that you try to connect with other pagan parents. There are several places for pagan parents to go on the Internet. I have listed some of my favorite sites in the Resources section of this book. For those of you without Internet access, there are metaphysical bookstores in most areas and a multitude of publications where you might find classes or groups, or even place your own ad. *Circle* magazine is a great place to find pen-pals, if secrecy is a high priority for you.

Most importantly, keep in mind that the gods and the spirits are always there for you when you need them. You are never truly alone. They will be your support system until you can find one in this reality. And they can help you connect with the right people for you. All you need do is ask. Whatever your reasons for creating a lack of human support at this time (and they may be karmic or subconscious), know that in raising healthy, loving pagan children, you are contributing to their personal spiritual growth as well as that of our entire society.

12

Rites of Passage

A vast number of pagans, particularly solitary pagans, do not follow a specific magical tradition that dictates how and when rituals must be done. As a result, modern pagans are opening to spirit guidance and their own intuition as they design their own rituals. For pagan parents, it becomes even more important to be able to create powerful rituals simply because these new traditions frequently do not spell out for us how rituals should be done with children.

A number of books on the market today detail elaborate rituals for just about every occasion. Some of these do contain rites of passage for children. If these rituals work well for you and your children just as written in a book, then that is wonderful, but often something is missing or it just doesn't seem to fit you. It is also quite common for your needs to change as you grow into your pagan path. Rituals that may have worked well for you in the beginning may not work as you progress along your path.

In these cases, you may prefer to design your own rituals, rather than searching through dozens of books to find one that does fit you. For this reason the ritual outlines that follow are as nondenominational and open as possible. These ideas will offer you a basic format that will spark your own creativity.

Rites of passage are, by definition, a marking of life changes. They are a ritual acknowledgement of the death of one chapter of life and the birth of another. Today, rites of passage are often superficial excuses to merchandise cards and presents. In fact, many rites of passage are completely overlooked by the majority of our society.

The main point to keep in mind when creating any ritual is to follow your feelings. While many books detail certain elements that should be included, this is not necessarily true for all people. If we are to truly empower ourselves to create from our hearts, we need to release those deeply ingrained feelings of "should." Open to yourself, the God and Goddess, and your spirit guides. Go with whatever feels right to you. If it works, that is excellent. If it doesn't, work with it a bit more. You will get it right for you and your child.

If your child is old enough to assist in any way with the creation of their own ritual, you will want to encourage them. This is especially recommended for the passage into adulthood. Not only is it wonderful training for a pagan child, but children are also less blocked by old and restricting beliefs. As a result they may be able to contribute powerful elements that truly speak to their souls. This is an important factor of any ritual.

In general, there are four major elements to any rite of passage. These are the invocation, experience/release, closure/grounding, and celebration.[1] In addition, there is the preparation for the rite. This preparation includes altar and room preparation but should also encompass personal preparation as well. Below I will discuss general preparation for ritual. Specific preparation for the individual rituals is included in those sections. This personal preparation is at least as important as the actual ritual itself.

---

1   Much of the following section detailing the elements of a general ritual are reprinted as they first appeared in *Shamanic Guide to Death and Dying*.

The first step is obviously the room and altar set-up. You may want to decorate the room for the occasion, or at least make space and clean up for the ritual. The altar should contain all the necessary ritual tools. Items that are related to the action of the ritual may be included on a separate table or elsewhere that is easily accessible.

It is a good idea to purify the area and the participants before the ritual. Many people smudge participants as they enter the Circle. This is a wonderful way to do the purification. In this way, participants leave behind stresses and everyday thoughts before entering the ritual space.

The next step is to delineate your sacred space in some way. Many pagans will cast a Circle. Others prefer to simply call on the Spiritkeepers of the directions. Druids will offer peace to the quarters before moving ahead with any ritual. Unless you are casting a formal Circle, this is a good way to get children involved in the creation of ritual.

Calling of the quarters is a relatively simple and short role for a child to take in a family ritual. It can also be combined with the study of the element associated with the direction they are Calling. As such, this will offer the child an additional understanding of that element.

This can also be done as a dual Call: adult with child. This takes a lot of the pressure off the child and can be a wonderful teaching tool. In addition, this method of Calling the quarters bring in a special, family-bonding type of feel to the ritual. In the very first year of the CraftWise conference[2] our opening ritual had one child and one adult Calling each quarter together. It was truly special and deeply touched many of those present.

The ritual is begun with the invocation of specific energies, deities, spirit guides, etc., and the stating of the ritual's purpose. This should be done in whatever manner feels right to you or is in keeping with your spiritual tradition. In a child's rite of passage, the child should be involved in the invocation of their particular helping spirits if possible.

---

2 See "Contact" section at the back of this book.

The experience/release element is essential to bring the focus of the ritual into reality. Without this portion, the rite is in danger of becoming a mental activity rather than a deep rite of passage. It is necessary for this to be done in a safe space because the emotional charge created may release deep and repressed emotions.

Many rites are designed with some type of action to physically manifest this element. If possible, all of the senses should be activated by this ritual action. Again, we use sensory input to bypass the analytical mind. I have seen many wonderful ritual actions from a cutting of symbolic cords to a purification by fire of photos or pieces of paper with things to release written on them.

The action of the rite makes it absolutely clear that we have the choice of remaining where we are, or passing through this symbolic action. We can remain stuck in old patterns or fully experience the rite to break us out of old stuff. This can be a powerful tool for internal change that will manifest as external change once the rite is concluded.

After this great release, we require closure and grounding of all this energy. This may be accomplished in many ways, from meditation to discussion to asking for support and guidance from spirit guides and deities. This is the perfect time to use any of the grounding exercises in chapter 4. Through this ritual element, we accept the new phase and our new identities.

Pregnancy

Ideally, you should be certain that you are ready to become a parent and are aware of the changes you can expect throughout your pregnancy and beyond. You have gone through the necessary personal preparation before becoming pregnant. Even if the pregnancy is a complete surprise, your choice of whether or not to terminate the pregnancy is the result of some personal work. Chances are if you are reading this book, you have decided to keep the baby, so that is the main focus in this section.

Pregnancy rituals are predominantly designed for the pregnant woman. While fathers-to-be are certainly affected, it is the woman who will experience major life changes during the pregnancy. She is the one whose body and lifestyle have been dramatically altered and she is the one who will be feeling the energetic effects of the incoming spirit.

Pagan Baby Blessing Ritual

Some pagan groups, particularly Goddess-focused groups, may have three separate rituals: one for each trimester. While this is a valid ritual process marking the physical and energetic differences of each of the trimesters, the ritual I have outlined below is simply to honor the fact that a conception has taken place and to ask for blessings throughout the pregnancy and delivery. It can easily be combined with a pagan (or pagan-friendly) baby shower.

> Set up the altar with pastel or Earth colors, flowers, candles. Spring flowers are best, if possible. Include some symbol of the Mother Goddess or the Earth Herself (include a Father or Fertility God if the father is included in this ritual). Smudge or burn incense. Have ready blessing oil, baby shower gifts, and Medicine pouches or other sacred objects for the child.
>
> Create a sacred space in your preferred manner.
>
> The ceremonial leader invokes the chosen gods and goddesses, the spirit guides of the parents-to-be, the spirit of the incoming child, and any other beings you wish to have present. The leader states the purposes of this rite: that you have gathered to honor _____ (mother/father's names) and celebrate her/their process of becoming a mother/father. You have also gathered to celebrate the return of this new being to this reality and his or her entrance into your family. Ask the guidance and protection of those invoked during this ritual and beyond, that your every action may honor them.
>
> The ceremonial leader anoints the mother/father with the blessing oil, saying that you bless these individuals with wisdom, patience, compassion,

strength, and any other quality you feel an ideal parent would possess.

The ceremonial leader thanks the incoming spirit on behalf of everyone present for choosing this family, for his/her presence in your lives, and for sharing his/her Earth journey with you.

Go around the circle (or go back and forth between mother and father if no one else is present) three times, offering prayers for an easy and healthy pregnancy and an easy, safe delivery.

The gifts are blessed and any sacred items are charged with the intent of this celebration.

First the mother (then the father, if present) goes before each quarter, presenting herself as a joyful mother-to-be and asks the blessings and protection of the Spiritkeepers of the directions. She (with the father, if present) then presents herself to Father Sky, Mother Earth, and the Great Spirit at the center of the Circle. She (they) asks for their blessings and their guidance and protection along this new path. She (they) promises to raise this child in honor and to teach him or her respect for All Life.

The mother/parents return to the circle. The ceremonial leader instructs everyone to hold a single thought in their minds, perhaps a happy, healthy baby and family, or the total focus of the ritual. Participants are directed to hold this thought as everyone intones the Om, or other sound that has power for you. Maintain the intonation until you feel the energy has built enough. Then the leader will give a sign and everyone should yell, releasing the thought into the universe.

Ground and center in your preferred manner.

The leader thanks and releases all beings invoked and closes the ritual.

Abortion

I include this section because many parents must deal with pregnant teenagers, and abortion is frequently the decision in these situations. Most followers of pagan paths support a woman's right to choose. While abortion may not be right for individual pagans, very few pagans would attempt to dictate another's actions based on personal feelings. The Goddess is not offended by a woman who makes an intelligent choice about her body and her ability to raise a child. We honor Her by the honesty of the choice.

However, as any woman who has had a child or an abortion will tell you, it is not simply a physical choice. This is not a decayed tooth that must be removed and discarded. Hormones and emotions are present that cannot be ignored or suppressed. In order for the woman to truly move forward from this event, these emotions must be dealt with in a loving and supportive manner. And while we may say that we perceive it as simply an embryo or fetus that has been eliminated, few women who have been through it honestly feel that way. Whether or not a spirit was ready to enter the body, it was a potential child and should be treated as such in an appropriate ritual such as the one that follows.

In addition, there needs to be an energetic healing, or the resultant damage to associated chakras can cause additional problems, including additional unwanted pregnancies. Unless you are proficient in energetic healing techniques, I would recommend using the Drum Purification Ceremony, spending as much time as is needed at each chakra, with particular concentration on the first, second, and heart chakras. Follow this up with some extra nurturing of the woman-child who had the abortion, as well as some in-depth discussions to determine why she created this. She may be encouraged to engage in some private journal-keeping.

No special preparation is required for this ritual. However, any child who needs an abortion that was not the result of a rape should at the very least receive counseling in the use of contraceptives and the facts about sexually transmitted diseases. I would also recommend some form of therapy (not necessarily professional or mainstream) to get to the root of why she created this situation in the first place and how to clear those causes before they bring her even more suffering.

If this pregnancy was the result of a rape, focus on the release of pain and suffering as well as any guilt she may feel. Make nurturing and helping her feel safe and loved a top priority. Then follow-up by getting her some form of counseling.

Abortion Healing Ritual

This ritual should be done in private with only the girl and her mother, or both parents if she feels comfortable with the presence of her father. If possible, the girl should be the one to lead the ritual, and instructions from this point on are directed to the girl, not the parent. Parents are present for energetic and emotional support.

Set up the altar with dark colors, especially dark red and black. Try to have some representation of the Maiden and Mother aspects of the Goddess, as well as a single, hard-boiled egg. If this ritual cannot take place outside, also have a small pot of earth, larger than the egg. Smudge or burn incense (myrrh is recommended).

Create sacred space in your preferred manner.

Invoke the chosen gods and goddesses, your spirit guides and any other beings you wish to have present. This is a good time to call upon the dark goddesses as well as the lighter ones. It is they who will need to show you how to be with the darkness of your shadow and to pass through the emotion of this time so that the light aspects can lead you back to yourself.

State the purpose of this rite—that you have come before the gods, goddesses, and your helping spirits to release the pain and suffering of the abortion along with those things that brought you to this point. You should also state quite honestly what those things may be and take responsibility for your actions. Ask their guidance and protection during this ritual and beyond that your every action may honor them.

Pick up the Mother Goddess symbol. Tell her everything you are feeling and ask for Her blessings. Tell Her that you recognize that you are not ready to be a mother and promise to be very careful about contraception or abstinence in the future. Do not make promises you do not intend to keep.

Pick up the Maiden symbol and speak to Her. Tell Her that now you are somewhere between Maiden and Mother. While you will never be the same child again, ask Her help in finding your way back to your joy in your youth.

Sit comfortably on the floor or a chair and allow your mother or parents to take over the ritual. At this point, the mother or parents should perform some form of healing on their daughter together. This may be the Drum Purification Ceremony, an energy sending, or simply a big family hug, as they send all their unconditional love into their daughter. They should be certain that any judgments or resentment are left outside the Circle, and follow this up by telling her how much they love her and how proud they are of her. They also will tell her of the strength, courage, etc., that they see in her.

Allow as much time as is necessary for the free flowing of emotion.

Ground and center in your preferred manner.

You (the daughter) then resume the ritual by taking up the hard-boiled egg. Speak to any spirit that may have been waiting to enter your womb and apologize for the confusion. Send it your love and say that when you are ready you would welcome that spirit into your family.

Then, see the egg as your own physical ovum and your potential for many types of creativity, including motherhood. Send your pain as well as your hopes and dreams into this egg. Then bury it in the pot of earth (or in the ground), asking the Earth Mother to cleanse your pain and bring your dreams to fruition. Ask Her help in transferring your fertility to other areas of life that are more appropriate at this time.

Speak from your heart as you thank your parents for their unconditional love and support.

Thank and release all beings invoked and close the ritual.

Birth

The preparation for a birth ritual clearly takes place over the course of approximately nine months. During this time, the expectant family will be preparing for the arrival of the baby in many ways and on many levels. Not all pagans hold specific rituals for a birth, and those that do often combine it with the Naming. Many prefer to wait anywhere from three days to three months for a Naming ceremony. As a result, I have outlined a combined Birth-Naming ritual.

Depending on your family and the circumstances surrounding the birth, waiting can be a good idea. New parents need not feel pressured to immediately hold a birth ritual when they have a million other things to deal with, including lack of sleep. Furthermore, you don't have to worry that the gods will not recognize your child without this ceremony. Should anything happen to this child before a ceremony is performed, that child's spirit will go on with the assistance of all her spirits as usual. The Old Gods and Goddesses would never turn their backs on a child simply for lack of a ritual.

Birth/Naming Rite

Set up the altar with pastel colors, flowers, candles. Spring flowers are best, if possible. Smudge or burn incense (rose, amber). Have ready blessing oils or water for "baptism," gifts for the child, any Medicine pouches or other sacred objects for the child. Be sure the mother and baby are comfortable and all potential needs are easily accessible, i.e./diaper change, milk, etc.

Create a sacred space in your preferred manner.

The ceremonial leader invokes the chosen Gods and Goddesses, the spirit guides and guardians of the child and his/her family, and any other beings you wish to have present. The leader states the purpose of this rite—that we have gathered to honor and celebrate the return of this being to this reality and his/her entrance into your family. Ask their guidance and protection during this ritual and beyond that your every action may honor them.

The ceremonial leader touches the water or oil to the child's forehead and names him/her. The leader than continues with the water or oil, blessing the child at each chakra point. You might choose to use blessings that correspond with the chakras, i.e., clarity at the third eye, love at the heart, etc.

The ceremonial leader thanks this being, _____ (child's name), on behalf of everyone present for choosing this family, for his/her presence in your lives, and for sharing his/her Earth journey with you.

Go around the circle (or go back and forth between mother and father if no one else is present) three times, offering personal blessings and promises of love and/or guidance that you are committed to give this child throughout his/her life.

The gifts are blessed and any sacred items are charged with the intent of this celebration.

The leader (or parent, if a parent is not the leader) takes the child to each quarter. The leader presents the child as _____ and asks the blessings and protection of the Spiritkeepers of the directions for this child. The child is then held out to Father Sky, Mother Earth, and the Great Spirit at the center. She or he is presented as _____ and blessings are requested. The parent promises to raise this child _____ in honor and to teach him or her respect for All Life.

The parent(s) once more offer their own blessings and promises to this child.

The leader thanks and releases all beings invoked and closes the ritual.

Parenthood Rite

The following ritual is designed for the new mother and/or father. It marks your entry into a new role as a parent and allows you a ritual space to ask for spiritual guidance and protection on this new path.

Set up the altar with pastel and primary colors, flowers, candles, symbols of mother/fatherhood, photos of you and your child(ren). Smudge or burn incense. Have ready blessing oils and your Medicine pouches, or a clear quartz crystal.

Create a sacred space in your preferred manner.

Invoke your chosen Gods and Goddesses (especially mother or father deities), your spirit guides and guardians, and any other beings you wish to have present. Ask their guidance and protection during this ritual and beyond, that your every action may honor them. State the purpose of this rite as a celebration and honoring of your passage into a new phase of life: mother/fatherhood. Ask the guidance of your deities and guides in this new identity of yours.

Touch the oil or water to your own chakra points, naming yourself as mother/father and bless yourself with each chakra point. You may wish to invoke the Mother/Father within you and specific qualities corresponding to each chakra.

Meditate on what parenthood means to you, on the specifics of your family, how you hope to grow through this experience, and what you hope to bring to your family.

Say to all you invoked and to your family members (who may or may not be present) what kind of parent you choose to be. Vow to these beings to be the best parent, teacher, student, and friend that you can be, and promise to remain open to spirit guidance for the greatest good of all.

Go to each quarter and present yourself as a new mother/father. Ask the blessings and protection of the Spiritkeepers of the directions on this new journey you taking. Present yourself to Father Sky, Mother Earth, and the Great spirit at the center and ask their continued blessings and presence along the way. Promise to be a living example of strength, balance, and love for your child(ren) and to create a family of honor and respect for All Life.

Thank and release all gods, goddesses, guides, and guardian invoked and close the Circle.

Adulthood

The passage into adulthood is one of the most overlooked events in modern society. There are any number of reasons for this, including the fact that most people are not really sure when a child is no longer a child. They are not allowed to vote or enlist in the armed forces until they are eighteen. The legal age of consumption or consent varies according to the state. But once a girl begins to menstruate and a boy has his first ejaculation, they can physically become parents. In most native cultures, this is the age of adulthood and young people are treated differently as a result. They are also expected to behave with more maturity as well.

We do our children a disservice when we turn these wonderful physical events into something to be ignored or feel ashamed of. These are the physical manifestations that follow a child's readiness to be entrusted with additional responsibility and to be no longer treated as a child. Unfortunately in modern society, our children are rarely prepared for adulthood except through intellectual learning in schools. Many are simply not ready to be treated as young adults in their early teens.

On the other hand, we cannot know what a child is ready for unless we give them the opportunity to show us. This is an age when many children rebel. Certainly much of this is due to the onset of puberty and all the confusion that comes with it, but often these children-who-are-no-longer-children need greater freedom, responsibility, and input into decisions regarding their own lives. This is part of the preparation and follow-up to the adulthood rites of passage.

In preparation for adulthood rites of passage, your children should have learned and begun to demonstrate that they are willing and able to handle the responsibilities associated with being a young adult. It is your responsibility to ensure that they have been taught about the realities of sexuality, drinking and drug use, driving, and anything else that combines freedom with responsibility and potential danger.

It is also recommended that you discuss what you know of men's and women's mysteries with the child. This generally includes gender-specific spirituality and how to work most effectively with the deities of your gender. It will also include more specific physical discussions, particularly with young women, as well as discussions on interacting honorably with those of the opposite gender. If the child has indicated that they are homosexual or bisexual, there will be similar discussions on honor coupled with discussions of the unique issues facing those of alternate sexual preferences.

I know there are many single parents out there who may find it difficult at best to have these types of discussions with a child of the opposite gender. However, without a trusted adult of the same gender as the child, it is the parent's responsibility. Ideally, you have been able to maintain open communication and trust with your child. Keep in mind that, while a father may not really understand the Moon Lodge, he may be the ideal person to discuss sexuality and boys with his daughter. Open to spiritual guidance and trust that you will communicate what needs to be said.

Even if there is no community or family Moon Lodge for your daughter to participate in, she should be encouraged to honor her Moontime. This is something that will require support and understanding from the entire family. The Moon Lodge can be vital to your daughter's self-confidence and self-esteem. In this way, menstruation becomes a sacred time for visioning, rest, and cleansing rather than the embarrassment or annoyance it has become in modern society. Young women need to be able to reclaim their power after so many thousands of years of repression and they need to be able to do so in a balanced way.

Menarche Ritual (Initiation into the Moon Lodge)
The following initiation ritual can be used by a group, if desired.

> Set up the altar with a red altar cloth and symbols of the Moon, the Goddess as Maiden and Mother, your Moon blood: for example red and white candles and flowers, a blood jar, pictures or symbols of the Moon as new and full.
>
> Drum each woman into the circle/smudge each woman as she enters.
>
> Create sacred space in your preferred manner.
>
> The ceremonial leader invokes the usual or chosen goddesses. She states the purpose of this rite: that we have gathered to honor and celebrate the entrance of
> _____ into the Sisterhood of Women and the Mysteries of the Moon Lodge. Ask their guidance

and protection during this ritual and beyond, that your every action may honor them.

The ceremonial leader brings the girl before the altar and instructs her in the sacredness of Circle and the Moon Lodge. There is a brief discussion on the strength and power of woman and the feminine energies. This is followed by one on the importance of balance in all things and of honoring the God within. The importance of honesty, community, and support among the Sisterhood is reaffirmed. The new woman is asked if she is ready for her role as a strong, creative woman and if she accepts her power. She is then presented with a special necklace, is anointed with special oils, or her face is painted with red moons. She is then blessed as a new Sister of the Moon Lodge.

The young woman then invokes her guides, guardians, Goddesses, calling upon one in particular to work through her this night and continue to work with her in the Mysteries as she comes into her power as woman. She offers her blessings to the Lodge and vows to uphold the sacredness and integrity of both the Lodge and herself.

She will then act as priestess and ceremonial leader for the rest of the ritual.

Meditation

Feel roots growing down from your body deep into Mother Earth. Extend your Self deep into Her center. Feel Her energy flowing up into the soles of your feet. Feel this grounding, empowering, beautiful energy flowing up filling your entire body. Breathe this energy into your entire being for a moment.

Raise up your arms and send out branches into the center of Father Sky. Extend your Self into His center. Feel this expansive, empowering energy

flowing down throughout your entire body. Breathe
this energy into your entire being for a moment.

Feel these two energies flowing through you at
once. Feel them meet and merge together in your
center. Feel their differences and how they balance
each other. They seem to dance throughout you.

You overflow with this energy. Feel it completely
surround your body. Send it out to your Sisters in
Circle. Send it beyond this circle out into the earth
and the multiverse. See this energy permeate all
things and connect you to all of Life.

The young woman speaks of the interconnections
of all life and how all our relations are sacred. She
speaks from her heart of the role of women in this
sacred plan and how she intends to fulfill her place in
that sacred plan. She allows any messages to come
through her (silently or aloud) from her special
Goddess.

Go around the circle three times sharing stories of
first blood and blessings for this young woman.

She is then presented with a basic red leather or
cloth bag with which to construct her own Moon
Medicine bag. She is given special herbs from the
Lodge to keep in her bag and she blesses these now
in Circle with her intentions as a sacred woman and
creative force. The rest of the bag will be completed
and kept in private by her alone.

Going around the circle, each woman presents the
new Sister with a gift and a secret or story about
being a woman. Each woman honors her as an equal,
although newer, woman in this Lodge and finally
offers a specific promise of continuing help or support for this new Sister.

The new Sister of the Lodge honors and thanks
her Sisters with renewed promises to be a living
example of female strength and to uphold the

integrity of the Lodge. She thanks and releases all
Goddesses, guides, and guardians invoked, and
closes the ritual.

Manhood Ritual

It is just as important for our young men to claim their power in
healthy and balanced ways. Over the last two thousand years or
so, the natural creativity, intuition, sensitivity, and nurturing
abilities of men have been repressed. They need to know that
protection and strength need not preclude integrity and love.

Menstruating women are automatically in a perfect space for
visioning each month. While women may certainly seek visions
at other times, the visionquest or "sitting out" of many cultures
was designed to bring men to that same place of psychic receptivity and altered states. This is excellent preparation for a young
man before his rite of passage, even if his visionquest must take
place in the backyard.

> Set up the altar with a dark blue or dark green altar
> cloth and symbols of the Sun, the God, and your
> helping spirits.
> Drum each man into the circle/smudge each man
> as he enters.
> Create the sacred space in your preferred manner.
> The ceremonial leader invokes the usual or chosen
> Gods. He states the purpose of this rite: that you
> have gathered to honor and celebrate the entrance of
> _____ into the Brotherhood of Men. Ask their
> guidance and protection during this ritual and
> beyond, that your every action may honor them. The
> ceremonial leader brings the young man before the
> altar and instructs him in the sacredness of Circle
> and the honor in the bonds between men. There is a
> brief discussion on the strength and power of man
> and the masculine energies. This is followed by one
> on the importance of balance in all things and of
> honoring the Goddess within. The importance of

honesty, community, and support among the Brotherhood is reaffirmed. The young man is asked if he is ready for his role as a strong, sensitive man and if he accepts his power. He is then presented with a special necklace, is anointed with special oils, or his body is painted with symbols of the God, creativity, strength, fertility, etc. He is then blessed as a new member of the Brotherhood of Men.

The young man then invokes his guides, guardians, and gods, calling upon one in particular to work through him this night and continue to work with him in the Mysteries as he comes into his power as a man. He offers his blessings to the Brotherhood and vows to protect and uphold the sacredness and integrity of himself and the Brotherhood.

He will then act as priest and ceremonial leader for the rest of the ritual.

Meditation

You are running through a forest. Faster and faster you run, feeling the strength and vitality of your body as you speed through the woods. You stop as you come to a clearing. In the center of the clearing is a huge man. He calls you to come to him. As you approach, he seems to shift his shape. You cannot tell whether he is human or animal.

Although he is a frightening sight, you continue to approach him. As you do, he grabs you by the shoulders and looks deep into your eyes. He probes your very soul as he asks you if you are ready to be a man. Answer him honestly and allow any emotion you may feel to flow forth.

As you stare into his eyes, you are pulled into his being. Within him, you experience tremendous strength. You know it is your responsibility to protect your loved ones. You look deeper and realize that it is also your responsibility to protect all beings and the Earth Herself.

Looking deeper, you behold a baby, then an injured deer with the greatest tenderness you have ever known. You realize that love and gentleness are strengths too.

Looking even deeper, you see the Goddess. She embraces you and you realize that you and She are One. You realize that balance is necessary in all things.

Suddenly, you are standing before the huge man and he no longer frightens you. He kisses you on the forehead and tells you how proud he is of you. Listen for any other messages he may have for you before returning to your body and the Circle.

The young man speaks of the interconnections of all life and how all our relations are sacred. He speaks from his heart of the role of men in this sacred plan and how he intends to fulfill his place in that sacred plan. He allows any messages to come through him (silently or aloud) from his special God. If he feels it is appropriate, he may share his experience of the meditation.

Going around the circle, each man presents the new Brother with a gift and a secret or story about being a man. Each man honors him as an equal, although newer, member of the Brotherhood and finally offers a specific promise of continuing help or support for him.

He then honors and thanks his Brothers with renewed promises to be a living example of male strength and to uphold the integrity of the Brotherhood. He thanks and releases all the gods, guides, and guardians invoked and closes the ritual.

Dedication Ritual

If you follow a specific tradition, it is very likely that this ritual will be spelled out for you. However, most pagans today do not follow a definite and established magical system. It is for you that I have outlined a dedication ritual. This ritual should only be held when children have attained a basic level of understanding of the family path and have decided for themselves that this is their path. It is written as a solo ritual, but parents may choose to either participate as ritual support, perhaps casting the Circle, or you may perform the ritual for the child, if you prefer.

Use your personal altar with symbols of your personal helping spirits and the deities you feel close to. Smudge or burn incense. Have blessing oil or water ready.

Create sacred space in your preferred manner.

Invoke your chosen Gods and Goddesses, your spirit guides, and any other beings you wish to have present. State the purpose of this rite: that you are here to dedicate yourself to your chosen path and to the gods of that path. Ask the guidance and protection of those invoked during this ritual and beyond, that your every action may honor them.

Sit in silent meditation for a few moments, reviewing what you know of this path and what led to your decision to follow this path. Be certain of your decision before moving ahead with the ritual.

Take up the blessing oil or water hold it between both hands. Offer it to those invoked and ask for their blessings.

Anoint yourself with the oil or water, blessing yourself with the qualities you want to bring to this path. You may choose to anoint each chakra point with blessings specific to that chakra.

Stand before each quarter, saying that you dedicate yourself to this path and to the spirits and deities of this path. Ask for their blessings and their guidance. Promise to live your life with honestly and integrity, honoring the Spiritkeepers with your every action. Then present yourself to Father Sky, Mother

Earth, and the Great Spirit or the God and Goddess at the center of the Circle. Ask for their blessings and their guidance. Promise to live your life with honesty and integrity, honoring them with your every action.

Thank and release all beings invoked and close the ritual.

Death

The issue of death is a complex one that cannot be covered in one section or even one chapter. However, death does affect children and it is important to deal with in this book. In chapter 8, I discussed how to handle the questions that will inevitably arise regarding death. In this chapter there are some very specific aspects of guiding children through the death of a loved one that I would like to address.

If you are faced with the death of someone close to a child or are responsible for creating a death rite of passage, I strongly recommend that you read my book *Shamanic Guide to Death and Dying*, or one of the others on the market today. There are several books that are specific to the pagan paths, but many of the mainstream books are valuable in their advice on how to help children through these passages or how to handle the loss of a child.

As I wrote in my book, the loss of a child strikes a heart-breaking, protective chord in most of us. The mere idea of a suffering child can send the media and society into a frenzy of anger and righteous indignation. For a parent, the loss of a child can be devastating. Most parents have a deeply ingrained resistance to even the thought of losing a child as a possibility.

One Wiccan woman whom I encountered online held an entire ritual for herself after the loss of her child. She used a perfect, unopened rose and a crystal egg to symbolize her child's innate beauty and unrealized potential. She called upon the Mother Goddesses to aid her in her grief and help her to find ways to go on living. At the conclusion of her Circle, she buried the rose and the crystal deep within the Earth. In doing this, she commended the body and spirit of her child to the Great Mother. She prayed to the Mother of All, asking that She carry her child's spirit to the next world with the enveloping love of a mother for her own child. As a mother myself, this beautifully simple ritual brings tears to my eyes.

Death rites of passage serve to bring closure and healing to both the living and dead. Well-constructed memorial services are designed to encourage the living to grieve openly and to provide a safe forum for them to do so. It is vital that we allow our children to grieve and to do so in their own ways.

In guiding children through the process of death and grief, we must be careful not to tell them how to feel or how to act. There is no right way to grieve, and children, like all of us, must find their own way. In this situation, a parent must become a guide and counselor, encouraging the child to talk about it, helping them to sort out their feelings, and allowing them privacy when they need it.

Since children may not always be able to tell us exactly what they are feeling, it is up to us to come up with creative ways to help them stay connected to their inner selves. Working with the water element can be a powerful means of preventing the blockages that can occur as the result of emotional trauma. Utilizing some form of creative outlet, such as music, mask-making, or sculpture, is also recommended as is making the most of physical release through sports or play.

Because of their natural creative openness, children can gain even more comfort and closure from rituals than do adults. Rites of passage, in particular, speak to them from the depths of their hearts and imaginations. Including children in the planning of these ceremonies provides them with the opportunity to do something concrete for the departed loved one and for themselves. This allows children a vital feeling of inclusion that is otherwise lacking for them at times like this.

Due to their relative lack of energy filters and their readiness to trust, children are generally very open to interdimensional energies, including communications from spirit guidance. Trusting in their intuitive suggestions for rituals can result in a simple, yet truly profound ceremony. They often have a way of innately *knowing* at a heart level, what is needed by those around them.

The death of a pet can affect a child very deeply. To most pagan families, pets are part of the family and we feel their passage as strongly as the death of most human loved ones. As family members, they deserve to have their own memorial services or funerals. This is a time for us to honor them and to say goodbye. It can be a safe forum from which to tell them how much they mean to us and to release their spirits lovingly.

It is unfortunate that the death of a pet is often ignored by the majority culture. People that react strongly to this type of death are often perceived as silly, weak, or just plain ridiculous. It is very important that pagan parents treat the death of a pet in the same manner as the death of a beloved human, particularly if your children were close to the animal. They may not be our physical children, but we often feel that they are our spiritual children. Furthermore, our children may bond to these animals as though they are siblings, especially young children.

Since death rituals for animals are generally handled as private family affairs, and there are not many books available detailing how to perform these, I have outlined two rituals for you to use as a guide.[3]

Burial Ritual for an Animal

Using incense, smudge, or a drum, purify the area and charge it with healing energy. If this animal disliked fire or smoke, omit those elements.

Once the grave has been dug, place some flowers or herbs in the base. You might choose to use forget-me-nots, roses, or other flowers you associate with everlasting love. Some beneficial herbs are sandalwood for its high spiritual energies, or sage (*Salvia* spp.) for its association with immortality,

---

3 Both of these rituals are reprinted as written in the "Pets and Death" chapter of *Shamanic Guide to Death and Dying*.

healing, and protection. Then place the body on top of these, and cover it with a few more of the flowers or herbs.

If you have chosen to place personal items, crystals, or other stones in the grave now is the time to charge them (if this has not already been done) with energy and place them in with the body.

Call upon the Spirits of the directions, the God and the Goddess to join with you in this ceremony. Ask that they bless your work. Request guidance, that your every action may honor them.

Call upon the spirit of the departed to join with you. Let him or her know the reason for this ceremony and make it clear that you honor them through it.

Offer a prayer, such as: "Through this ceremony, we commend the body of our beloved _____ to the Earth as we entrust his [or her] spirit to the Lord and Lady. We gather here to honor his [or her] memory and to send him [or her] our blessings for a joyous reunion with All of Life."

The leader leads the gathering in a special prayer or song at this point. I would only recommend that this focus on the continuity of life and love as well as celebrate life, freedom, and rebirth.

If one person has been designated to replace the earth in the grave, do so now. Alternatively, you may choose to take turns placing a shovel full of earth in the grave. However you choose to organize this, make each step a sacred one.

With each consecutive shovel-full, offer a prayer to the Earth who receives this body, to the being who is now on his or her way to a new life, and to the Great Spirit, God, or Goddess who will receive his spirit. Continue to offer prayers for peace, love, release, and anything else you choose, until the grave is full.

Holding hands and forming a circle, if you can, sit or stand around the grave. Allow yourself to feel every emotion you experience. Feel comfortable expressing these emotions as an offering of honesty and respect for this departed animal.

Go around the circle and take turns offering prayers, good wishes, stories, jokes, and whatever you feel. Continue this until all present feel some sense of release.

Offer one final prayer:

"Although we grieve for the times we will no longer share in this world, we rejoice in your freedom. We are grateful for the sharing of our lives during your time here in this world. Your memories and gifts live on within each of us as we freely release you to your next world. We send you heartfelt blessings of peace, love, and joy. We say not good-bye, but fare well until we meet again."

Memorial Service for an Animal

This ritual is excellent for use as part of an ashes-scattering after a cremation. If you know that this animal disliked smudge or smoke, omit those elements unless this ceremony takes place at least a month after the animal's death.

Prepare the area with any flowers or decorations you prefer. Set up a simple altar with a photo of the departed in the center, surrounded by personal effects and items symbolizing the Earth and Great Spirit or God and Goddess.

Using incense, smudge, or a drum, purify the area. Charge it with healing and loving energy.

Set up a central altar on a blanket inside or outside, at the animal's favorite spot. Place a picture of the animal in the center and surround it with items that were special to this animal or items that are symbolic of this animal's favorite things, places, and people. Also on this blanket, have a bowl of earth. As is true with the human rite, the earth is our Earth Mother to whom this animal's body has returned.

Clear those attending with your drum or smudge as they enter. The ritual leader should explain the symbolism of the altar and other decorations to those attending. Allow everyone some time to look over the altar and get comfortable.

Sit or stand in a circle. The leader states the purpose for this ritual and invites the spirit of the animal to join in. Any other deities or spirits you wish to invite should be called at this time.

Go around the circle, speaking your prayers for this animal. Share stories and feelings about your time together or your grief. Everyone should be made comfortable to say what they feel. Go around the circle at least three times, until everyone feels some sense of release and closure.

Ground and center in your preferred manner, if necessary.

Conclude with specific prayers and blessings of release, peace, and love. Allow everyone time to let this animal know how honored they were to have shared this life, how grateful they are for the blessings of that relationship, and how much they will always love that animal. Encourage everyone present to release their ties to this animal so that she or he may easily move onto the next world.

Some families will choose to honor this animal's memory by giving a home to another animal in need. If this is the case, let the departed animal know that this is what you have chosen to do and ask for his or her blessing in this. Promise to honor and love the new animal as family, yet make it clear that no one will ever replace this departed animal in your hearts.

Finish up by doing something that may have been special to this animal. If this animal loved to hike in a particular place, go there for a walk; if this animal tended to be a couch-potato, lie around all day. Be aware during this time of the possibility that this animal may decide to be with you.

I would like to end this chapter with the following ceremony to create a special Medicine bundle or altar to the memory of the departed, whether human or animal. This can be extremely beneficial in the acknowledgement of the time it may take for us to completely release our bonds to the departed and to heal from these wounds. It offers both children and adults a concrete method of hanging on and then finally releasing the loved one when they are ready. This brings an element of control back into the situation in that you do not need to release the altar or bundle until you decide to.

This is a common process among indigenous peoples for the remembering and gradual easing of grief. Generally speaking, these altars or bundles are kept and honored for one year after the death of the loved one. At the end of that year, the honored items are ceremonially either burned or buried in recognition of the end of a mourning period and to fully release the loved one to the next world.

Creation of a Memorial Altar or Medicine Bundle Ceremony

If this ceremony is for an animal that disliked smudge or smoke, omit those elements unless the ceremony takes place at least a month after the animal's death.

Select the items you wish to include in this altar or Medicine bundle. These may include a lock of hair, a photo, items that were special to the departed, and anything else that you feel is important, including any symbols relating to the spirit guides of the departed. If you have chosen to create a Medicine bundle, also select the bag or cloth to be used to contain the bundle items.

Put together and bind your Medicine bundle or set up the altar.

Purify the ritual space and all the ritual items, using either the smudge ceremony or the drum purification ceremony.

When purifying any leather or other animal parts to be used in the construction of the altar or bundle, be sure to release and honor the spirits of these animals. Thank them for the gifts of their bodies and make an offering to their spirits of some kind. This may be anything from a donation to a wildlife refuge to a direct offering of food or water.

Call upon the Spirits of the directions, the God and the Goddess, or the Great Spirit to join with you in this ceremony. Ask that they bless your work. Request guidance, that your every action may honor them.

Call upon the spirit of the departed to join with you. Let her or him know the reason for this ceremony and make it clear that you honor them through it. Ask their assistance in creating this altar/bundle.

Holding your hands out over the items to be used, bless them with the memory of your departed loved one. "This altar/bundle will be honored as the symbolic representative of _____. Through this altar/bundle, we maintain a physical connection to you and you continue to share a physical space within our home. This altar/bundle will be an instrument of love and healing for all of us and will be ceremonially released when we no longer need its energy.

"In creating this altar/bundle, we acknowledge that we have not yet released all ties to our departed

_____. We ask the blessings of the God and the Goddess or the Great Spirit and all our spirit guides in our time of grief and healing. Guide us that we may fully heal and rejoice in this glorious transition."

Thank all those spirits who joined with you in this work, particularly the departed, spirit guides, and the God and the Goddess or the Great Spirit. Release them and let them know they are always welcome at your home.

At the end of the year, or whenever you feel the time is right, you will ceremonially bury or burn these items. The burial ritual given above may be easily altered for this purpose. This basic outline can also be used for a burning. Rather than commending the altar/bundle to the Earth, you will ask that the fire purify and cleanse your grief and anything still binding this spirit to our world. Request that the spirit of your loved one be released by the fire; and that the smoke carry him or her directly to the God and the Goddess or the Great Spirit.

Conclusion

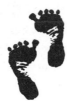

Our Future

I wrote this book for many reasons. One of those reasons was in the hope that pagan parents can lead the way in raising happy, healthy, connected children. Society is sadly lacking in respect, honor, and community and we have the opportunity to begin to return that to our reality, through how we live our lives and how we raise our children.

Our children truly are our future. We are foolish if we think that we have no responsibility for the state of the world. It is not someone else's problem or someone else's fault. It is certainly not the fault of the children. There is plenty of blame to be had but far too little responsibility being accepted. For the last few thousand years, our species has fallen further and further from honor.

In a misguided effort to control our world, we have completely divorced ourselves from the cycles of Nature and from all other life on this planet. We can no longer feel our interconnections with All of Life and with a Great Spirit. Therefore, we believe that we are not affected by any actions taken toward another being, or toward the Earth itself. We work hard and play hard and our children often lose in the process. So many of us are unprepared to meet the challenges of our own lives, how can we hope to guide our children through theirs?

As I wrote in the introduction, pagan parents are pioneers. We are responsible for creating community, even if it is limited to the pagan community. Pagan parents are working to raise conscious children that have a better chance to avoid the trap of modern commercialism and modern "progress."

God is not dead to pagans, nor is the Goddess. We feel Them everywhere. They are the trees, the rocks, the buildings, the other people. They are Us and we recognize that. They are our children and we must treat them as such. We teach our children, through word and action, that when we respect the Earth and other beings, we respect ourselves and everyone wins.

Pagan parents have the opportunity to guide a new generation back into a more sacred way of living on this Earth. When we walk in balance and with integrity, we become powerful examples of strength and sensitivity; power and grace. And when we combine that with complete, unconditional love and play, we open the doors to truly beautiful relationships with our children. We become the parents we always wanted, and always dreamed of being.

This is the hope of our world. As parents, we are in a unique position to contribute to the future of our world and our families. Only through self awareness and living with integrity can we hope to give our children the tools to create a preferred reality. As pagan parents, I know we are all working and praying toward that end.

With this in mind, I would like to end with "The Mabon's Prayer," from the Order of Bards, Ovates, and Druids.

> I come to this place as a child of future generations.
> My gift is the gentle flame of hope that each new life
> brings into this world. I, and those who follow me,
> ask that those of you who gave us life protect this
> sacred flame. You who are the earthly guardians of
> wisdom unite together in peace and harmony to
> protect this planet, our home. This I ask for the
> children of the world.

Recommended Reading

Health and Healing

General

The Anatomy Coloring Book, by Wynn Kapit and Lawrence M. Elson. Canfield Press.

How to Raise a Healthy child . . . In Spite of Your Doctor, by Robert S. Mendelsohn, M.D. Ballantine Books.

Smart Medicine for a Healthier Child, by Janet Zand, LAc., O.M.D.; Rachel Walton, R.N.; and Bob Rountree, M.D. Avery Publishing Group.

Healing Stones

Color and Crystals, by Joy Gardner. The Crossing Press.

Love is in the Earth: A Kaleidoscope of Crystals, by Melody. Earth-Love Publishing House.

The Women's Book of Healing, by Diane Stein. Llewellyn Publications.

Homeopathy

Homeopathy for Pregnancy, Birth, and Your Baby's First Year, by Miranda Castro. St. Martin's Press.

Homeopathic Medicine at Home, by Maesimond B. Panos, M.D. and Jane Heimlich. Jeremy P. Tarcher, Inc.

Herbs

Natural Healing with Herbs, by Humbart Santillo, B.S., M.H.
Hohm Press

Wise Woman Herbal for the Childbearing Year, by Susun S. Weed.
Ash Tree Publishing.

Body Work

Chinese Pediatric Massage Therapy, by Ya-li Fan. Blue Poppy
Press.

Infant Massage, by Vimala Schneider McClure. Bantam Books.

Kundalini Yoga for Strength, Success, & Spirit, by Ravi Singh.
White Lion Press.

Shiatsu Therapy: Theory and Practice, by Toru Namikoshi. Japan
Publications, Inc.

Diet & Nutrition

The Complete New Guide to Preparing Baby Foods, by Sue Castle.
Bantam Books.

the low blood sugar handbook, by Edward and Patricia Krimmel.
Franklin Publishers.

The Self-Healing Cookbook, by Kristina Turner. Earthtones Press.

Sugar Busters! by H. Leighton Steward; Morrison C. Bethea,
M.D.; Sam S. Andrews, M.D.; Luis A. Balart, M.D.
Ballantine Books.

Vegetarian Mother Baby Book, by Rose Elliot. Pantheon Books.

Energy Work

The Energy Within, by Richard M. Chin, M.D., O.M.D.
Paragon House.

Hands of Light, by Barbara Brennan. Bantam Books.

Reiki: Universal Life Energy, by Bodo J. Baginski and Shalila
Sharamon. Life Rhythm Publications.

Wheels of Light, by Rosalyn L. Bruyere. Simon & Schuster.

Breathing

Science of Breath, by Swami Rama, Rudolph Ballentine, M.D., and Alan Hymes, M.D. Himalayan International Institute of Yoga Science and Philosophy.

Pagan Paths

Celebrating the Great Mother, by Cait Johnson and Maura D. Shaw. Destiny Books.

Circle Round, by Starhawk and Diane Baker and Anne Hill. Bantam Doubleday Dell Publishers.

The Family Wicca Book: The Craft for Parents and Children, by Ashleen O'Gaea. Llewellyn Publications.

New Moon Rising: Reclaiming the Sacred Rites of Menstruation, by Linda Heron Wind. Delphi Press.

The Pagan Family: Handing the Old Ways Down, by Ceisiwr Serith. Lewellyn Publications.

Wheel of the Year, by Pauline Campanelli. Llewellyn Publications.

Death and Dying

Bereaved Children and Teens, edited by Earl A. Grollman. Beacon Press.

On Children and Death, by Elisabeth Kübler-Ross, M.D. Simon & Schuster.

The Pagan Book of Living and Dying, by Starhawk, M. Macha Nightmare, and the Reclaiming Collective. HarperSanFrancisco Publishers.

Pet Loss: A Spiritual Guide, by Eleanor Harris, Llewellyn Publications.

Shamanic Guide to Death and Dying, by Kristin Madden. Llewellyn Publications.

Miscellaneous

Sleep Issues

The Family Bed, by Tine Thevenin. Avery Publishing Group, Inc.

Helping Your Child Sleep Through The Night, by Joanne Cuthbertson and Susie Schevill. Doubleday.

Solve Your Child's Sleep Problems, by Richard Ferber, M.D.

Parenting and Discipline

How to Keep Your Kids from Driving You Crazy, by Paula Stone Bender, Ph.D. John Wiley & sons, Inc.

The Strong-Willed Child, by Dr. James Dobson. Living Books.

Time-Out For Toddlers, by Dr. James W. Varni and Donna G. Corwin. Berkley Books.

Contacts

General

Circle Network News
P.O. Box 219
Mt. Horeb, WI 53572
www.circlesanctuary.org   Email: circle@mhtc.net

CraftWise conferences
P.O. Box 2277
Milford, CT 06460
Telephone (203) 874-6963
www.CraftWise.com   Email: FDalton367@aol.com

Covenant of Unitarian Universalist Pagans
8190A Beechmont Avenue #335
Cincinnati, OH 45255-3154
www/cuups.org   Email: CUUPS@ aol.com

Military Pagan Network
P.O. Box 253
Ellicott City, MD 21041–0253
Telephone (410) 750-3327
John Machate, Coordinator/CEO
www.milpagan.org/   Email: coordinator@milpagan.org

Pagan Educational Network
P.O. Box 1364
Bloomington, IN 47402–1364
[please send business-sized SASE for snail mail requests]
www.bloomington.in.us/~pen/
Email: pen@bloomington.in.us

Order of Bards, Ovates, and Druids
P.O. Box 1333
Lewes, East Sussex
BN7 1DX, England
www.druidry.org   Email: office@obod.co.uk

Parenting Websites

The Pagan Parenting Page Website
www.jazgordon.com/pparent   Email: Jaz@jazgordon.com

Witches Voice
www.witchvox.com/witches/xparent.html
Teen pages: www.witchvox.com/xteen.html

COG Pagan Parents Reading Guide
Email: parents@cog.org

Eunomia
www.members.xoom.com/trtlgrrl/eunomiahome.htm
Email: eunomia@xmission.com

Global Pagan Parents & Families Contact List
www.geocities.com/Heartland/Fields/5464
Email: kethera@geocities.com

Half Moon Hill
www.geocities.com/Athens/Oracle/5595
Email: halfmoonhill@hotmail.com

Kethera'sDomain
www.geocities.com/Athens/Acropolis/6376
Email: kethera@geocities.com

My Little Corner of the World: Self-Esteem pages
www.mylittlecorner.com/sesteem.html
Email: rhiannon@mylittlecorner.com

Pagan Parenting Forums and Chats
www.customforum.com/paganparenting
Email: silvrskys@geocities.com

Raven's Haven
www. geocities.com/Rainforest/Vines/2958
Email: RavenWays@aol.com

Silvrskys' Pagan Corners
www.geocities.com/Athens/Forum/9180/
Email: silvrskys@geocities.com

Legal Resources

American Civil Liberties Union
ACLU
125 Broad Street, 18th Floor
New York, New York 10004–2400
www.aclu.org

Americans United for the Separation of Church and State
www.au.org

Earth Religions Legal Assistance Network
www.conjure.com/ERAL/eral.html

Foundation For Religious Tolerance
www.religioustolerance.net/

The Electronic Frontier Foundation (strictly Internet)
www.eff.org/

Lady Liberty League (LLL)
P.O. Box 219
Mt. Horeb, WI 53572
www.circlesanctuary.org/liberty/   Email: circle@mhtc.net
Telephone (608) 924-2216, FAX (608) 924-5961

Military Pagan Network

Military Pagan Network Inc.
Dept. of Harassment Affairs
Director: Stephenie Urquhart
1634 Moran Road
Choctaw, OK 73020
www.milpagan.org/

Ontario Consultants on Religious Tolerance
US Postal Address:
  OCRT
  P.O. Box 514
  Wellesley Island, NY 13640-0514

Canadian Postal Address:
  OCRT
  Box 27026
  Frontenac PO, Kingston, ON
  Canada K7M 8W5
  Email: ocrt_qu@cgo.wave.ca
  Fax: (613) 531-9609

Religious Rights Contact List
  www.geocities.com/Athens/9802/rights.html

United States Constitution
  www.law.cornell.edu/constitution/constitution.overview.html

U.S. Bill of Rights
  www.law.cornell.edu/constitution/constitution.billofrights.
  html

Witches League for Public Awareness (WLPA)
  P.O. Box 909
  Rehoboth, MA 02769
  www.CelticCrow.com/   Email: hernesson@aol.com

The Witches' Voice Inc.
  P.O. Box 4924
  Clearwater, FL 33758–4924
  Telephone (813) 723-0734 (press Star button for fax)
  Witches Voice direct URL:
    www.witchvox/white/w_legal_aid_links.html
  Email: WebMaster@witchvox.com

Witches Anti-Discrimination League
  P.O. Box 821
  Connersville, IN 47331
  wadl@webworks2000.net

Glossary

Asatru: The worship of the Nordic pantheon; roughly translated as "belief in the Old Gods."

Astral Body: The spirit or energetic double that travels freely during trance states and dreaming.

Astral Travel: to travel in spirit only without the physical body.

Aura: the personal energy field; that which permeates and surrounds the physical body.

Body soul: A shamanic term for that part of the spirit or personal energy field that remains with the physical body as long as it lives.

Chakra: an energy vortex or center of activity for the subtle, life force that permeates and animates the physical body. They are believed to be interrelated with the parasympathetic, sympathetic, and autonomic nervous systems.

Deathwalk: the psychopompic shamanic journey after physical death into the next World.

Deathwalker: a shaman who deals with the dying and the dead; a psychopomp: one who guides the departed beyond this life into the next world and/or connects them with their spirit guides after death.

Devas: Nature faeries, generally seen as very small and often amorphous.

Empathic: one who psychically receives the feelings and emotions of other people.

Empathetic: one who can understand or relate to the way another feels.

Free soul: a shamanic term for the astral body.

Hologram: a three-dimensional image; each piece of the hologram contains the image of the whole.

Homeopathy: a system of healing based on the concept of "like cures like."

hundredth-monkey phenomenon: referring to the book by the same name, *the hundredth monkey,* by Ken Keyes. The idea is that once a certain critical percentage of a population has learned or developed an ability, the remainder of that population will instantly (or "overnight") develop the same ability.

Incarnation: the process of entering physical form; rebirth

Kundalini: generally dormant energy that is said to reside at the base of the spine. It is often compared to a sleeping serpent. It is a vital energy, both static and kinetic, that is one's power; one's fire of enlightenment and awakening.

Nagual: the mysterious, Otherworldly aspect of Self.

Norse: referring to the Nordic or Scandinavian peoples.

Polyamoury: nonmonogamous.

Psychometry: the ability to obtain psychic impressions from inanimate objects.

Quickening: The time when a pregnant woman first feels the movement of her baby; usually occurring around the fourth month of pregnancy.

Saami: the indigenous people of northern Norway, Sweden, Finland, and the Russian Kola Peninsula; commonly known as Lapps or Laplanders.

Santeria: a similar religion to Voudoun; principally based on the beliefs of the Yoruban peoples who were brought to the

Americas as slaves. *Santo* means saint and refers to the African gods that were assimilated as Christian saints.

Santero: a practitioner of the Santeria religion; usually male; Santera usually denotes a female practitioner.

Scrying: a method of divination using a glass or bowl of water as a focal point.

Shadow side: a shamanic term for the place within where we hide those aspects of Self that we would rather not acknowledge.

Shamanism: an ancient spiritual path characterized by the shamanic journey, or conscious and controlled astral travel.

Sidhe: the Great Elves or Faery folk of the ancient Celts; generally seen as human size or larger and very powerful.

Soul fragmentation: the energetic blocks or loss of energy and memories that result from trauma.

Soul retrieval: a shamanic process to retrieve and reintegrate lost and blocked soul fragments.

Spirit Guides: any interdimensional beings that teach, guide, and guard humans.

Telepathy: wordless, psychic communication.

Thoughtform: a psychic creation that has form and, with enough energy, may develop a life of its own.

Tonal: the rational, everyday aspect of Self.

Universal energy field: the energy or Spirit that permeates and connects all things in all worlds.

Voudoun: also referred to as Vodou or Vaudoun; synchretized religion combining aspects of indigenous West African and Haitian beliefs with Catholicism.

References

Blue's Clues @ 1998 Viacom International

Brennan, Barbara. *Hands of Light*. New York: Bantam Books, 1988.

Bruyere, Rosalyn L. *Wheels of Light*. New York: Simon & Schuster, 1994.

Castro, Miranda. *Homeopathy for Pregnancy, Birth, and Your Baby's First Year*. New York: St. Martin's Press, 1993.

Centers for Disease Control Website, http://www.cdc.gov

Fan Ya-li. *Chinese Pediatric Massage Therapy*. Boulder, CO: Blue Poppy Press, 1994.

Health and Human Services Press Office Website, www.hhs.gov

Madden, Kristin. *Shamanic Guide to Death and Dying*. St. Paul, MN: Llewellyn Worldwide, 1999.

Panos, Maesimond B., M.D., and Jane Heimlich. *Homeopathic Medicine at Home*. Los Angeles: Jeremy P. Tarcher, Inc, 1980.

Sanchez, Victor. *The Teachings of Don Carlos*. Santa Fe: Bear & Company. 1995.

Santillo, Humbart, B.S., M.H. *Natural Healing with Herbs*. Prescott Valley, AZ: Hohm Press, 1985.

Swami Rama, Rudolph Ballentine, M.D., and Alan Hymes, M.D. *Science of Breath*. Honesdale, PA: Himalayan International Institute of Yoga Science and Philosophy, 1979.

Zand, Janet, LAc, OMD, Rachel Walton, RN, and Bob Rountree, MD. *Smart Medicine for a Healthier Child*. Garden City Park, NY: Avery Publishing Group, 1994.

Index

☽ REACH FOR THE MOON

Astrology & Your Child

A Handbook for Parents

Gloria Star

(formerly titled *Optimum Child*)

Many who face the challenges of parenthood have wished for a handbook on each child. Well, that handbook exists. It is the astrological chart! The horoscope symbolically indicates a child's physical, mental, emotional, and spiritual needs. It is an excellent tool for allowing children to be who they really are, and for helping them to develop their fullest potential. *Astrology & Your Child* is written for parents new to astrology, as well as experienced astrologers.

Since a child's expression of the Self is not yet mature, the astrological symbols must be interpreted with this in mind. Just as psychologists have put forth theories dealing specifically with the behavior and developmental stages of children, astrologers must also redefine their usual adult focus with dealing with children.

A brief table of where the planets were when your children were born is included in the book so that even if you don't have their individual birthcharts, you can find out enough to begin to help them develop their potential.

1-56718-649-1, 312 pp., 7½ x 9⅛, 84 charts   **$17.95**

Pagan Rites of Passage

Pauline Campanelli
illustrated by Dan Campanelli
(Formerly titled *Rites of Passage*)

If you have ever held a newborn child in your arms and wanted to rejoice with the deities over the birth but didn't know what to do, or if you've felt frustrated at the funeral of a loved one by a minister's empty words, then this book is for you.

Pagan Rites of Passage is a complete and cohesive system of rites that draw upon ancient Pagan traditions of many cultures to celebrate the inevitable life transitions of those on the Pagan path. As well as describing traditions and offering ideas for the passager and participants, this book will tell you about charms, amulets, gifts, and altar decorations you can make in preparation for a rite. Hundreds of traditions and rites are provided, including birth and Paganing; coming of age and initiation; handfasting and parting; midlife and priest or priestesshood; cronehood/ elderhood; death and many more.

This book was written for beginner or advanced practitioners, solitaries or covens, with rituals general enough to be adapted into any tradition. Your life's cycles are connected to the seasons of the year and the cycle of the sabbats—now you can celebrate them with new knowledge, confidence, and joy!

1-56718-111-2, 288 pp., 7 x 10, illus., photos $14.95

Shamanic Guide to Death and Dying

Includes Meditations & Rituals

Kristin Madden

Throughout history and across the globe, societies have called upon their shamans to assist the dying, the dead, and those loved ones remaining in physical life. The shaman, as deathwalker, is responsible for guiding us through our journeys to the next world. This book, written by a modern shamanic deathwalker, offers personal experience and practical examples of the process through life into death and rebirth, along with suggested methods for you to use in your own experience.

Shamanic Guide to Death and Dying will take you on a journey beyond this reality. It will show you the continuity of life after the death of the physical body, and will help you to reconnect with departed loved ones and your own spirit guides.

- Find out what really happens at the moment of death, and to what worlds we travel after leaving this body
- Experience actual deathwalks for humans and animals through the eyes and ears of modern deathwalkers
- Explore your own past lives and learn about the effects of other lives on your current incarnation
- Create and facilitate rites of passage and other ceremonies using the outlines provided
- Find out why children are more open to the Other worlds and how to encourage the development of their abilities and self-esteem
- Learn to assist your pets through their passages

1-56718-494-4, 288 pp., 7½ x 9⅛   **$16.95**

Dandelion Fuzz Wishes:
Elemental Air Magic for Young Children

For the baby or toddler, dandelion fuzz can be the tool for their very first natural magic. Dandelions grow in almost all areas and most of us are familiar with making wishes while blowing the fuzz from them at the end of their season. This is very similar to the wish-spells associated with blowing out birthday candles. Just as in any form of magic, belief and emotion are vital to the success of a dandelion fuzz wish and with very young children, a parent may need to initially provide this.

Dandelion Fuzz Wish

Before going outside to find a dandelion in fuzz, decide on the wish you and your child will be making. Then go outside with that wish in your minds and ask to be led to the dandelion that wants to help make that wish come true.

Ask before picking the dandelion of your choice. When permission is given, pick it with a prayer of thanks. If your child is able, have him or her say thank you along with you as you pick the flower.

Hold the dandelion by its stem and have the child hold it gently with you. (An older child can hold the plant alone.) Repeat the wish out loud. If your child is old enough, tell them to imagine the wish growing really big in their head. Then blow the wish out into the dandelion fuzz, and watch as it is carried off into the air.

Tell your child that the wish is now part of the fuzz and the air will carry it to the Great Spirit or God and Goddess.

About the Author

Kristin Madden is Karl's mom and was raised in a shamanic home. With her family, she has explored many Eastern and Western mystic paths. She is a shamanic deathwalker as well as a Druid and tutor in the Order of Bards, Ovates, and Druids. She is the author of Shamanic Guide to Death and Dying and has served on a Master's degree thesis committee for a program on the use of visual imagery and parapsychology in therapy with ADD/ADHD children.

To Write to the Author

If you wish to contact the author or would like more information about this book, please write to the author in care of Llewellyn Worldwide and we will forward your request. Both the author and publisher appreciate hearing from you and learning of your enjoyment of this book and how it has helped you. Llewellyn Worldwide cannot guarantee that every letter written to the author can be answered, but all will be forwarded. Please write to:

Kristin Madden
℅ Llewellyn Worldwide
P.O. Box 64383, Dept. 1-56718-492-8
St. Paul, MN 55164-0383, U.S.A.
Many of Llewellyn's authors have websites with additional information and resources. For more information, please visit our website at
www.llewellyn.com.
Please enclose a self-addressed stamped envelope for reply, or $1.00 to cover costs. If outside U.S.A., enclose international postal reply coupon.